fondazione MUSEI SENESI

Fondazione Musei Senesi
Guides / 13

# Siena

## The Palazzo Pubblico
## The Civic Museum
## The Torre del Mangia

*Edited by*
Letizia Galli

SilvanaEditoriale

*cover*
The Campo with the Palazzo Pubblico
and Torre del Mangia
(photo by Bruno Bruchi)

Silvana Editoriale

*Produced by*
Arti Grafiche Amilcare Pizzi Spa

*Direction*
Dario Cimorelli

*Art Director*
Giacomo Merli

*Copy Editor*
Lorena Ansani

*Layout*
Donatella Ascorti, Nicola Cazzulo, Floriana Pellegrino

*Production Coordinator*
Michela Bramati

*Editorial Assistant*
Elena Piaggesi

*Iconographic office*
Deborah D'Ippolito, Alessandra Olivari

*Press Office*
Lidia Masolini - press@silvanaeditoriale.it

Fondazione Musei Senesi
Guides /13
Siena
The Palazzo Pubblico, the Civic Museum, the Torre del Mangia

City of Siena

Provincial Administration
of Siena

Monte dei Paschi di Siena
Foundation

*With the support of*
Region of Tuscany, Integrated
Culture Plan 2009
Monte dei Paschi di Siena
Foundation

*Series editor*
Luigi Di Corato
Fondazione Musei Senesi

*A book edited by*
Letizia Galli

*Editorial coordinator*
Elisa Bruttini
Fondazione Musei Senesi

*Texts*
Mauro Civai (M. C.)
Letizia Galli (L. G.)
Paola Gepponi (P. G.)
Veronica Randon (V. R.)

*Photos*
Bruno Bruchi, Siena
Fabio and Andrea Lensini, Siena
Archivio Fondazione Musei Senesi

*Translation*
Susan Scott

*Acknowledgements*
Stefano Amidei, Alessandro Bagnoli, Duccio Balestracci, Matilde e Paolo Corbini, Alberto Cornice, Antonio De Martinis, Gianni Falciani, Susanna Fratiglioni, Stefano Gentilini, Fabio Pacciani, Luca Rossi, Cecilia Sani, Laura Vigni

*Special thanks to*
Simone Bezzini, Emanuela Carpani, Maurizio Cenni, Marcello Flores, Gabriello Mancini, Enrico Rossi, Marco Saletti, Cristina Scaletti, Mario Scalini

*Siena's Palazzo Pubblico is without question one of the best-known and most important Gothic public buildings of the late Middle Ages in Italy. Built in little more than a decade, between the thirteenth and fourteenth centuries, at the behest of the Government of Nine, it holds important state rooms, enriched with extraordinary fresco cycles, the works of major artists, all Sienese in origin but sought after, in various ages, all over Europe. Masterpieces like* The Virgin and Child Enthroned in Majesty *and* Guidoriccio da Fogliano *by Simone Martini or The* Capture of Giuncarico Castle *attributed to Duccio, or the illustration of the* Allegory *and the* Effects of Good and Bad Government *by Ambrogio Lorenzetti are still able to bear witness to indelible chapters in the history and art of Italy and beyond.*
*But Palazzo Pubblico, together with the Campo that embraces it so gently, does not just document the sublime moment of its design and construction, which coincides with the most luminous age Siena ever knew. It is perfectly able to bear witness, more effectively and immediately than anything else, to the unique development of Sienese history, with its most glorious and triumphant moments but also the most bitter and painful. The many objects on display in the Civic Museum which gives life to the grand frescoed chambers accurately illustrate the city's constant efforts to pursue two fundamental priorities: one aesthetic, applying beauty to every manifestation and every activity it carries out, and that of* Good Government, *an elusive myth but here in Siena reached various times thanks to the creation and constant updating of rules as rigorous as they are just, inspired by the best principles of living in society and by good sense.*
*If, then, visitors dare to climb up to the top of the Torre del Mangia, the symbol of Siena par excellence, their experience will be enriched by the unparalleled view of the vast lands of Siena, so magnificently diverse but all the result of a harmonious union between the quality of their design and respect for their original sites.*
*This guide, new in concept, is well able to interpret these fundamental aspects and transmit them effectively to its undoubtedly attentive and numerous readers.*

Maurizio Cenni
*Mayor of Siena*

*Along with the majestic Torre del Mangia, the Civic Museum is the best-known and most treasured part of Siena's celebrated Palazzo Pubblico. Its fresco cycles on religious and civic themes are universally known masterpieces, loved by specialists and the general public alike. It is a museum with a complex balance, one where it is not always easy to reconcile preservation concerns with respect for the original characteristics and current uses of the building, especially in light of the large number of visitors who come each year to see it. A system of symbols still living, sought after and loved by the local community that has found in it over the centuries one of its most successful forms of representation, the mirror of a* civitas *that continues even today to identify with it. In this duality, the Civic Museum of Siena becomes a paradigm of the debate on the contemporary role of museums, which must go from being "passive museums," limiting their activity to the display and conservation of the permament collections awaiting the arrival of visitors, to being "proactive museums," places that are able to 'speak' to all and to narrate their secrets and those of the communities that generated them, offering a unique experience.*
*An "education central" at the service of society and its development, which has the courage to find a new fulcrum: no longer the objects on display, but the local community and visitors.*
*In this perspective, even while remaining the pride of the* communitas, *the ideal museum becomes one that is accessible and welcoming, strong in the importance of its cultural, but also educational and social role, at the center of its territory and capable of offering valuable cultural services, in continuity with tradition but also in full awareness of the needs of the present, capable of responding to the demands of the new communities.*
*This guide aims at being a new kind of tool, conceived for visitors, whether beginners or experts, in which information and curious facts, art and life, history and legend all come together to provide an incisive support for a tour of the museum and to whet their curiosity to know more.*

Gianni Resti
*President*
*Fondazione Musei Senesi*

Luigi Di Corato
*General director*
*Fondazione Musei Senesi*

# Contents

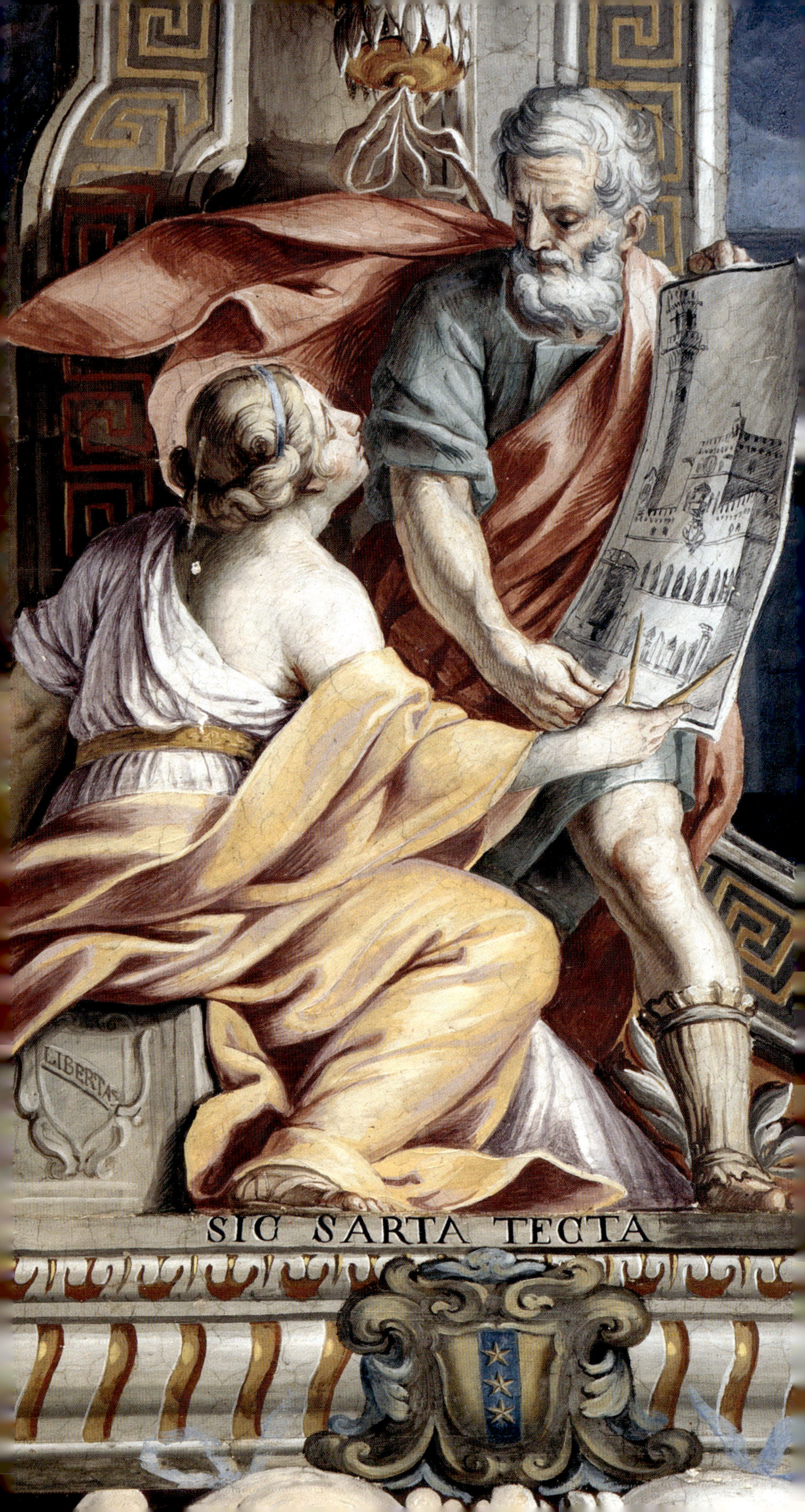

LIBERTAS
SIC SARTA TECTA

## History
# The Palazzo Pubblico and its Museum

*Mauro Civai – Director of the Civic Museum*

Deifebo Burbarini: *Urban Architecture Looking Over a Plan of the Palazzo Pubblico*, detail
Bilanceria di Biccherna (Mayor's office)

The Palazzo Pubblico has always been a real source of pride for the Sienese, probably since the time it was first conceived by the Magnificent "Signori Nove" (Nine Lords) who wanted it to be majestic and at the same time elegant and rich on the interior with painted stories which could demonstrate to everyone the confident trust and high political culture of that enlightened ruling class. In its rooms, given over to politics and administrative functions, many noble examples were meant to orient the activity of the governors and point out the right path to citizens.

But such a grand work could not have been conceived in this extraordinary way if not intended to astound everyone who had occasion to enter its Gothic portals and walk through its stately rooms. And so many people over the centuries – ambassadors and reigning sovereigns, high prelates but also ordinary and maybe modest pilgrims – must have received this enormous impression which not a few of the most illustrious visitors wrote down in deeply-felt, admiring pages of memoirs.

The precise, fully-achieved idea of allowing non-Sienese and the public in general to visit the city's Town Hall, at least at chosen times when its rooms were not in intensive use, coincides with the completion of the unification of Italy. The achievement of the new unitary State, to which Siena adhered quickly and enthusiastically, restored dignity and a desire for development to a city that had never completely metabolized the dramatic loss of its ancient independence and the domination, albeit rather mild, of its eternal antagonist Florence.

Under Savoy rule, Siena became an Italian city like all the others, indeed probably even more meaningful than most of the other urban realities, thanks to its intact urban structure that makes it an invaluable witness, well-suited to representing the highest levels of what the national community, even though broken up into a thousand pieces, was able to build earlier.

The Sienese were immediately proud to show off their treasures once again; along with the Accademia gallery, which already housed many of the greatest masterpieces coming

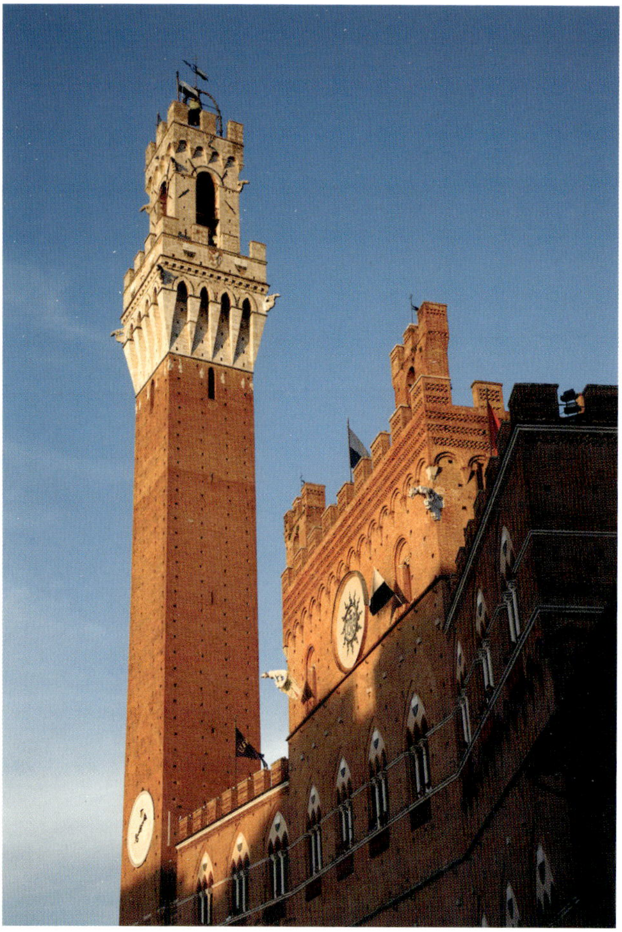

The Palazzo Pubblico with the Torre del Mangia

from the monasteries in and around Siena, and the Cathedral, an unparalleled treasure chest of Italian art, especially sculpture, by opening the Town Hall to the public the rooms could be shown where the governors of Siena arrived at the decisions and laws that for centuries were able to guarantee the very high level of Sienese civilization.

Immediately after 1860, it thus became possible to tour the Palazzo Pubblico on certain days. The rooms on the various floors, even those on the so-called *piano nobile*, were still occupied by administrative offices and thus furniture and supplies. Under Simone Martini's painting of *The Virgin Enthroned in Majesty*, the enormous wooden bench used for meetings of the Court of Assizes of Siena limited the view of the imposing fresco and hid the signature of the great Sienese artist, a favorite of popes and of Petrarch, as well as its hendecasyllabic dedication, somewhat worn but with the date "1315" prominently displayed and readily visible.

The Sala della Pace ("Room of Peace"), too, presented itself to these early tourists as suffering from countless injuries,

bearing witness to the lack of consideration in which the golden age of Sienese painting had been held by the occupants of the palace, but more generally by public opinion, in the preceding centuries, who thought of it as barbarous and primitive and preferred to pursue a modernity that was often vacuous but, as in every age, also necessary.
Despite this fact, those austere rooms continued to speak, better than any other place, to whoever walked through them of the many men who had carried out their functions in them and the many events that had taken place there, making Siena great, trying above all to keep the city completely or as much as possible independent.
Between the late nineteenth and early twentieth century, the Sienese thus took back completely their most important public building and its value as a witness to the past, and also as a sign of awareness of the great contribution it could make to the city's image in the future, deciding to place inside it the monument the city intended to dedicate to the advocate of Italian unity, Vittorio Emanuele II.
This monument was conceived not as a large statue, maybe on horseback, as most of the other Italian cities had done, but rather as a series of painted stories that would trace his splendid course on earth and remain to narrate his greatness for all time. But they had to do this on the ancient walls that displayed the deeds of the Signori Nove, the mercenary captain Guidoriccio da Fogliano, Pope Alexander III, and all the others who directly or indirectly, in reality or only ideally, were fathers of the Sienese fatherland.
When, too, right as the twentieth century began, the idea took shape, following the example of other cities and in the wake of universal expositions already in vogue, of planning a great exhibition to show the world for the first time the incomparable richness of Sienese art, it was a fairly simple matter to decide to hold it in the Palazzo Pubblico. This undertaking was extraordinarily demanding and was made possible only after the municipal administration bought Palazzo della Ciaia, on a street next to Piazza del Campo, and move there all the court offices which until then had been housed in the Palazzo Pubblico.
The show was a great success, well beyond the rosiest predictions: in that long-ago 1904, 50,000 visitors from all over Europe came to Siena, despite the truly dismal transportation connecting the city to the rest of the world, to admire the some 8,000 masterpieces crowded into every room on the various floors of the Palazzo Pubblico, with really innovative installation ideas, thanks also to the involvement of the first great Italian museologist, Corrado Ricci,

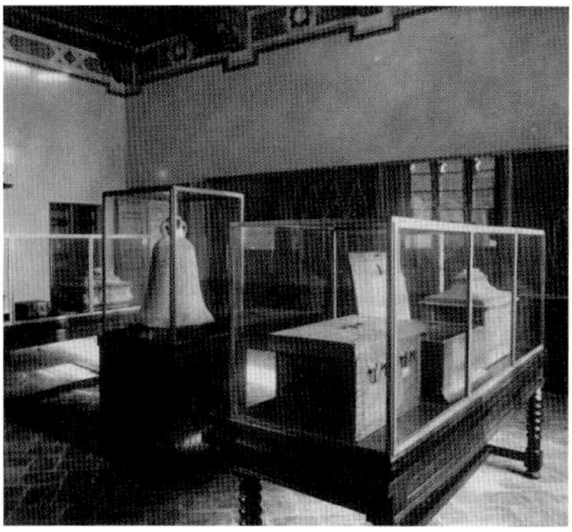

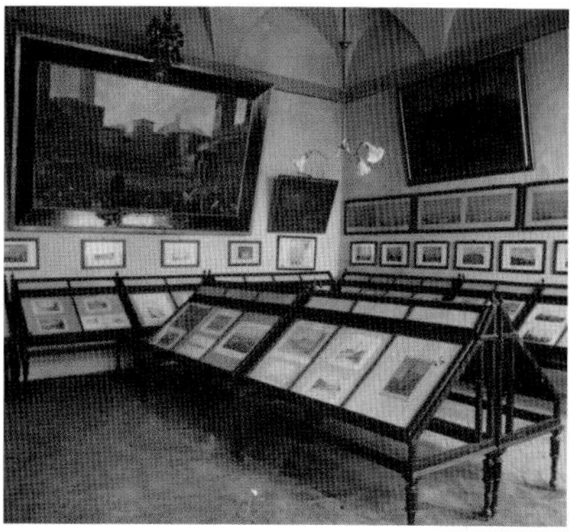

Some of the museum rooms in the 1930s. Historic Archive of the City of Siena

at the time director of the Uffizi gallery in Florence.
Thanks to the *Exhibition of Early Sienese Art*, Siena achieved full status as a leading art center, on the same plane as Florence, Rome, Venice, and Naples, just to give an idea, and the ever-increasing number of tourists pouring in began to consider the pottery and other "souvenirs" of Siena to be objects of real value. Many began to be more and more convinced that Siena's Town Hall should be made the most of by using it as a museum and moving most of the offices still housed in it to other locations. It was in this perspective, which was being encouraged and pushed by the city's intellectuals but ran into budgetary problems on the municipal and national levels, that the decision was made in any case to open the monumental rooms of the palace to the public, starting 1 October 1907, with an entrance ticket costing 50 lire.
The economic situation in that period and obviously also World War I caused a twenty-year delay, to 1922, in opening the Prints or Topographical Museum on the top floor. This museum, which was forcefully championed by the most outstanding Sienese leader of the time, the *podestà* Guido Bargagli Petrucci, housed an exceptional gallery of images of the city and its territory which offered a complete journey back through Sienese history. These were for the most part paintings, drawings, and prints coming from the Biblioteca Comunale, the natural repository of historical evidence of all kinds, thanks to the generosity of numerous donors and the far-sightedness of its earliest librarians, among them Giuseppe Ciaccheri and Luigi de Angelis, who were active between the second half of the eighteenth century and the first part of the nineteenth.
It took several years more, necessary mainly for moving out some employees and certain offices who were reluctant to leave, to create also the so-called Numismatic Museum in the large rooms around the Cortile della Podestà. Here were

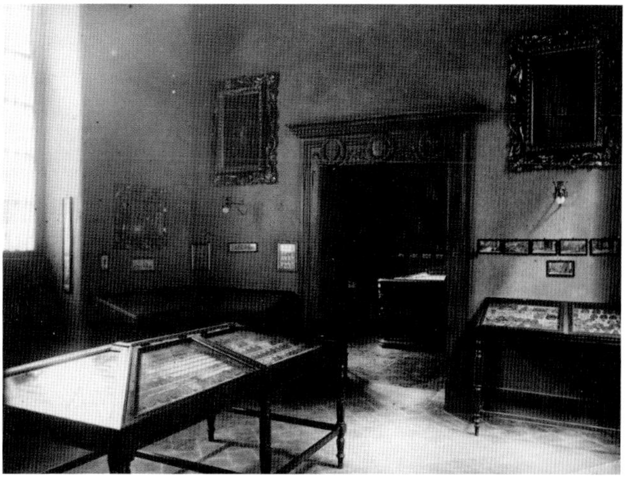

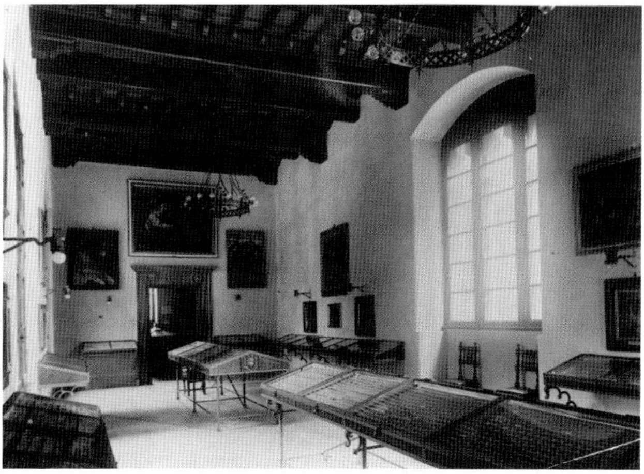

placed the extensive collections of ancient coins, starting with examples from ancient Rome and continuing through the Byzantine empire, the Middle Ages, and the Renaissance. Besides coins, the substantial, rare collections of ancient seals, Renaissance and baroque medallions, and trademarks were all lined up in neat rows in austere wrought iron display cases.

The collections of coins and seals also came from that enormous storehouse, the Biblioteca Comunale. Alongside these, other examples of painting, sculpture, and work in precious metals were gathered together to place in the museum, the majority of which were made for the palace itself, but a goodly number were also bought on the antique market to add to the Civic Museum's holdings.

A great triumph of civilization was being turned into a noble setting. It remained unaltered until the 1960s, when the room called the Sala dei Pilastri, adjacent to the Sala della Pace (or Sala dei Nove), was renovated and its contents

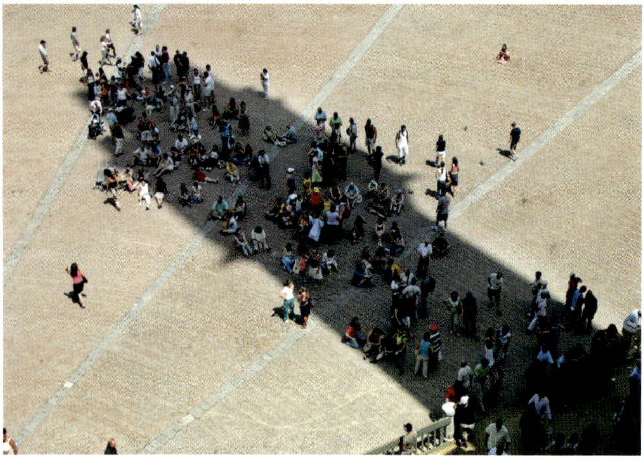

Piazza del Campo marked by the shadow of the Torre del Mangia

The Palazzo Pubblico on an early twentieth-century postcard

rearranged, with the important addition of some seminal works, first and foremost the fifteenth-century "Golden Rose" by Simone da Firenze, a precious sign of the gratitude and affection Pope Pius II always had for the city where his family, the Piccolomini, was born and based.
The current state of the museum, which on one hand in the most recent three or four decades has witnessed major structural improvements, including the demanding, complex restoration of its principal fresco cycles, and on the other has seen a significant decrease in its exhibition space, still suffers to some degree the problems of coexistence with the part of the Town Hall still occupied by the municipal administration and the executive offices. But despite this fact, the Civic Museum is the most visited museum in Siena and the one most present in the imagination of those who look at, or at least dream of, this city.
Pausing in the ample embrace of Piazza del Campo and resting in the shadow of its tall tower still today is an extraordinary experience, just as it was for Albert Camus when, as a young student, he arrived in the city after walking across the gentle ridges of the Sienese clay fields. Then to go stand in front of the immortal masterpieces of the Sienese school, from the Gothic period to the Renaissance and even later, and perhaps to venture up to the top of the Torre del Mangia, is a fitting conclusion for an itinerary among the most evocative anywhere, and of all time.

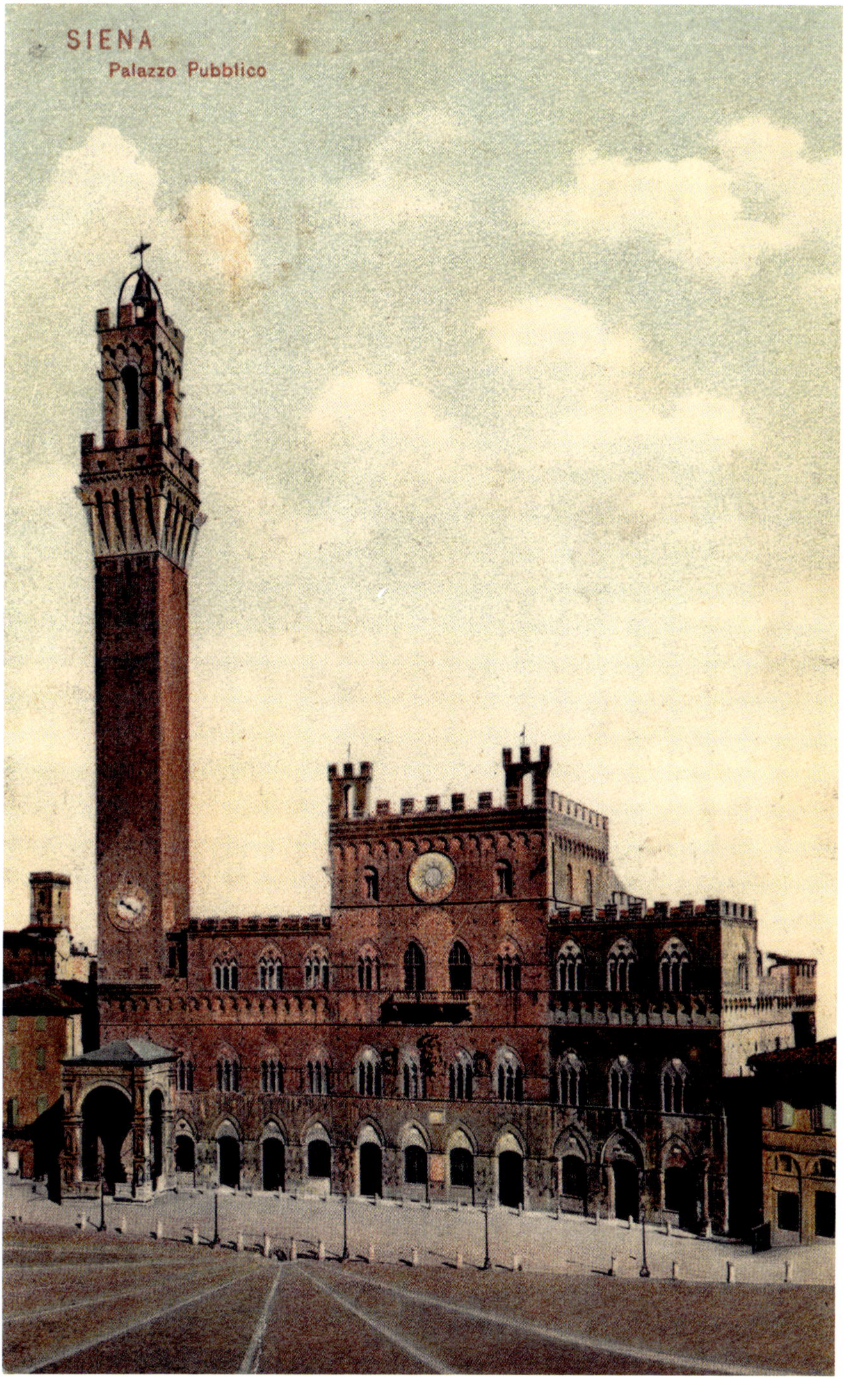
SIENA
Palazzo Pubblico

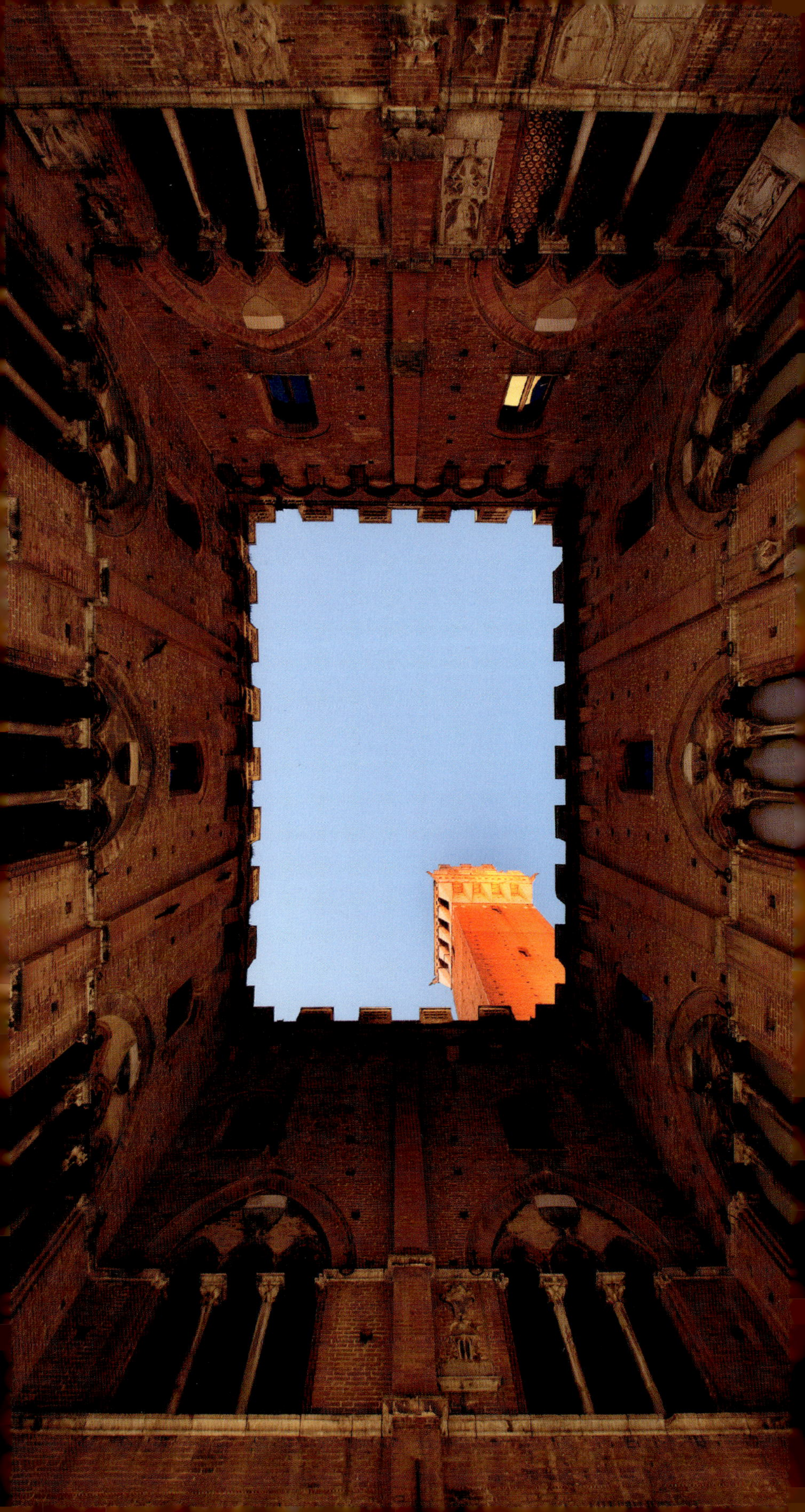

## The Course through the Museum

# The History of Siena Painted on the Walls

*Letizia Galli*

An evocative view of the Torre del Mangia seen from the Cortile del Podestà

Horses in the *Entrone* during the days of the Palio

The Cortile del Podestà, through which visitors walk to the entrance to the Civic Museum, is a spacious, stately atrium in the style of the fourteenth century. Standing in the middle, one has an evocative view of the Torre del Mangia, framed photographically by the merlons of the crenellation atop the palace. On the left side of the courtyard are the stairs leading to the ticket booth for the Torre del Mangia and on the back wall are two doors to the Teatro dei Rinnovati.

For the Sienese, however, what is familiarly called the *Entrone* (the Big Entrance) is not just any courtyard. During the days of the Palio, it holds the horses and jockeys, and here they spend the last minutes before the race. Enclosed and calm, protected from the noise in the square, strictly forbidden to all but a very few people, it is pervaded in those moments by a magical, mysterious atmosphere, while with the last-minute agreements, final finishing touches to the horses and exhortations to the jockeys, the efforts are made to put in place the last squares of the mosaic which, in reality, only the hand of Fortune will bring to completion with the longed-for victory in the race.

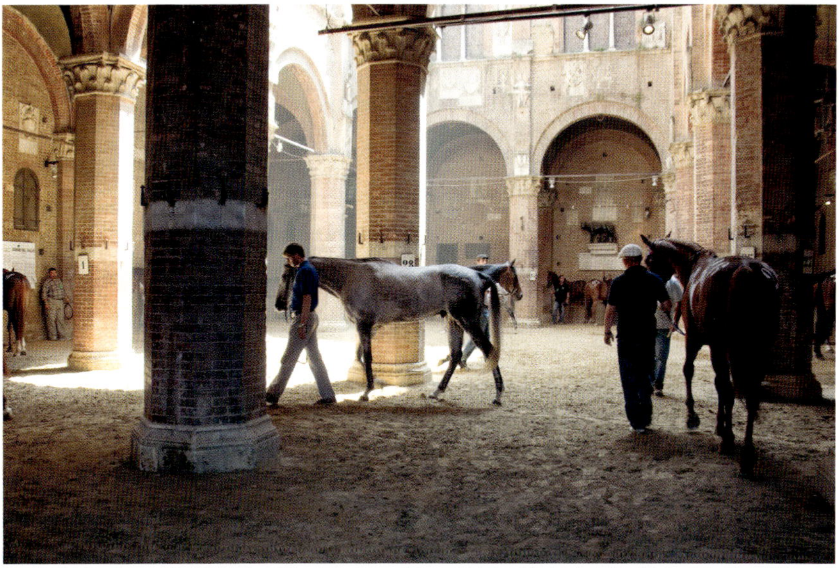

A curious note

# *Mangia*, Ringer of the Hours

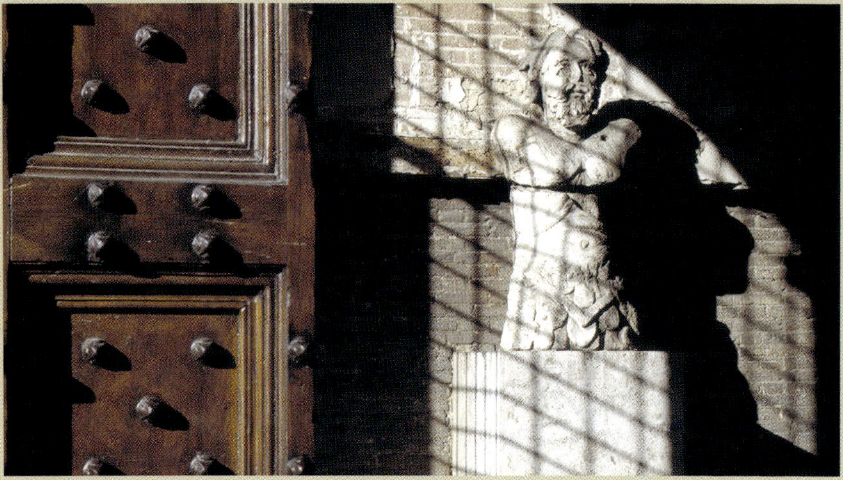

In the discreet shadows of a corner of the Entrone is a strange travertine sculpture, the broken-off torso of a bearded man in the guise of a proud warrior. This is Mangia, a sculpted depiction, made in the second half of the eighteenth century by the Florentine sculptor Angiolo Bini, of the legendary bell-ringer in the civic tower, which became known as the Torre del Mangia, "Mangia's tower," because of him.

When the first bell was placed on the just-finished tower, a certain "Giovanni di Balduccio" was hired to ring the hours. It seems he was a wastrel, and because of this he was called "Wage-eater," or more simply "Eater." His name, or rather nickname, was later transferred to the mechanical automaton installed in 1400 to strike the hour, replacing the human bell-ringer, after a mechanical clock had been installed in the tower in 1360.

In reality, nobody knows exactly why the tower took the name of Mangia, if not for the simple reasons just mentioned. However, it is certain that the mechanical automatons which one after the other were placed on top of the tower to strike the hours marking off the days of the Sienese were all called by the same name, until the end of the eighteenth century when the last Mangia was taken down and never replaced. Abandoned in a storeroom and then found again by chance, Mangia now stands here, slightly hidden, but always vigilant – a mute and legendary figure never forgotten by his fellow citizens.

(L.G.)

The statue of *Mangia*

The stairs leading up to the museum.
In the display case, the bronze bell originally in the church of San Cristoforo

The entrance to the Civic Museum is just off the Cortile del Podestà. On the first floor of Palazzo Pubblico, it takes visitors into the heart of what was and still is the emblematic place of this city and its history.

The museum is rich and rather spread out, so at least one hour should be set aside for even a hurried tour giving an overview of the art and objects displayed there.

In the broad historical and artistic context unfolding before the visitor, the suggested itinerary will necessary follow a chronological criterion, starting from the early fourteenth and ending in the late nineteenth century.

In the stairwell, on the landing of the first flight of stairs are fifteenth-century treasure chests. The bronze bell in the showcase dates to 1109 and comes from the church of San Cristoforo, where the Sienese government used to meet before the Palazzo Pubblico was built.

Continuing up the stairs and turning left past the bookshop, cross three rooms (the Sala del Risorgimento, Sala di Balìa, and Anticamera del Concistoro) to enter the so-called Sala del Mappamondo (Map Room).

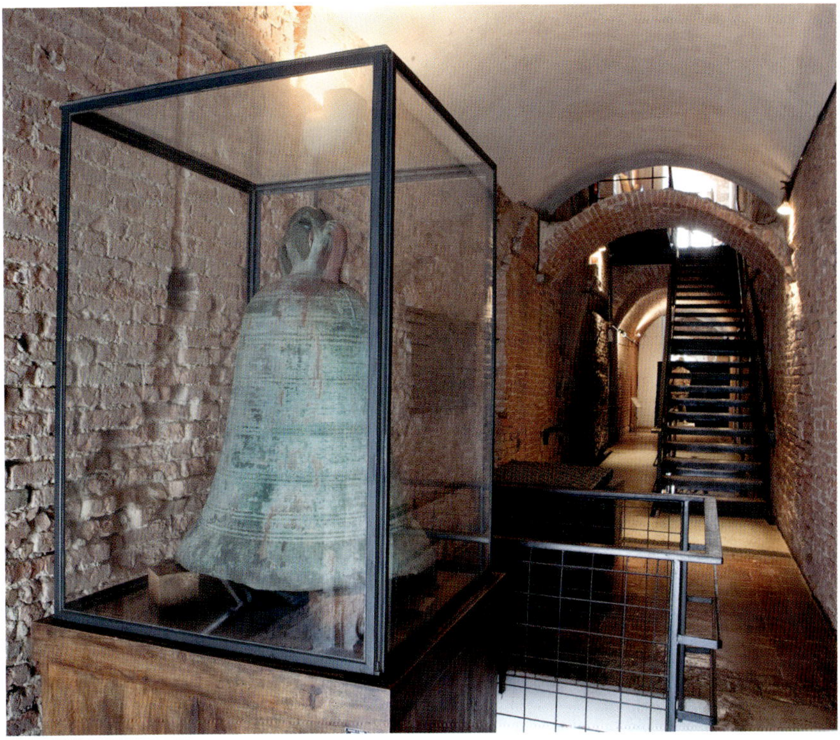

## The Sala del Mappamondo

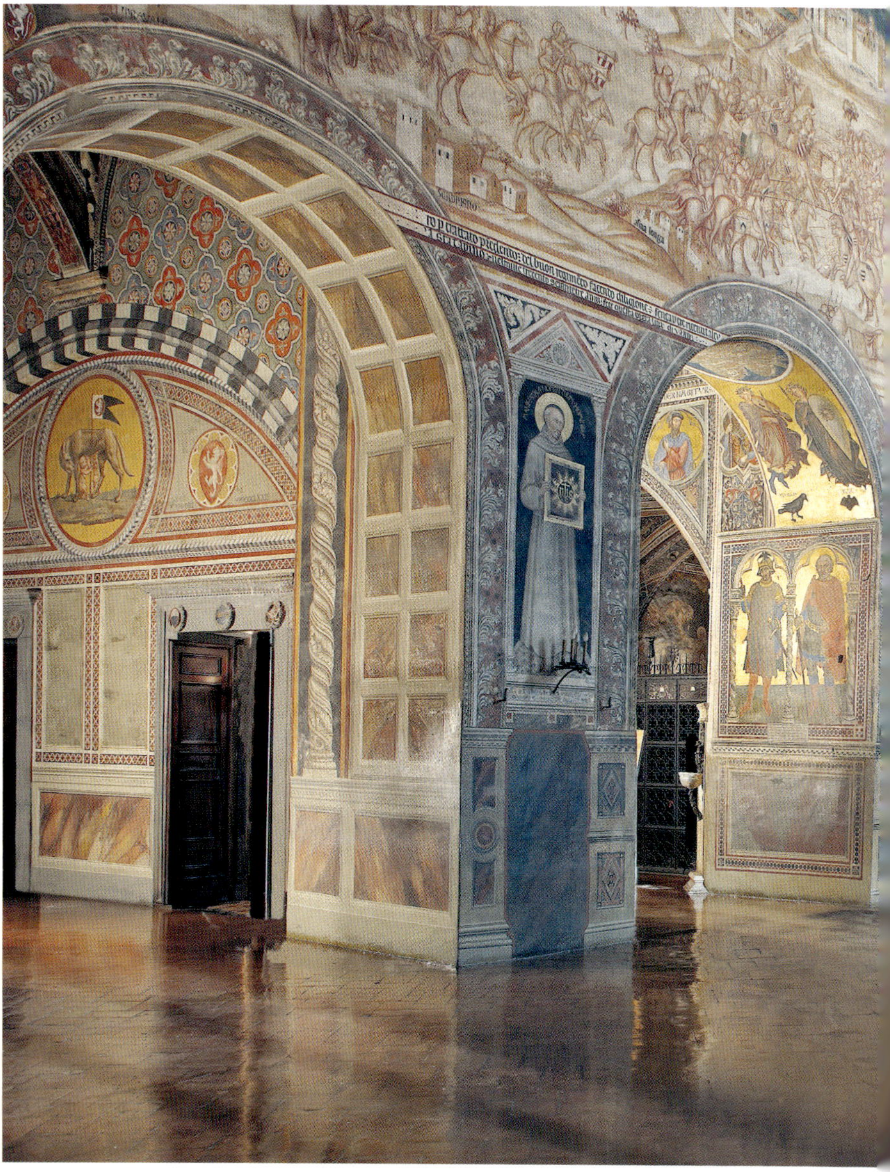

The Sala del Mappamondo, or "Map Room"

This room was created inside the palace to hold the meetings of the General Council, which was also called the "Council of the Bell" because a bell was rung to convoke the meetings. The map of the world (*mappamondo*), now lost, was a large wooden disc, whose surviving parts were still visible in 1752; it revolved around a central pivot, as can be intuited by the traces left in the center of the wall. A map on paper or parchment, or perhaps cloth, was attached to this "wheel," on which Ambrogio Lorenzetti painted in 1344 the lands known at the time, with special

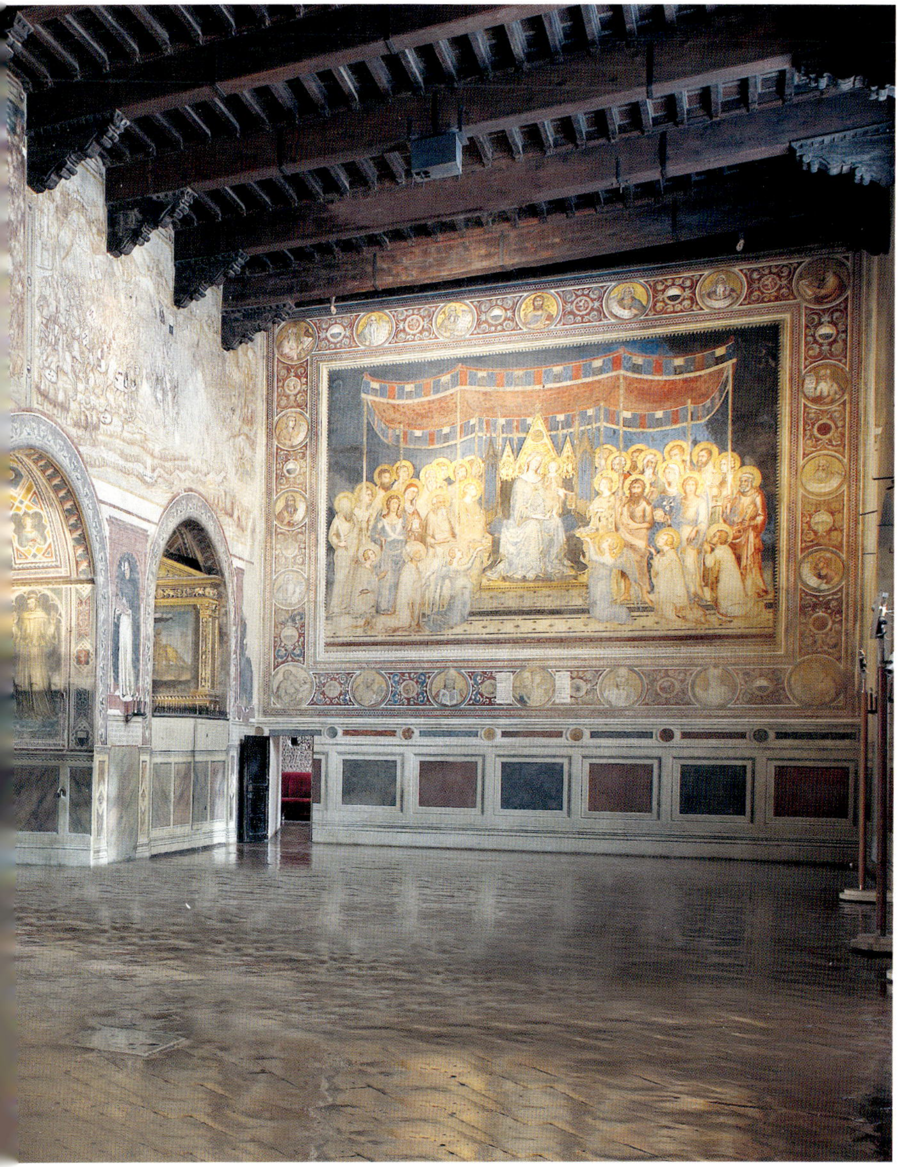

attention to Italy and the possessions of the state of Siena. The frescoes, on sacred and profane subjects, which over a span of three centuries entirely covered the walls of the large room, range in import from the highly sacred, devotional value of the *Virgin and Child Enthroned in Majesty* (the *Maestà*) to the more strictly political nature of the horseman *Guidoriccio* depicted among the conquered castles, but they all transmit the same message: that of a rich, powerful and proud city, but at the same time humble and meek in the face of divine might.

# The Protagonists
## Simone Martini

Simone Martini, *The Virgin and Child*, Siena, Pinacoteca Nazionale

Simone Martini, *Blessed Agostino Novello and Four of his Miracles*, Siena, Pinacoteca Nazionale

The prevalent opinion among critics by now is that Simone, whose work represents the summit of the Gothic style in Sienese painting, was born in Siena around 1284 and trained as an artist in the flourishing workshop of Duccio di Buoninsegna around the turn of the fourteenth century. His earliest production, unanimously recognized as the parts of the *Maestà* in Siena's Palazzo Pubblico preceding the readaptation of 1321, the *Virgin and Child* (no. 583) in the Pinacoteca Nazionale in Siena, and the *Virgin of Mercy* in Vertine, in the Chianti region, show the strong influence of Duccio. Even though still young, Simone must have already been a successful artist when the government of the Nine decided to give him the commission for the *Maestà*, the most emblematic painting in the large audience chamber of Siena's seat of government. In the first version of the fresco, finished in 1315, Simone already presents an original, fully formed style, uniting reminders of the Sienese school with an up-to-date knowledge of Gothic art from beyond the Alps and suggestions from Giotto. The intensification of this latter aspect as he worked on this painting, his first masterpiece, makes it extremely likely that Simone was working at the same time on the decoration of the Saint Martin chapel in the Lower church of San Francesco in Assisi (concluded in 1317), which would have enabled a more direct approach to the art of Giotto. During the interval between the *Maestà* in Siena and the frescoes in Assisi, he probably painted the polyptych originally destined to the church of Sant'Agostino in San Gimignano (now dismantled and divided among Italian and foreign museums) and the cartoons for the mosaics in the side apses of Pisa cathedral, as well as the gabled altarpiece showing *Saint Louis of Toulouse Crowning his Brother Robert of Anjou*, made for the canonization of the saint on 7 April 1317. Before 1321, the date of the reworking of the *Maestà*, Simone must also have painted both a polyptych, reported as having been at one time inside the Palazzo Pubblico in Siena and now divided among various foreign museums, and the much more complex altarpiece made for the church of Santa Caterina in Pisa, which the seventeenth-century annals of the adjacent Dominican convent report was done in 1319-1320. He then worked in Orvieto where, as the head of a booming, well-organized workshop, he produced three

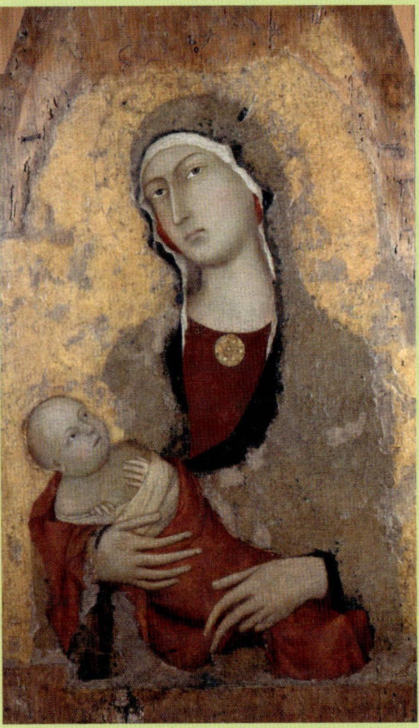

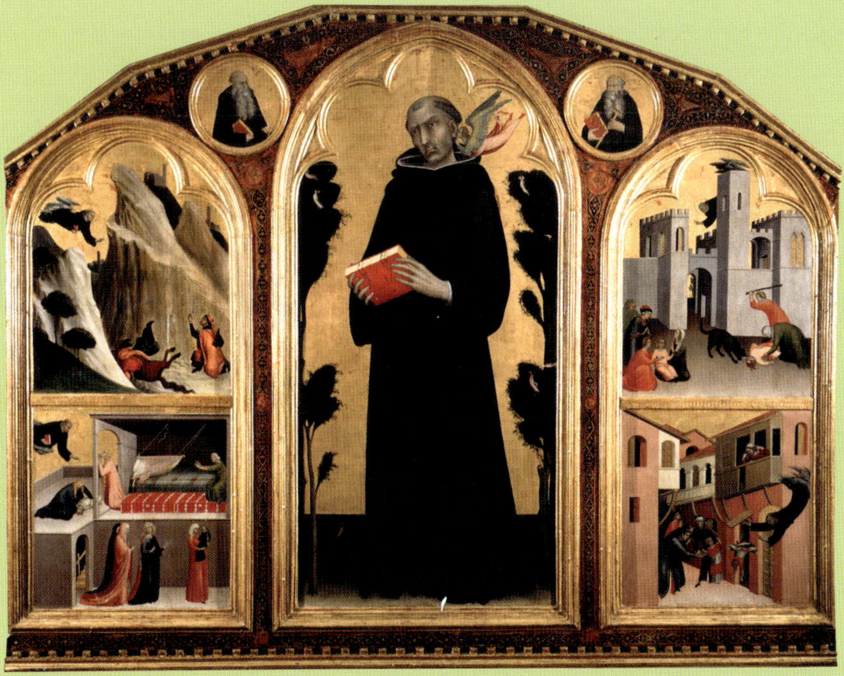

polyptychs: for the Dominican church, commissioned by bishop Trasmondo Monaldeschi, and for the churches of Santa Maria dei Servi and San Francesco. The paintings in Orvieto, similarly to the more or less contemporary panel painting of *Blessed Agostino Novello and Four of his Miracles*, probably originally above the tomb-altar of the saint erected in 1324 inside the Augustinian church in Siena, and the wing of a diptych showing *Saint Ladislaus of Hungary*, of 1326, show his increased interest in the three-dimensionality of the figures and the study of space. He was active again in the Audience Chamber of the Palazzo Pubblico in Siena in 1328, when he painted the large fresco of the mercenary soldier *Guidoriccio da Fogliano*, which is usually linked to a series of payments made to him by the government of Siena for painting frescoes of the castles of Montemassi and Sassoforte. In 1333, by now about to leave for the papal court at Avignon, from which he would never return, Simone signed, together with his brother-in-law Lippo Memmi, *The Annunciation with Saints Ansanus and Massima* for the altar dedicated to Saint Ansanus inside the cathedral, his last masterpiece made for his homeland. In France, Simone appears in documents for the first time in 1336, when Petrarch, his close friend during those years in Avignon, mentions him in some of his writings. Unfortunately, little remains of the final phase of the master's activity in Avignon. After the destruction in 1828 of the fresco of *Saint George and the Dragon* in the church of Notre Dame des Doms and the loss of the famous *Portrait of Laura* made for Petrarch, all that survives of Simone's certain late work are the small *Passion Polyptych*, dismantled and divided among various foreign museums, the miniature on the frontispiece of the *Aeneid* now in the Biblioteca Ambrosiana in Milan, the frescoes on the tympanum and portal of the church of Notre Dame des Doms in Avignon, and the *Holy Family* in the Walker Art Gallery in Liverpool, which bears the date 1342.

Simone probably died in Avignon in 1344, the year reported by Giorgio Vasari as appearing in his now lost funerary epitaph.

(V.R.)

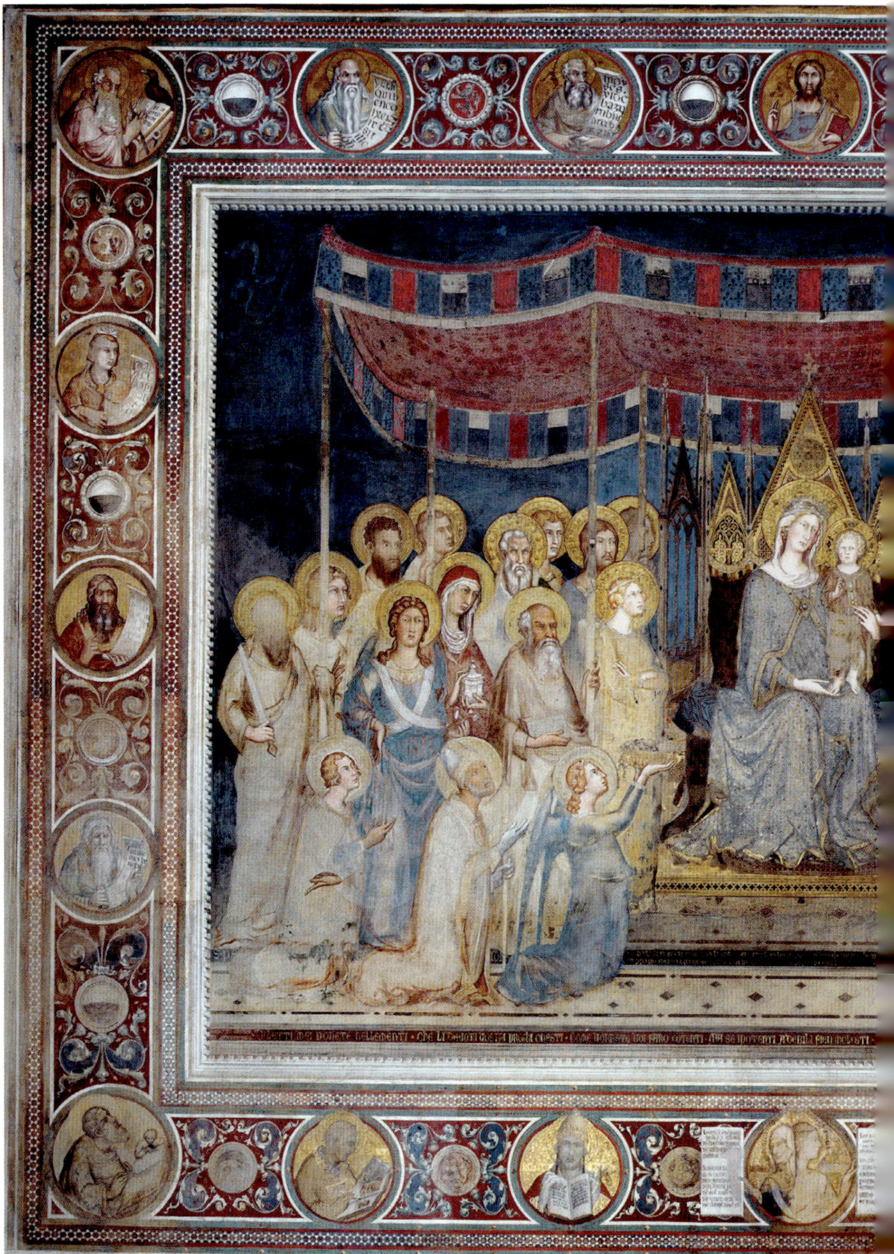

***The Virgin and Child Enthroned in Majesty*, by Simone Martini**

Simone Martini (ca. 1284-1344) worked for the Commune of Siena starting in 1315, but a large part of these works has been lost. The painting generally called the *Maestà* (1315-1321), commissioned for the most important room in Palazzo Pubblico, is his earliest autograph work.

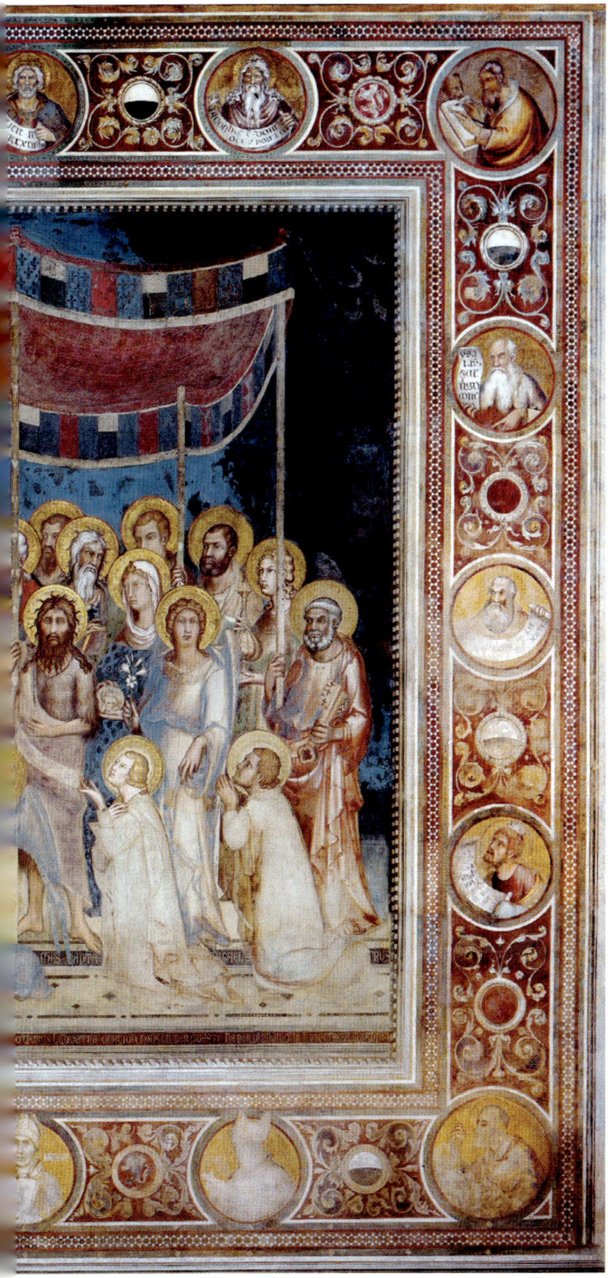

Simone Martini,
the *Maestà*

The grand fresco, which takes up an entire wall of the room, shows the Virgin Mary enthroned, holding the Child, and surrounded by angels and saints. Around the whole scene, set under an elegant canopy tent, is a painted frame decorated with medallions showing Christ giving his blessing, prophets, the evangelists – recognizable in the corners by their iconographic symbols – and the emblems of the Commune of Siena, with the black and white Balzana and the coat of arms of the Sienese people,

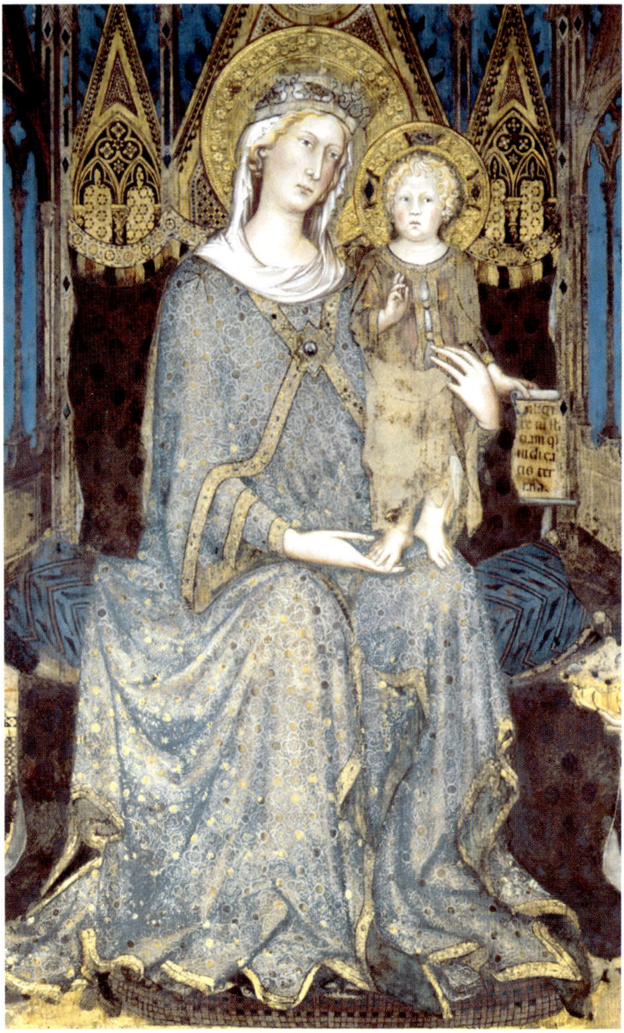

Simone Martini, the *Maestà*, detail

a rampant lion on a red field. The artist's signature is found in what remains of an inscription incised into the plaster, unfortunately only partially visible, in the center of the wall under the lower edge of the fresco, which reads "S...A MAN DI SYMONE" [S…A (Siena) by the hand of Simone]. The date, 1315, is also painted in capital letters in a section of the cornice painted around the *Maestà*, which reads "MILLE TRECENTO QUINDICI VOLTO / E DELIA AVRA' OGNI BEL FIORE SPINTO / ET JUNIO GIÀ GRIDAVA I' MI RIVOLTO / SIENA A MAN DI SIMONE M'HA DIPINTO". The dedicatory tercet, containing the fresco's date ("One thousand three hundred fifteen") and the name of its author ("the hand of Simone painted me"), alludes also to the period of the year when it was painted, between the spring, when Delia makes the flowers bloom, and the end of June, the month dear to Juno.

A curious note

# Painted Arms for the *Maestà*

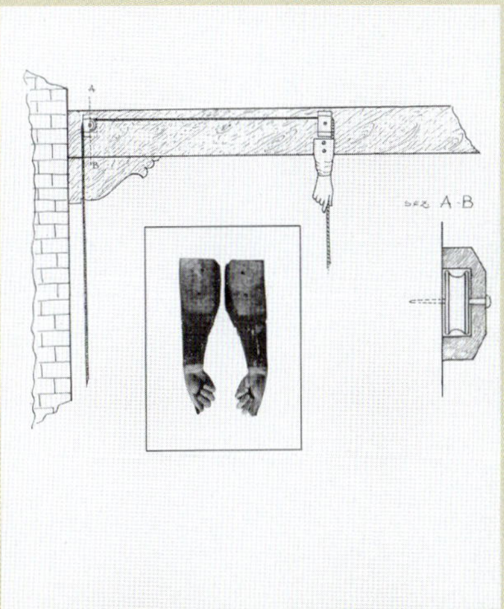


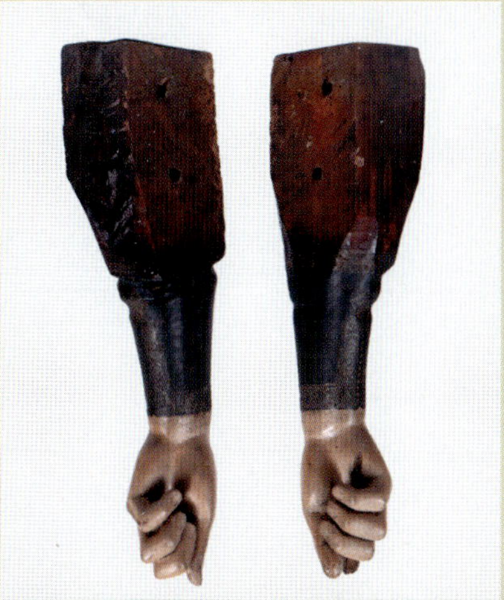

If you stand in front of the *Maestà* by Simone Martini and lift your eyes up high, you will see two wooden forearms handing from the ceiling. These are part of the mechanism used to raise and lower the votive lamps kept burning in front of the sacred image of the Virgin. They are true wooden sculptures, even though made for an unusual purpose. The chains supporting the lamps ran from the pulleys above, which were attached to either side of the fresco, through the curved fingers and palm of the hands. The hands are supported by two forearms, meticulously sculpted and painted, with sleeves forming soft folds and adorned with little buttons at the wrists. The paint, now somewhat faded, must have once been bright and colorful, with the lacquer red of the sleeves, embellished by decorations, juxtaposed to the pink flesh of the hands with their slender, elegant fingers. The great attention to the making of these objects, destined to a practical use and hardly visible, is astounding. But this may be explained by the fact that in any case these were part of the devotional apparatus for the *Maestà*. The date of these two precious pieces, which can be attributed to an artist in the circle of Simone Martini, must not be too distant from that of the *Maestà* itself, since it is very likely that they were attached to the ceiling using the same scaffolding mounted for the painting of the fresco.

(L.G.)

Explanatory drawing for attaching the wooden forearms to the ceiling, first half of 14th century

Wooden forearms, first half of 14th century

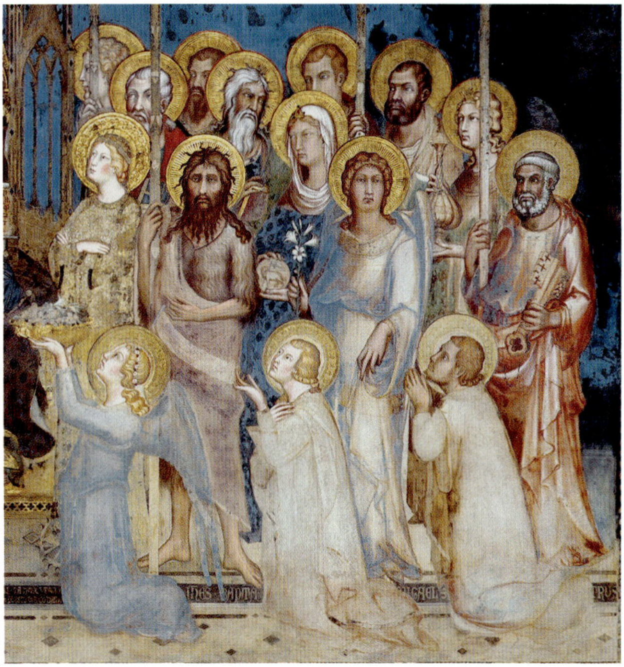

Simone Martini, the *Maestà*, detail

Simone himself and his workshop assistants returned to the painting in 1321, at the patron's request, adding an inscription at the base of the throne. As we said above, the Virgin Mary is placed in the center of the picture, sitting on an elegant throne with Gothic lines and decorations; on her left are Saints Catherine of Alexandria, John the Evangelist, Mary Magdalene, the archangel Gabriel, and Saint Paul, and on her right Saints Barbara, John the Baptist, Agnes, the archangel Michael, and Saint Peter. Kneeling at their feet and turning towards the Virgin are Siena's four patron saints, from left Ansanus, Sabinus, Crescentius, and Victor, introduced by two angels offering roses and lilies, to invoke divine protection for the city and its inhabitants. The great innovation of this painting lies in the composition of the scene, set under a canopy whose poles mark off the portion of space in which the figures are positioned. A crowd of figures surrounds the Virgin, an elegant, refined lady. Even though forced into a small space, the people do not jostle each other but are lively and vivacious in their facial expressions and poses. Seen from the back of the room, the picture, set under a pavilion with a colored tent like at a knightly tournament, with soft but lively colors and lit by the gleams of the gold of the haloes and decorations, seems to evoke more the atmosphere of a secular court than a solemn sacred procession. But the intent of the governors of Siena who commissioned this painting was unquestionably a devout one, renewing Siena's faith and love for the Virgin.

# A Comparison of Three Versions of the *Maestà*

*Madonna dagli Occhi Grossi*, 13th century, Siena, Museo dell'Opera

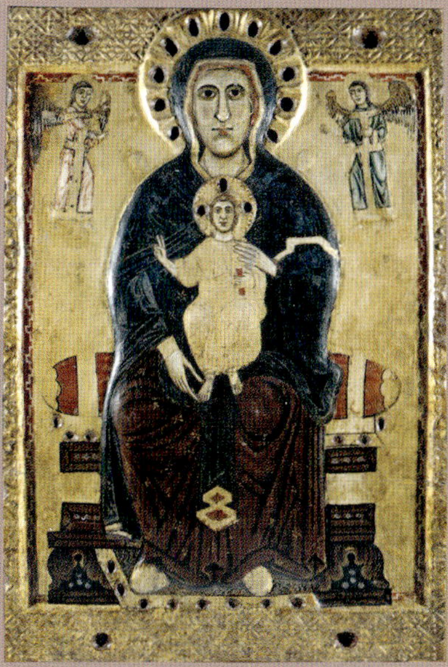

The close tie binding Siena to the Virgin Mary, often manifested in the course of the Middle Ages by the epithet of *civitas Virginis* (the Virgin's city), has ancient roots. The story is told that on the eve of the Battle of Montaperti, fought in 1260 against the Florentine army, the Sienese went in solemn procession into the cathedral, where they offered the keys to the city to the icon of the Virgin Mary which is now kept in the Museo dell'Opera and known as the *Madonna dagli Occhi Grossi* ("Madonna of the Big Eyes"), thus turning the city over to the Mother of Christ. As a result of the Sienese victory, the Virgin was honored with a new image, still venerated today inside the cathedral with the title of the *Madonna del Voto* ("Our Lady of Vows"), and became the official advocate of the city of Siena. The preferential relation between the Sienese and their heavenly protector was reiterated a few decades later in the inscription on the step of the throne where Mary sits in the great altarpiece painted by Duccio between 1308 and 1311 for the cathedral's high altar, known familiarly as the *Maestà*; probably following an indication by the city authorities, it asks her to protect Siena and the artist who painted the picture. Duccio's *Maestà* manifests an eminently sacred meaning in its severe abstract aspect of a neo-Byzantine icon aloof from the public, even though the exaltation of the civic value of the painting is made clear not only by the inscription and the presence of Siena's patron saints shown interceding at the foot of the Virgin's throne, but also by the meticulous description of its transport from the artist's workshop to the cathedral, accompanied by the highest officials of the commune and all the population, passing meaningfully across Piazza del Campo, the place that is the symbol of secular power.

Despite the apparent resemblance deriving from the analogous subject, a radically different concept is expressed only four years later in Simone Martini's *Maestà*. Even though respecting the obligatory nature of Duccio's model, the fresco in Palazzo Pubblico presents a more complex iconographical program which adapts the sacred subject to specific demands of political ethics. This added value therefore makes it necessary for the scene not only to have great impact, but also be a believable representation of reality. People entering the room were not supposed to find themselves in front of an unchanging image of a distant and unreachable

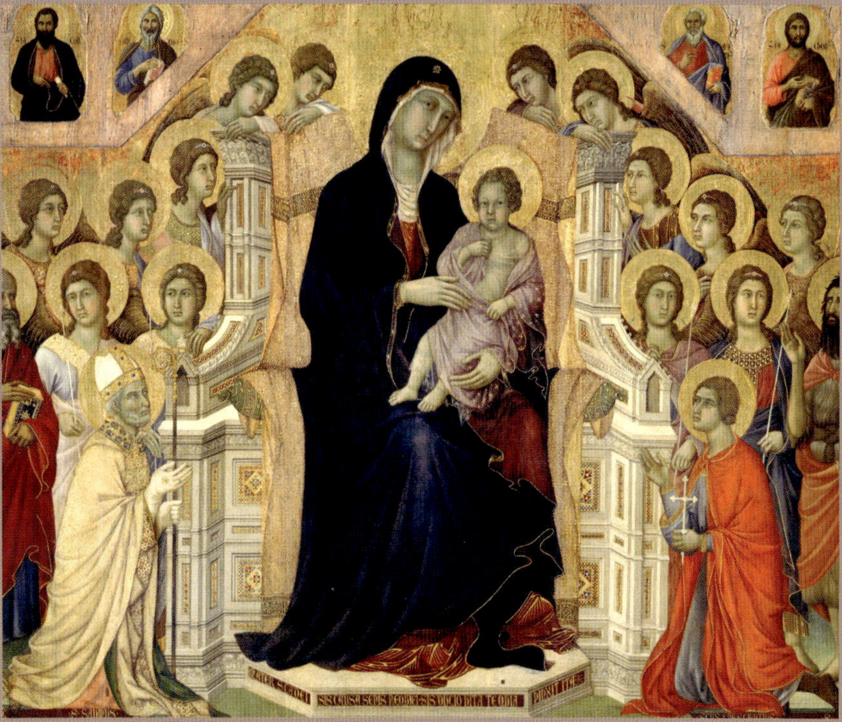

paradise, but the welcoming, real depiction of a court. Within the bounds of the fresco, the close connection between the central image and the communal government of Siena who commissioned it is made clear in the iconographical program of the frame. Here we find pictures of Christ giving his blessing, the Patriarchs, Prophets, Evangelists, and Doctors of the Church, alternating with civic emblems: a Sienese coin (a silver *grosso*), the She-wolf nursing the twins, the Balzana, and the rampant lion which is the symbol of the Sienese people. As a reinforcing element, like on an official document on parchment which concluded with the seal of the person responsible for its text, the great fresco presents, painted at the bottom, the seals of the Republic of Siena and the Captain of the People, which authenticate both the sacred image and its political content. The most pronounced innovation introduced by Simone in this *Maestà* is nonetheless represented by the fact that the Queen of Heaven is no longer portrayed as the passive object of prayers and requests, but in the active role of dispenser of ethical and moral precepts. The picture's meaning is not entrusted solely to the mute eloquence of the image, but made explicit by the addition of written rhymed texts in the vulgate, which by facilitating understanding simulate a dialogue between the Virgin Mary and the observer. The first inscription, in which the Virgin answers the four patron saints of Siena, kneeling in the foreground at the foot of her throne in the act of asking her intercession to save the city, has these words: "My beloved, keep in mind that the devout honest prayers, as you wish, I will grant. But if the powerful cause harm to the weak, burdening them with shame or damage, your prayers are not for them or for anyone who deceives my land." Thus it contains a direct warning, addressed in particular to the members of the magistracies and the representatives of the three districts of the city who met in the great hall of the General

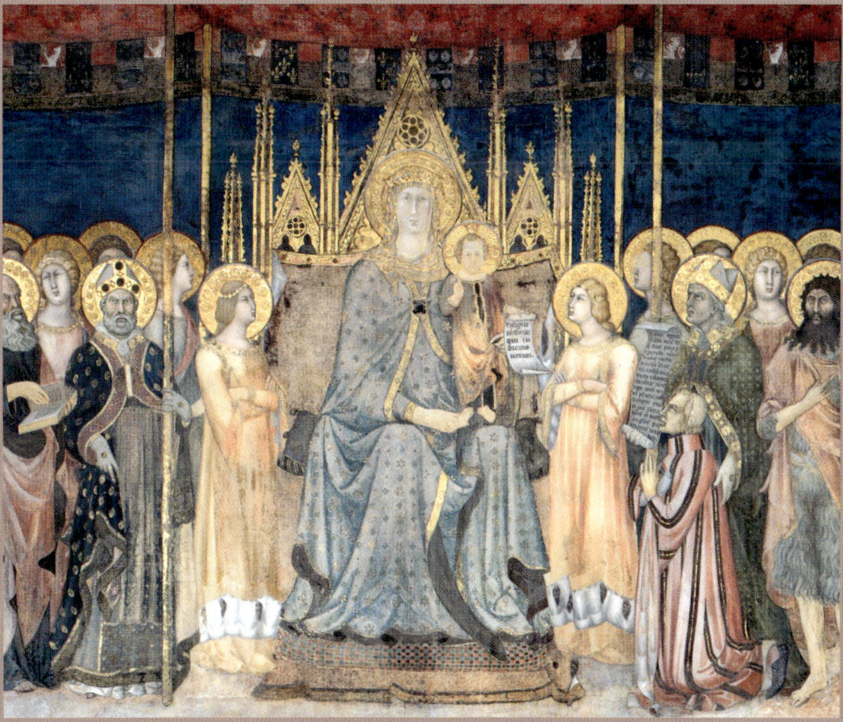

Council, admonishing them to respect justice and its correct administration in the observance of human and divine law. In the second inscription, placed on the step between the two kneeling angels ("The angelic little flowers, roses and lilies which adorn the heavenly meadow do not please me as much as good counsel.
But sometimes I see someone who because for his own position disdains me and deceives my land and when he speaks the worst is praised the most. Let each one whom these words condemn look out"), the Virgin severely censures those who put private interests before the good of the entire community, foreshadowing the theme that a few years later would form the guidelines for the fresco cycle painted by Ambrogio Lorenzetti in the adjacent room, the Sala della Pace ("the Peace Room"). Its great innovative effect on art, inviting secular aspect, and the public destination of Simone's *Maestà* made it immediately an unavoidable example which conditioned many artists and patrons eager to emulate the governors of Siena. Thus, just two years after the first version of the *Maestà* was finished, the *podestà* Nello di Mino Tolomei commissioned Lippo Memmi, Simone's brother-in-law, to paint a smaller replica in San Gimignano's Palazzo Comunale. But even though Lippo's *Maestà* is the vehicle of strong civic significance, its message appears weaker than that of the prototype. None of the dedicatory inscriptions appended to the picture succeed in creating a dialogue between the Queen of Heaven and her audience, and the inclusion of the patron in the picture seems to bring down to an individual level the higher universal message of Simone's *Maestà*.

(V.R.)

Duccio di Buoninsegna, the *Maestà*,
Siena, Museo dell'Opera

Lippo Memmi, the *Maestà*, detail,
San Gimignano, Palazzo Comunale

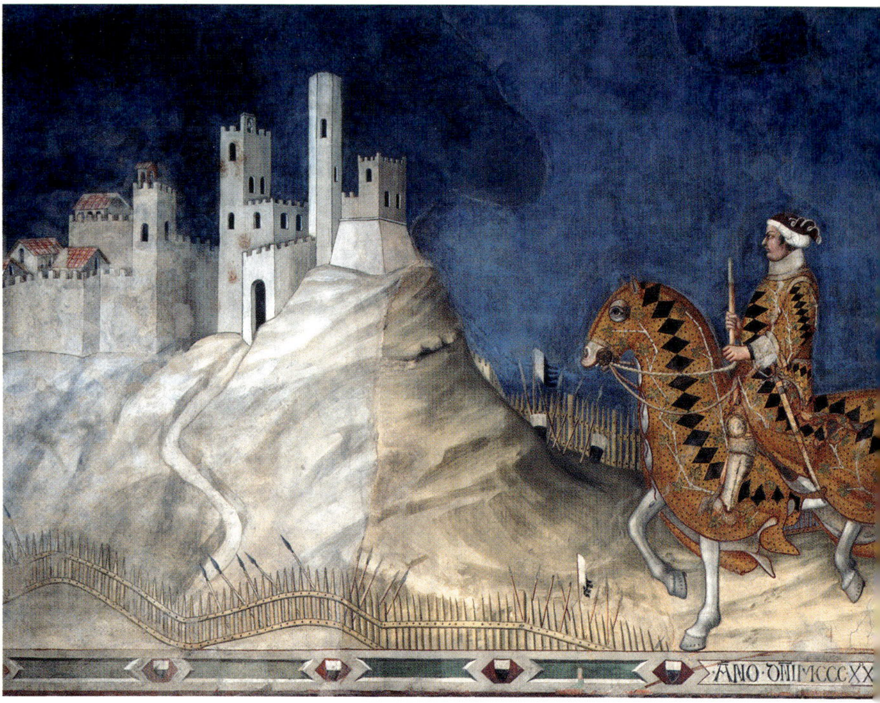


## Guidoriccio

The paintings on the wall opposite the *Maestà*, at the other end of the large Sala del Mappamondo, are perhaps one of the most interesting features of the Palazzo, certainly the one that is most debated and mysterious. They were painted over a stretch of time from the early fourteenth to the early sixteenth century, the period when the two patron saints of the city, *Saint Victor* and *Saint Ansanus*, were painted by Sodoma in 1529, partially covering other paintings already present on the wall.
It is just this problem of overlapping, dating, and identification, both of artist and subject, that is the subject of debate concerning these frescoes in recent years.
On the top section of the wall, Simone Martini was commissioned in 1328 to paint Guidoriccio da Fogliano, captain of the Sienese troops, shown on horseback in the center of a bare, deserted landscape among turreted castles and military camps. The scene shows the siege of Montemassi castle in the Maremma area, captured by the mercenary leading the Sienese troops. Montemassi appears on the left of the painting, perched on a hilltop, with its towers, village, and castle keep.

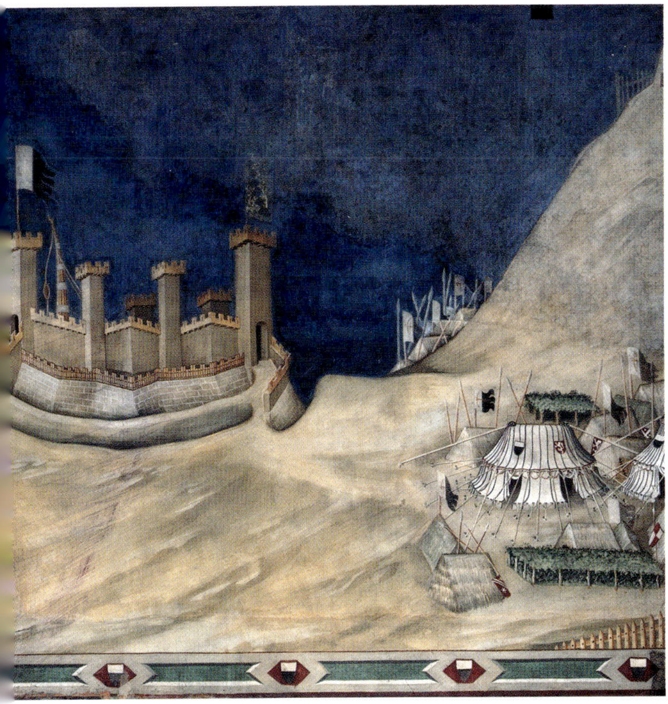

Simone Martini, *Guidoriccio da Fogliano*

On the hill facing Montemassi, the structure that some have identified as another castle, perhaps Sassoforte, seems in reality to be a *battifolle*, in essence a temporary wooden fort, used for the siege: in its center can be seen the top of the so-called '*pertica del trabocco*,' a medieval war machine made up of a bundle of flexible poles maneuvered by ropes, used like a slingshot to launch big rocks a considerable distance.
Below the *battifolle* is the Sienese soldiers' camp, with their tents over which the Sienese banners are flying, straw huts, and a vineyard. The battlefield is enclosed by a long wooden fence running the length of the fresco.
Guidoriccio, the victorious captain who had conquered these two castles for the Republic of Siena, merited the tribute of the Sienese and a portrait that undoubtedly has brought him more glory and fame than his military exploits.
Simone Martini shows him proud and elegant in his golden yellow tunic decorated by bands of black lozenges and leafy tendrils, and the matching horsecloth on his mount, equally stately with its parade gait. Originally the armor and horsecloth were covered by silver leaf, which has since been lost, although the imprints of the decorations applied to the wet plaster are still visible.

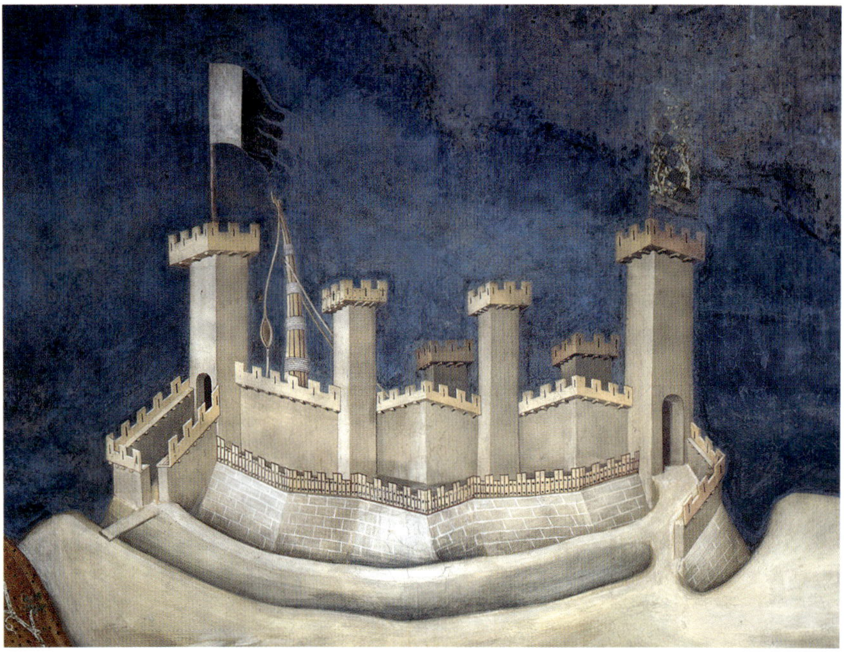

Simone Martini, *Guidoriccio da Fogliano*, detail of the battifolle

The image is on the borderline between a realistic, precise representation of a historically documented event and the transfigured celebration of a symbol.
The physical features of Guidoriccio, a noble from Reggio Emilia who lived for a while in Siena and died there in 1352, are a faithful likeness; his slightly chubby body, fleshy protruding lips, and short fat neck made this one of the earliest civilian portraits of the Middle Ages, and the landscape, too, resembles the reality of southern Tuscany, as does the setting of the scene.
But it is a superficial realism. The knight rides past, solemn and haughty, while around him all is deserted and silent, in a suggestive suspended unreal atmosphere, against the almost monochromatic background, marked off only by the contrast between the ochre of the countryside and the gray of the stone against the uniform deep blue sky.
Guidoriccio looks ahead and passes, proud and indifferent, as does his horse, erect and disdainful in his improbable gait (only two feet touch the ground and both of these are on the same side).

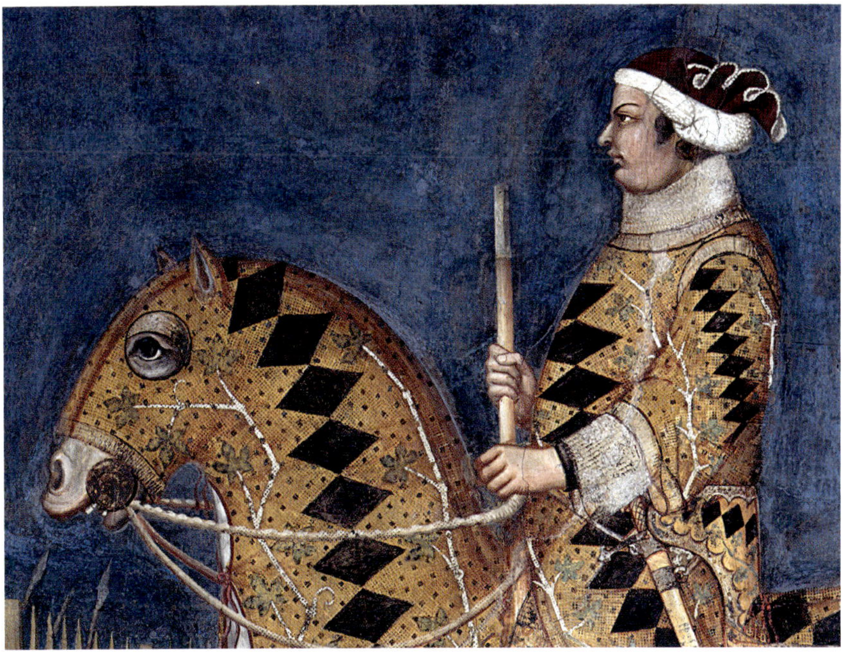

Simone Martini, *Guidoriccio da Fogliano*, detail

## Two Men and a Castle

The discussion among scholars about the attribution and date of the fresco arose at the beginning of the 1980s as the result of the sensational discovery, under a layer of plaster, of a painting earlier than the *Guidoriccio*, which partially overlaps the newly discovered one.
This older fresco is very beautiful and of high quality, but its subject and authorship are difficult to identify. It shows two figures in the foreground, with a fortified castle behind them. The work certainly fits into the iconographic program initiated at the beginning of the fourteenth century by the commune of Siena to present pictures of the castles conquered by the Republic of Siena in the Council Hall, celebrating its victories and victors, as in the case of Guidoriccio, in keeping with a didactic-informational intent that has few equals in Italy in this period, a sort of civilian, secular 'painted chronicle' which would reach its apex in the adjacent Sala della Pace, frescoed a few years later.
At the time of the discovery of the earlier painting, scholars split into two camps. The fresco was attributed to Simone Martini, who presumably depicted Guidoriccio's conquest of Arcidosso, but the names of Pietro Lorenzetti and Memmo di Filipuccio were advanced, even going so far as to hypothesize that the painting in question was a sixteenth-century reworking of an earlier painting.

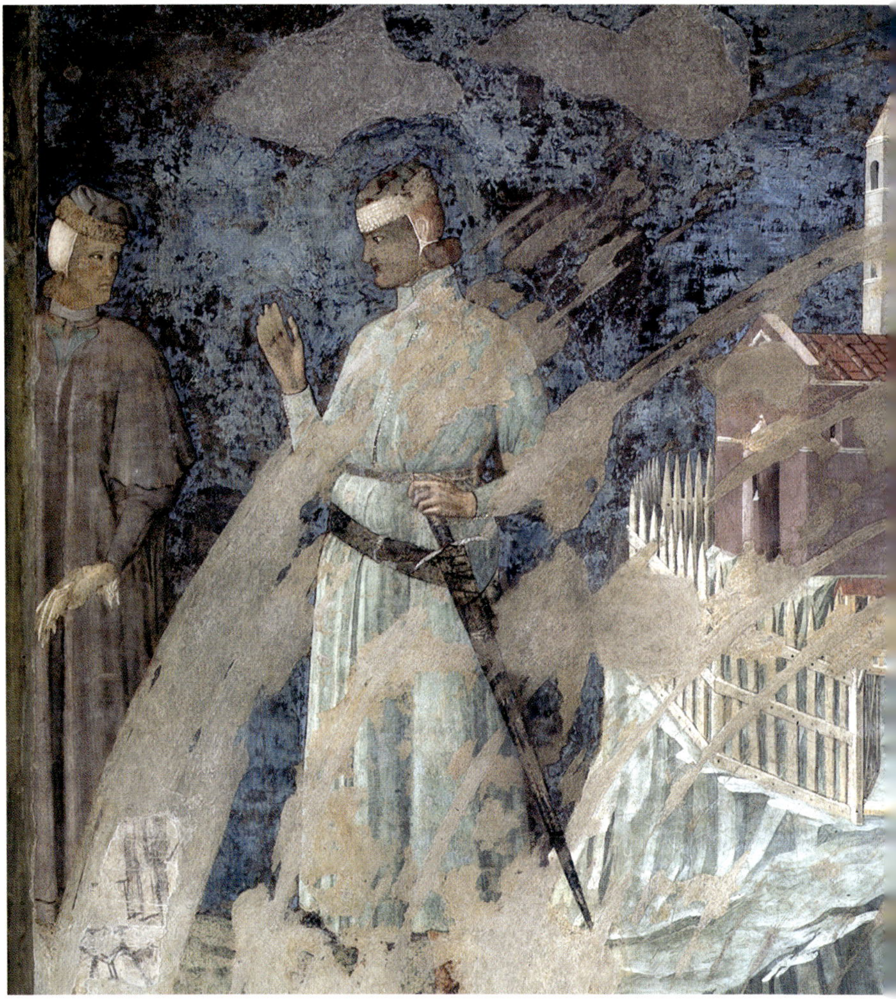

Among the host of proposals, the most accredited and accepted still today is that this is *The Consignment of Giuncarico Castle*, painted by Duccio.

Duccio di Buoninsegna, *Consignment of Giuncarico Castle*

This would be one of his few works in the fresco medium, dated in a late phase of his career, presumably around 1314, before his death in 1319.

The castle of Giuncarico, identified as the one in the fresco, was conquered in that year; it was destroyed, but it was located on the top of a steep hill like the one in the painting, and had a church next to it. The figures are probably the lord of Giuncarico Nello di Paganello and a member of the Nine come to take possession of the castle, which appears fortified but with the fence and castle gates open, and no sign of damage or soldiers, which seems to suggest

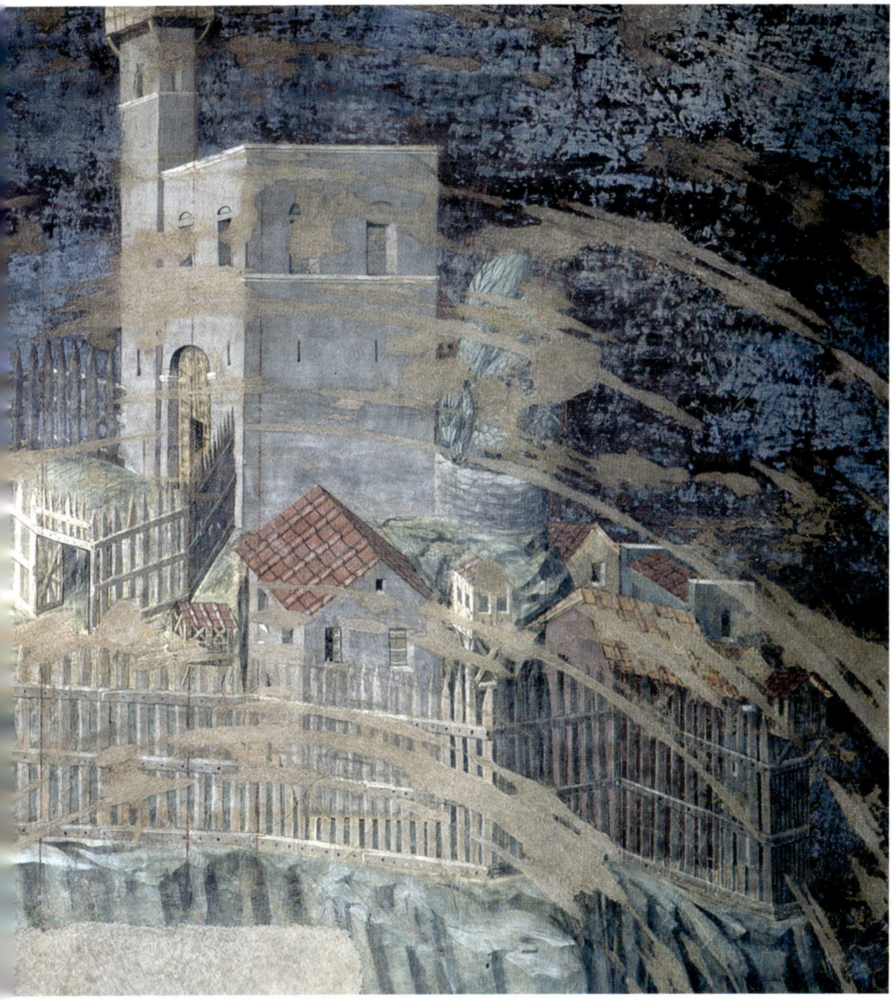

more an act of submission than a surrender after a siege, as in fact really happened. It is possible that besides the two figures still shown, also the *podestà* of Siena and other members of the city government were depicted, but were later covered up by the sixteenth-century fresco.
Barring further discoveries, at the moment this is the oldest painting in the building, and is also one of the earliest depictions of a real landscape, not tied to other scenes, in what seems to be a very early version of a "history painting."
Relatively well preserved as to color and the surviving image, the painting was damaged by the circular abrasions caused by what was, in all probability, the revolving map which gave the room its name.

# The Protagonists
## Duccio di Buoninsegna

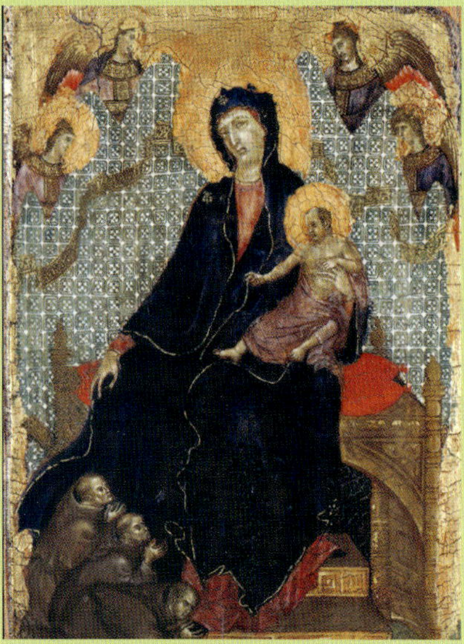

The earliest recorded mention of Duccio di Buoninsegna, the founder and undisputed leader of the Sienese school of painting in the fourteenth century, concerns some payments to him in 1278 from the Commune of Siena for the decoration of twelve chests to hold public documents for safekeeping. His birth date must therefore have been around 1255. Later payment records, at intervals from 1279 to 1295, testify to his assiduous work in these years on minor commissions for the Commune of Siena, while the many fines he accumulated reveal a disorderly life and restless temperament. Duccio had already been working for some time when he received, from the Compagania dei Laudesi at Santa Maria Novella in Florence, the prestigious commission for the *Rucellai Madonna*, now in the Uffizi and the largest thirteenth-century Italian panel painting to survive to our day. Its strong Gothic component betrays the influence of northern artists working in Italy at the end of the thirteenth century. Duccio's stay in Florence is connected also with the wall paintings in the Saint Gregory chapel in Santa Maria Novella, brought back to light only at the beginning of the twentieth century. Duccio's presence in Florence in those years is certainly tied to his apprenticeship in Cimabue's workshop, as can be deduced from his earliest surviving work, the *Gualino Madonna*, which, like the other paintings assigned to his early phase (the *Madonna of Crevole* and the *Crucifix* showing the living Christ in the Salini collection), is characterized by the absence of Gothic elements and the rarefied, elegant sense of color which would become one of the distinguishing traits of his work and indeed of all Sienese painting at least until the sixteenth century. The little *Madonna of the Franciscans* in the Pinacoteca of Siena, in which the poses of the three friars still show strong echoes of Byzantine art, must also have been done shortly before the large panel in Florence. Among the few works that can be attributed to Duccio and dated with certainty in these years is the large round stained-glass window in the apse of Siena cathedral showing some *Stories from the Life of the Virgin Mary*, connected with two documents dated 1287 and 1288 which bear witness to the date of the commission. Divided into nine compartments, the window presents, for the first time in Sienese art, the motif of an architectonic throne, taking the place of the large wooden chairs of the Byzantine tradition, an innovation innate to the new concept of painted

Duccio di Buoninsegna, *The Madonna of the Franciscans*, Siena, Pinacoteca Nazionale

Duccio di Buoninsegna, *Stained glass window*, detail, Siena, Museo dell'Opera

space deriving from Giotto, who was also a disciple of Cimabue in the same years when Duccio was in his workshop. Sometime around the date of the window, this innovation would be repeated in the small *Maestà* in the Kunstmuseum in Bern. Duccio's next phase showed a further evolution of his style in the direction of a greater softening of the chiaroscuro and color, which become more subdued and less transparent. These aspects, which first appear in works like the *Virgin and Child* in the Galleria Nazionale dell'Umbria, the portable triptych in the National Gallery in London, the triptych belonging to the Queen of England, and the small panel formerly in the Stoclet collection, would reach their peak in the great altarpiece painted for Siena Cathedral. Among the lost works painted in this same period, especially important is a *Maestà* painted in 1302 for the chapel of the Nine inside Siena's Palazzo Pubblico, which represents an obligatory prototype for some paintings by his closest disciples in Siena. Works like the winged triptych in the Museum of Fine Arts in Boston, showing the *Crucifixion* in the center and *Saints Nicholas and Gregory the Great* on the sides, and polyptych no. 28 in the Siena Pinacoteca can be assigned to the intermediate period between the lost *Maestà* of 1302 and the one painted for Siena Cathedral. The first document which has come down to us concerning the great altarpiece, painted on both sides with pictures of the *Virgin and Child in Majesty* and *Episodes from the Life of Christ* for the high altar of the Cathedral, is dated 9 October 1308; the work

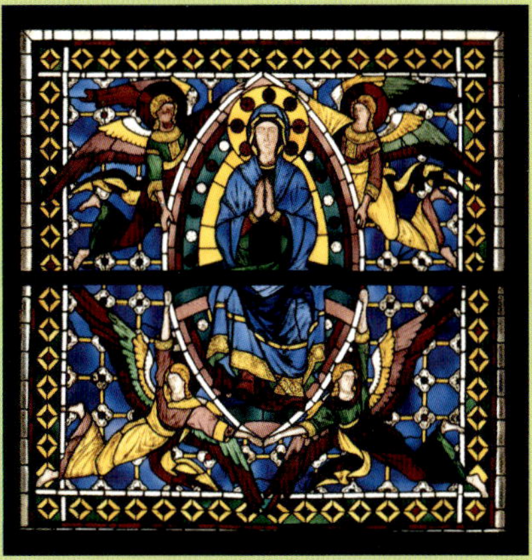

was already finished by June 1311. The true masterpiece of the artist's maturity, the painting to which Duccio proudly added the dedicatory prayer *Mater sancta Dei/ sis causa Senis requiei / sis Duccio vita / te quia pinxit ita* ("Holy Mother of God, bring peace to Siena and life to Duccio, because he painted you like this), despite the reductions it has suffered in the course of time, is unanimously considered a milestone of Italian art of all time because of its richness and complexity. The master's final phase, after the *Maestà*, resulted in the polyptych no. 47 in the Pinacoteca, the fresco of *The Delivery of a Castle* linked with the document in which on 30 March 1314 the General Council of the Republic of Siena resolved to have the castle of Giuncarico painted inside the main room of Palazzo Pubblico, and the *Maestà* for the cathedral of Massa Marittima, a replica of the one made for Siena Cathedral. Duccio was already dead by 1319, the date when his sons renounced all rights to their inheritance because of their fathers' many debts.

(V.R.)

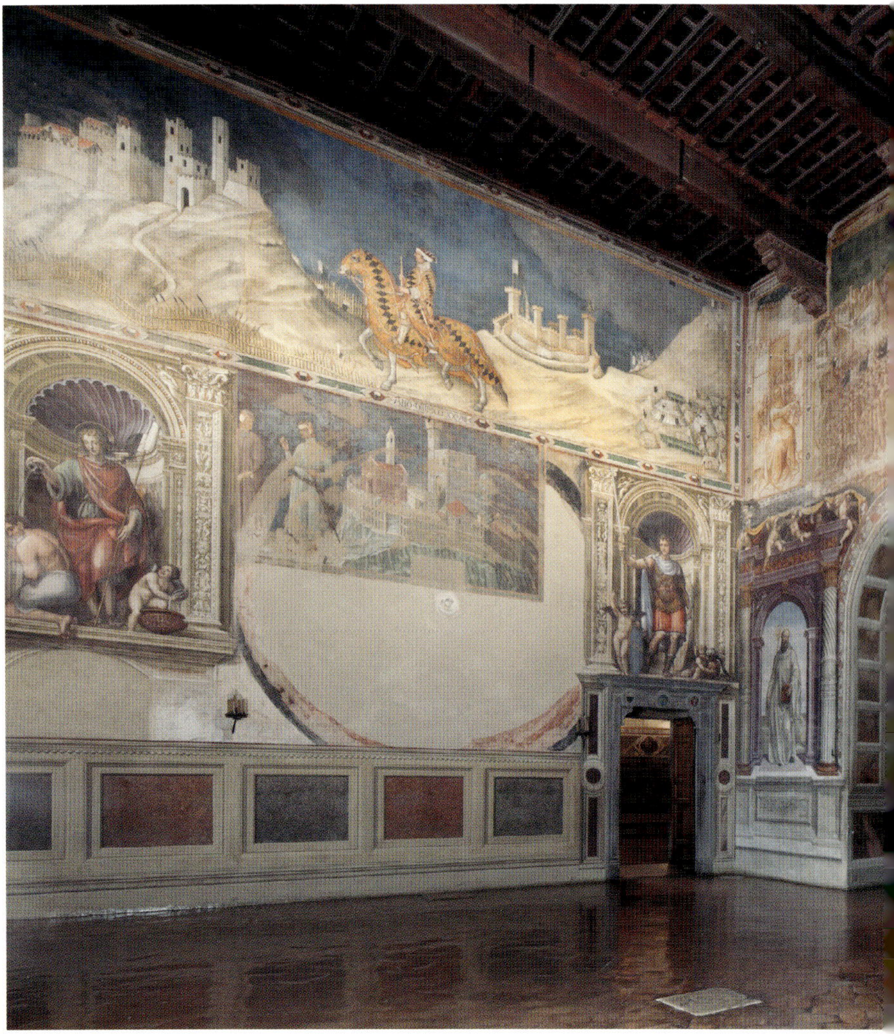

**The Battles**

The room's other wall presents in the upper section a monochrome depiction of two battle scenes, the *Battle of the Chiana Valley* (on the left), won by the Sienese and frescoed by Lippo Vanni in 1363, and the *Battle of Poggio Imperiale* (1480), a clash between the Sienese and the Florentines, won by the Sienese on 8 September 1479.
The *Battle of the Chiana Valley* commemorates the victory by the Sienese troops, led by Count Giordano Orsini, over the Bretons in the 'Company of the Hat,' commanded by Niccolò da Montefeltro, in the Chiana valley in the southern part of the territory of Siena, looking towards Arezzo. This was an important event for the Republic of Siena, since it came at a crucial time in local history, when the city, still suffering from the social and economic aftereffects of

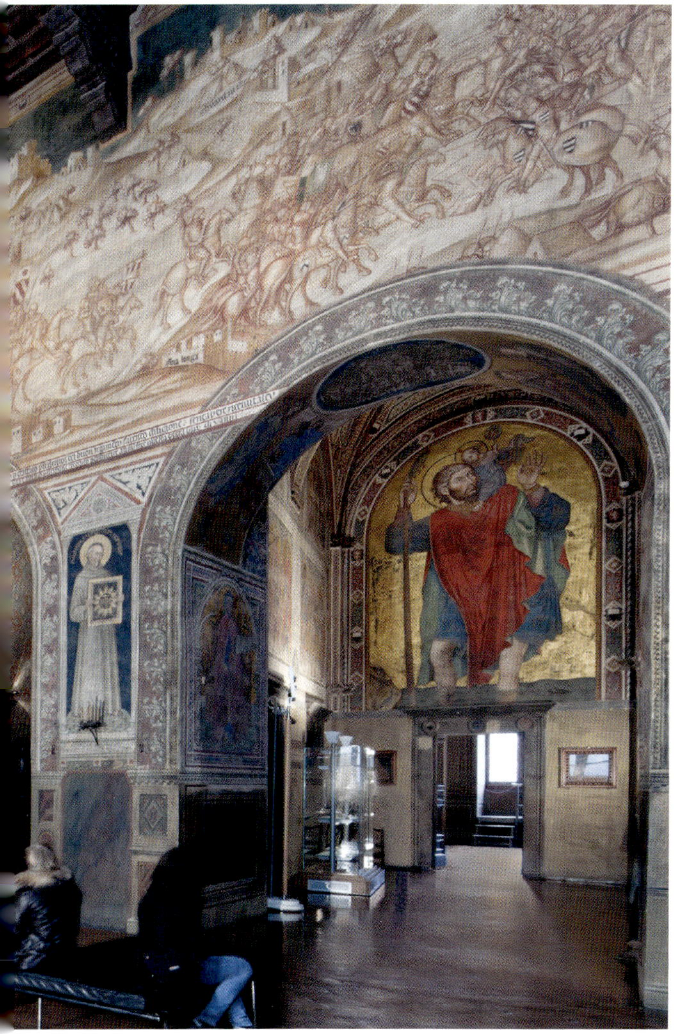

The Sala del Mappamondo (on the right, the wall showing the battles)

the terrible plague that struck it in 1348, went through a severe political and institutional crisis because of the fall in 1355 of the Government of the Nine, which had been in power since 1287. The victory in a major battle thus becomes an event to be commemorated, and as such worthy of being immortalized in the main room of Palazzo Pubblico, in keeping with the established trend of fixing in images the most important and meaningful elements of civic and religious glory.

The large fresco of the battle, painted in monochrome with dark-brown earth (*terretta*) on a blue background, is divided into two overlapping planes. The valley serves as background for the scene of the fighting, with the castles and villages marked with their names, well-known places that still today preserve the same names, like Farnetella, Travale, Scrofiano, Bettolle, and Sinalunga or "Asina Longa."

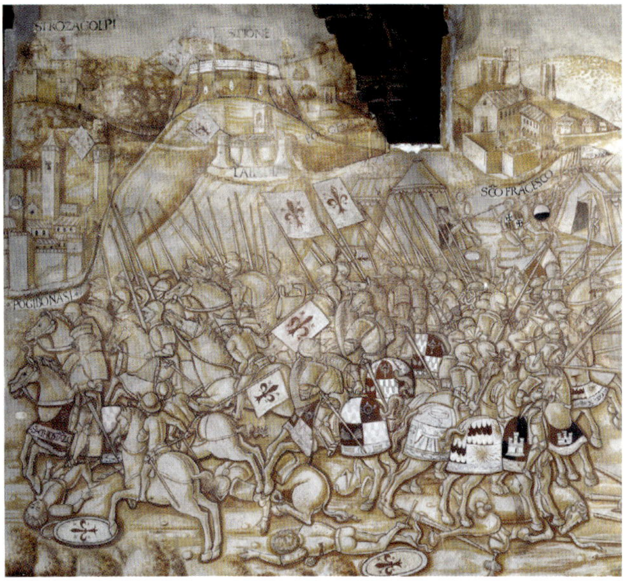

Giovanni di Cristofano Ghini and Francesco d'Andrea, *Battle of Poggio Imperiale*

While the authenticity of the places is attested by their names, the same is not the case for the landscape, which remains generically anonymous and does not resemble in any way the actual appearance of the Sienese countryside offered by Lorenzetti a few years earlier in the nearby fresco cycle of *The Effects of Good and Bad Government*. Lippo Vanni does not seem interested in this aspect and if anything appears more affected, as is probably proper that he would be, given the subject of the picture, by the progress of the battle, which he shows us in two salient moments, like a serial story. In the first part he depicts the Sienese troops as they present themselves on the battlefield: the archers, infantry, and captains on horseback holding their flags, preceded by the drummers. Immediately afterwards is the battle itself in the midst of its fervor, with the Sienese and their allies breaking through the enemy lines, great bursts of gunfire, body-to-body combat, and the precipitous flight of the vanquished. A little more than a century later, the wall was completed with another "victorious" commemoration, but we know that in reality other scenes of this sort, or at any rate of "civic memory," were painted in the Council Chamber, but have since been lost.

*The Battle of Poggio Imperiale* was painted in 1480 by Giovanni di Cristofano Ghini and Francesco d'Andrea, following the same monochrome technique as the adjacent painting, the same compositional scheme of labeling the castles and places, and showing the salient episodes of the scene of the clash. This too was an important battle for the Sienese, won against their eternal bitter enemy, Florence. Poggio

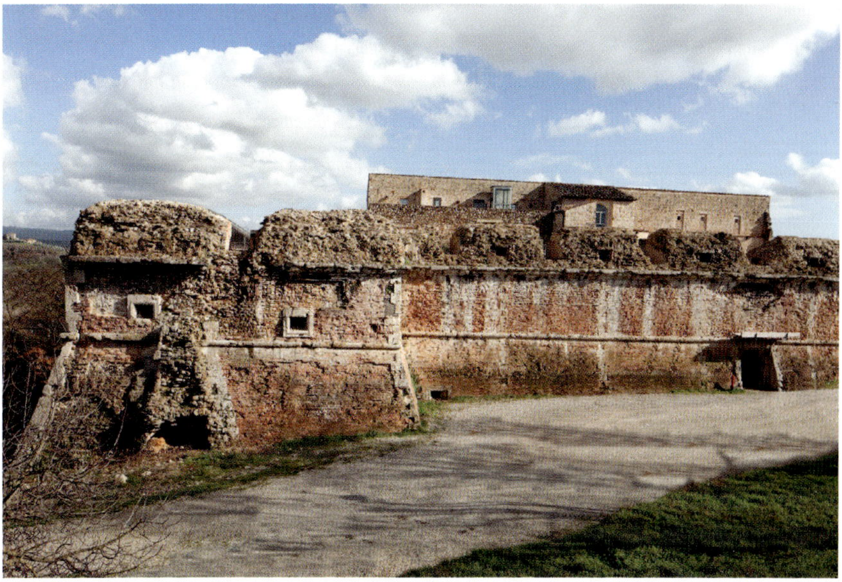

The Poggio Imperiale fort at Poggibonsi

Imperiale is a monumental fort located above the town of Poggibonsi, on a site chosen by Henry VII to build a city. His project remained unfulfilled, but it was taken up again by Lorenzo the Magnificent and never finished, due to his death in 1492. In 1479 it was the Florentines' most advanced outpost in the direction of Siena, and the Sienese managed to win it back, regaining control of the Elsa valley and part of Chianti.The decoration of the room was later completed during the fifteenth century with some figures of Sienese saints and blessed painted on the pilasters. Starting from right, next to the wall holding the *Maestà*, is *Blessed Ambrogio Sansedoni* (by a Sienese artist, 16th-17th cen.) receiving grace from the Holy Spirit, in keeping with his usual iconography, and holding the city of Siena, reflecting the great efforts he made to restore it to papal protection after it had allied itself with the emperor. Next is *Saint Catherine* (by Lorenzo di Pietro, known as Vecchietta, 1461), one of Siena's two emblematic saints, delicate and sweet, holding a book and a lily alluding to her purity. On the next pilaster is the other great Sienese saint, *Saint Bernardine* (by Sano di Pietro, 1450), frescoed in the year of his canonization and portrayed with his usual gaunt facial features and holding a wooden panel with the monogram of Christ, which has become his principal iconographical attribute. The parade of Sienese saints is brought to a close by *Saint Bernardo Tolomei* (by Giovanni Antonio Bazzi, known as Sodoma, 1533), just recently canonized, the founder of the Olivetan order and of Monteoliveto Abbey near Siena.

# The Sala della Pace

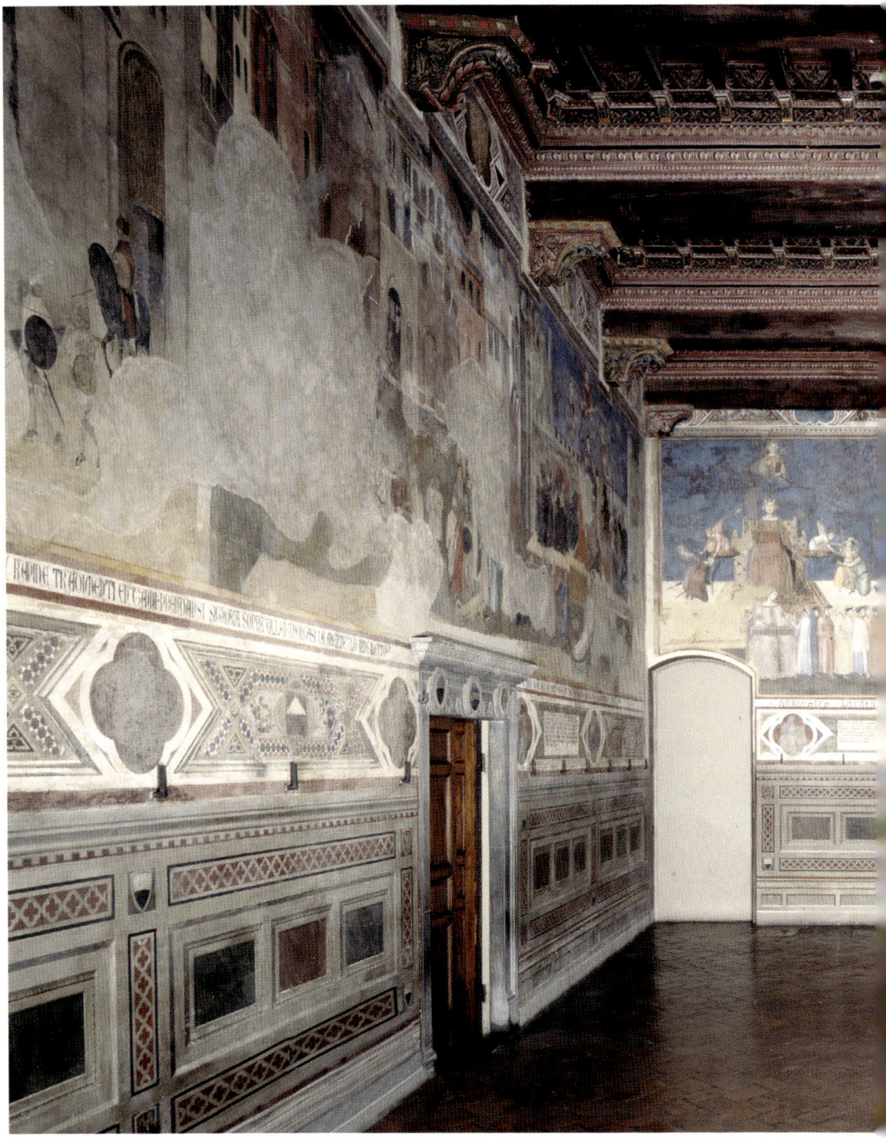

The Sala della Pace

This room, entered through the Sala del Mappamondo, is called the *Sala della Pace* ("Peace Room") or *Sala del Buongoverno* ("Good Government Room") from the subjects of the paintings on the walls; it was earlier known as the "Room of the Crossbows" because it was used as an armory.

The most appropriate name, however, could be the one referring to the council of the Nine, who governed Siena from 1287 to 1355 and commissioned this great and famous civic and political medieval manifesto.

In 1337, when Simone Martini had already left for the

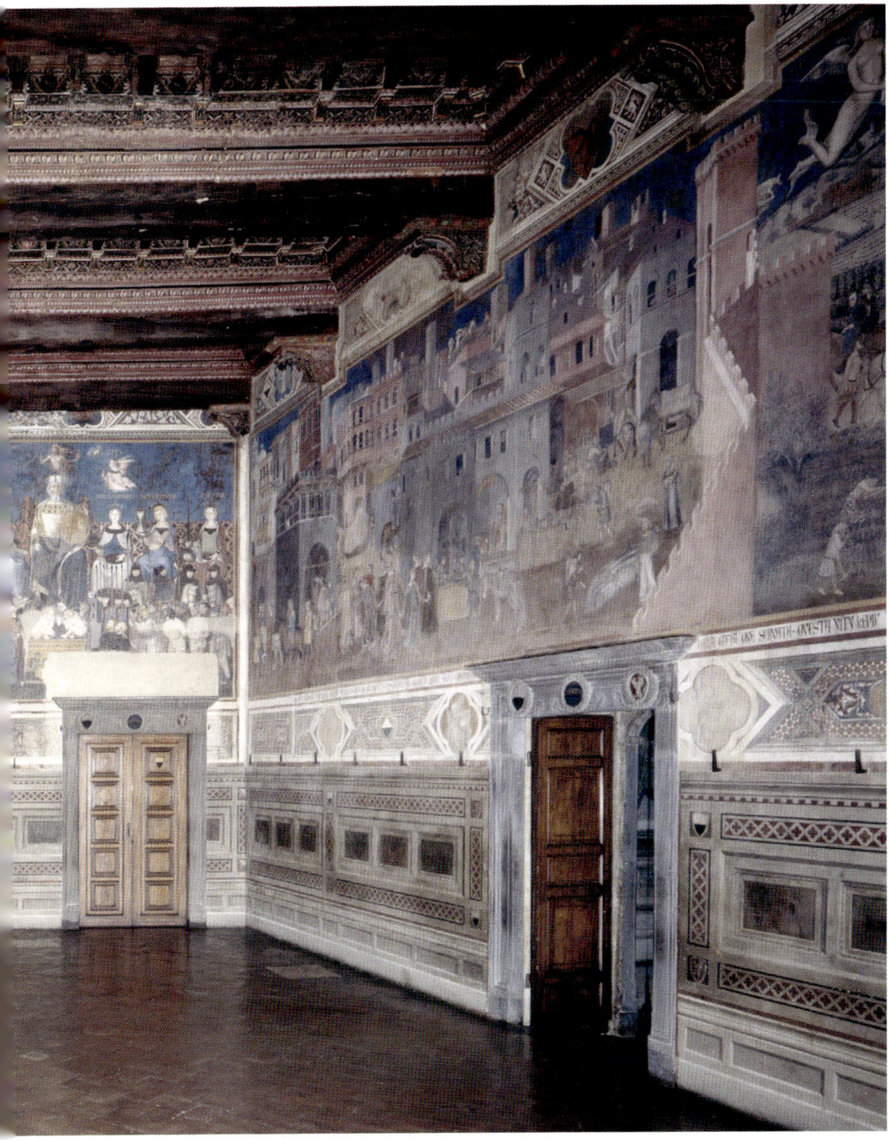

papal court in Avignon, the Nine commissioned the leading painter of the moment in Siena, Ambrogio Lorenzetti, to decorate an entire room of the palace. The subject matter was a strictly secular theme: he was to illustrate good and bad government and the effects they produced on the city and the countryside. Ambrogio Lorenzetti executed the work between 1338 and 1339, creating one of the most important secular cycles in the history of art, still preserved, the first in central Italy and a unique example of the instructional painting so beloved in the Middle Ages.

# The Protagonists
# Ambrogio Lorenzetti

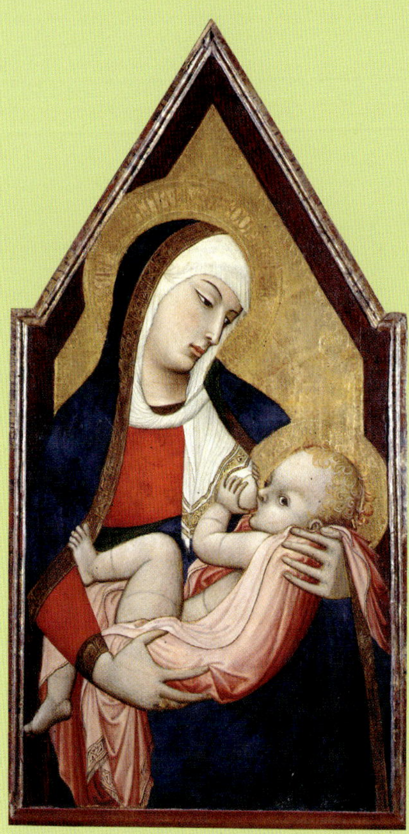

*Ambrosius Laurentii de Senis Hic Pinxit Utrinque* ("Ambrogio Lorenzetti of Siena here painted both walls"). With these words, Ambrogio Lorenzetti, one of the undisputed protagonists of early fourteenth-century Sienese painting, proudly proclaims his authorship of the complex fresco decoration of the Sala della Pace in Palazzo Pubblico in Siena, which would earn for him the epithet of "learned painter" given him by Lorenzo Ghiberti. While we know that he was the younger brother of Pietro, also a famous painter, very little is documented of his life and works, aside from the positive opinions of early biographers like Ghiberti or Giorgio Vasari. A highly original artist within the context of Sienese painting, dominated from the early decades of the fourteenth century by Simone Martini and his thriving family workshop, Ambrogio revealed as early as *The Virgin and Child Enthroned* at Vico l'Abate, of 1319, his first known work, an unusual attention to the orientations of the Florentine school, with particular reference to Giotto and the sculptor Arnolfo di Cambio. Documented in Florence in 1321, throughout that entire decade Ambrogio alternated time in Siena, where in 1324 he is reported as resident in the Camporegio neighborhood, with long stays in Florence, where he joined the guild of physicians and apothecaries (to which painters also belonged) between 1328 and 1330. In the first half of the 1320s he painted two frescoes, of *The Martyrdom of the Franciscans in Morocco* and *Saint Louis in Front of Pope Boniface VIII*, for the chapter house of the convent of San Francesco in Siena. Besides the calibrated construction of space he learned from Giotto, these manifest Ambrogio's interest in human physiognomy and the various styles of the clothing worn by the characters. In 1332 he was in Florence again, where he painted a triptych for the church of San Procolo (now in the Uffizi), which, like the *Nursing Madonna* in the Museo Diocesano d'Arte Sacra in Siena painted more or less at the same time, show that his style was becoming more elaborate, in the direction of the Sienese Gothic art of Simone Martini. This same

Ambrogio Lorenzetti, *The Nursing Madonna*, Siena, Museo Diocesano di Arte Sacra

Ambrogio Lorenzetti, *The Annunciation*, Siena, Pinacoteca Nazionale

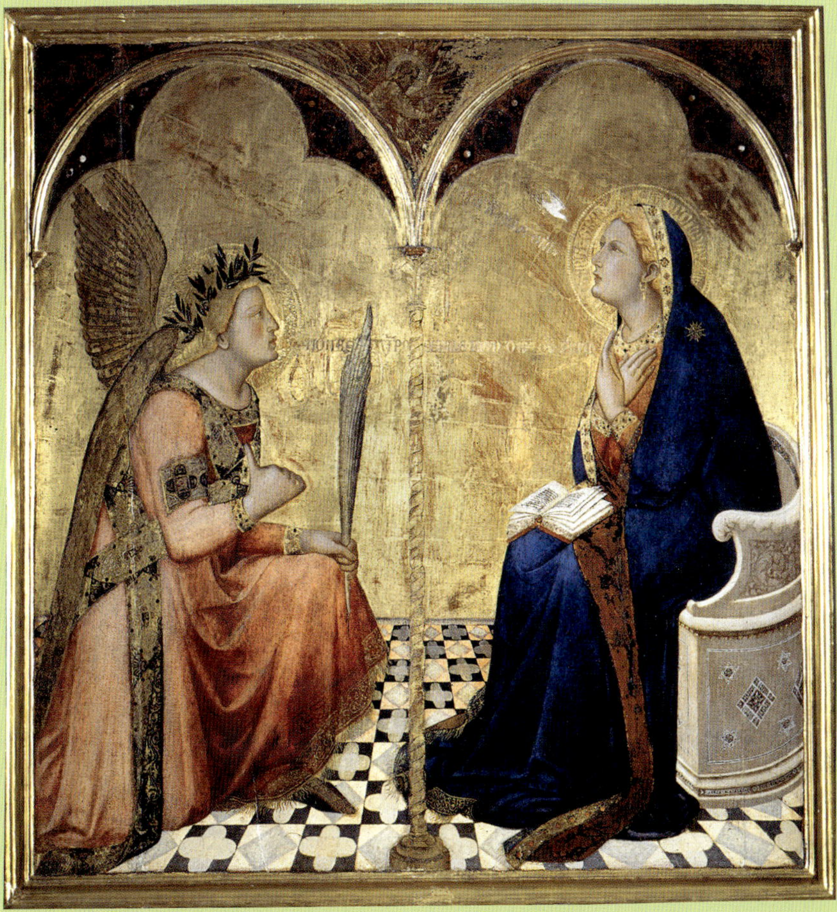

church in Florence was the destination also of two small panels with four *Stories from the Life of Saint Nicholas*, examples of the artist's mature work in their complex perspectival depiction of a medieval city and the meticulous description of individual details, foreshadowing the later urban views of *Good Government*, the apex of his work in this regard. In 1334, Ambrogio's name appears among those of the witnesses to an act drawn up inside the Cistercian abbey of San Galgano, near Siena, in whose Gothic chapel, annexed to the nearby Romanesque rotunda of Montesiepi, he painted a fresco cycle of *Stories of Saint Galganus*, *Saint Michael the Archangel*, a *Virgin and Child Enthroned in Majesty* (*Maestà*), and an *Annunciation*. By now at the peak of his career, the artist was called, probably in 1338, on the occasion of the general meeting of the Hermits of Saint Augustine in Siena, to paint a *Maestà* in the

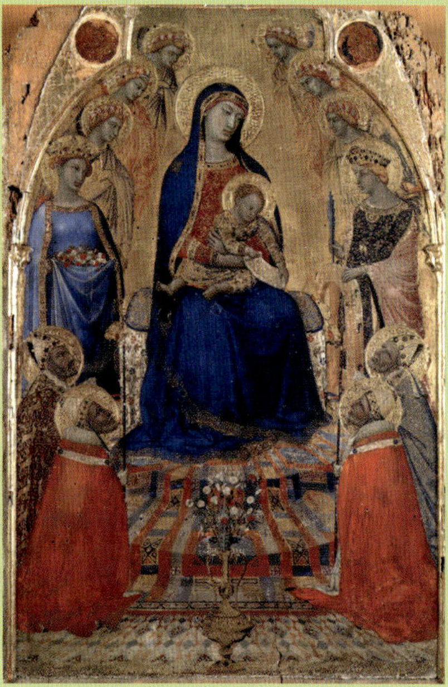

local church of Sant'Agostino, still there and similar to the design of the slightly earlier *Maestà* in Massa Marittima, and *Stories of the Creed* and of *Saint Catherine of Alexandria* on the ceiling and walls of the chapter house, which have unfortunately been gone for some time. In that same year, Ambrogio was engaged in frescoing, in the Sala dei Nove of Palazzo Pubblico in Siena, the allegory of *Good and Bad Government* and the *Effects on Town and Country*, his undisputed masterpiece because of the complexity of its composition and its high instructional content, executed, as can be deduced from the notations of payments that run from February 1338 to March 1339, in less than a year and a half; this enterprise confirmed him as the best artist in the city and the Sienese government's 'official painter.' Unfortunately, very little of his work done after the frescoes in the Sala dei Nove has survived to our day. Lost is the large *Mappamondo* installed in 1345 in the room which still bears its name in Siena's Palazzo Pubblico, which was plausibly decorated with a map of the castles conquered by the Sienese. The surviving evidence of Ambrogio's late activity is thus only the *Presentation in the Temple*, signed and dated 1342, now in the Uffizi but originally in Siena Cathedral, and the *Annunciation* in the Pinacoteca in Siena, painted in 1344 for the Gabella (tax) authorities, both of which present a waning of Gothic rhythms and an emphasis on the study of perspective. Like so much of the Sienese population, Ambrogio too seems to have fallen victim to the Black Plague of 1348. The last documentary mention of him appears in the *Memorie* and *Entrate* of the Compagnia della Vergine Maria in Siena, which record the date of his will, drawn up on 9 June 1348, indicating his death in the course of that year.

(V.R.)

Ambrogio Lorenzetti, *The Virgin and Child Enthroned*, Siena, Pinacoteca Nazionale

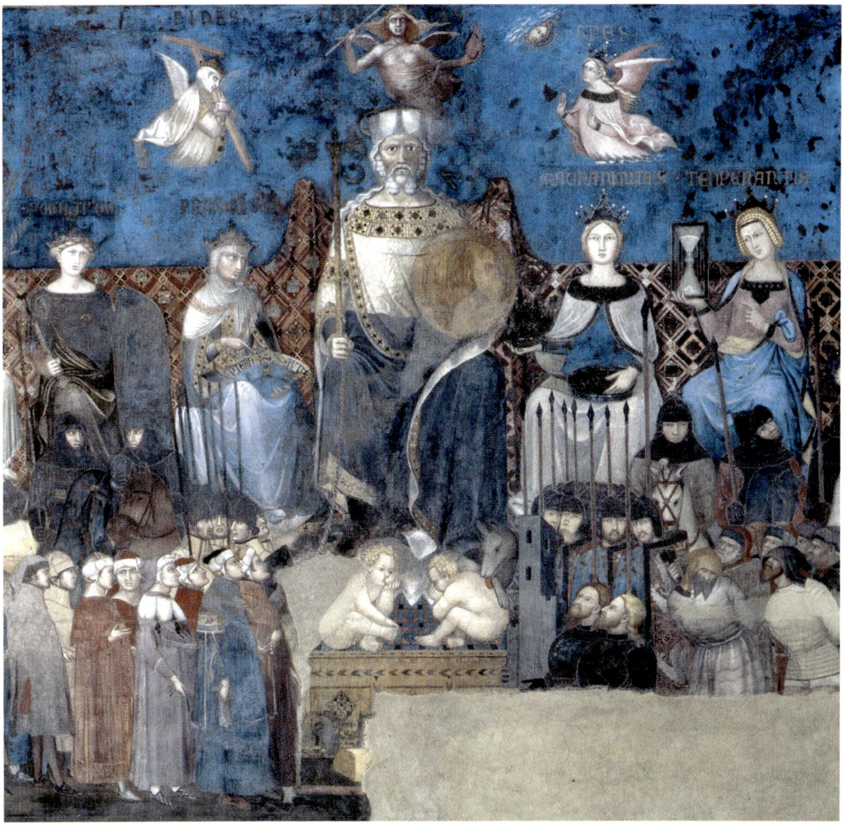

Ambrogio Lorenzetti, *The Allegory of Good Government*, detail of *Good Government*

The wall facing visitors entering the room shows Bad Government and its effects. But to follow the narrative thread and understand fully its deepest meaning, expressed in the symbols and details of the pictures, you should turn to look at the wall on your right.
Facing the natural light pouring in through the window, Ambrogio painted the allegorical representation of Good Government, setting it in a sort of grand room dominated by the bearded, stately figure of Good Government and the female figure of Justice, seated on thrones. In the upper left part of the fresco, Knowledge holds a large scale, on which two angels are handing out *commutative* justice, compensating one person and cutting off another's head, and *distributive*, offering favors and money, while Justice, who keeps the two sides of the scale in balance, lets fall two ropes which Concord joins together, holding in her lap a carpenter's plane for smoothing out disagreements. The rope is grasped by 24 citizens who pass it along, as they look towards the symbol of the Commune of Siena, i.e., Good Government, seated on the throne wearing the colors of the Balzana (black and white), with the she-wolf nursing the twins, symbol of the city, at his feet.

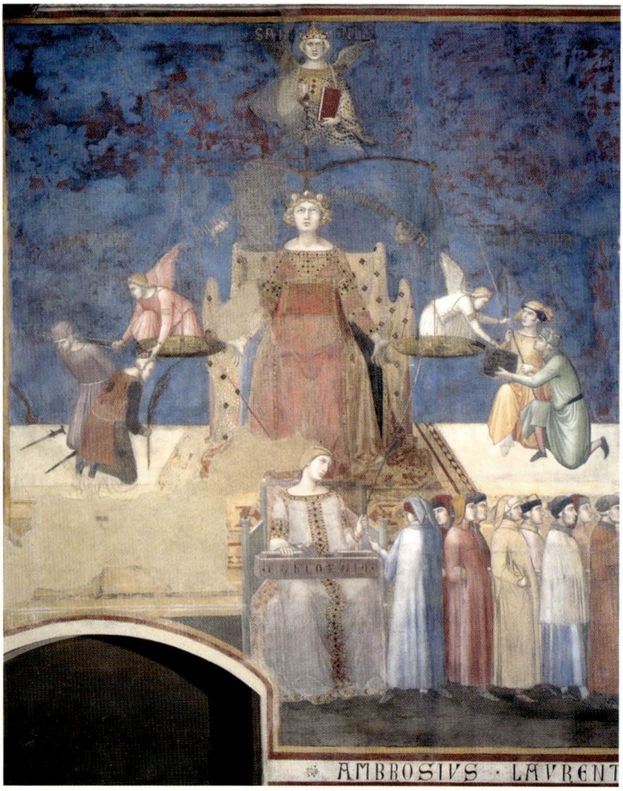


Ambrogio Lorenzetti, *The Allegory of Good Government*, detail of *Justice*

Ambrogio Lorenzetti, *The Allegory of Good Government*, detail of *Peace*

Floating above his head are the three theological virtues, Faith, Hope and Charity, to combat the vices illustrated on the next wall, and seated next to him are the four cardinal virtues, Fortitude, Prudence, Justice, and Temperance, joined here by Peace and Magnanimity. Peace, the very popular lady dressed in white who has lent her name to the entire room, is shown on the left, leaning languidly on cushions, under which have been placed, partially hidden, weapons and shields. Next to her is Fortitude, with soldiers at her feet and a mace and shield in her hand, to reiterate the principle that firmness, even armed strength, is necessary for defending the peace. Prudence, next to her, is shown as a mature queen, a symbol and an admonition to govern wisely.

To the right of the figure representing Good Government are Magnanimity with a tray of coins on her lap, Temperance holding an hourglass, and Justice holding a cut-off head and a sword. At their feet, in the bottom part of the painting, on the right armed soldiers guard some prisoners, while two kneeling lords offer their castles.

The message of the allegory of Good Government is clear: to govern with wisdom under the protection of the Christian virtues, operating in favor of the peace and

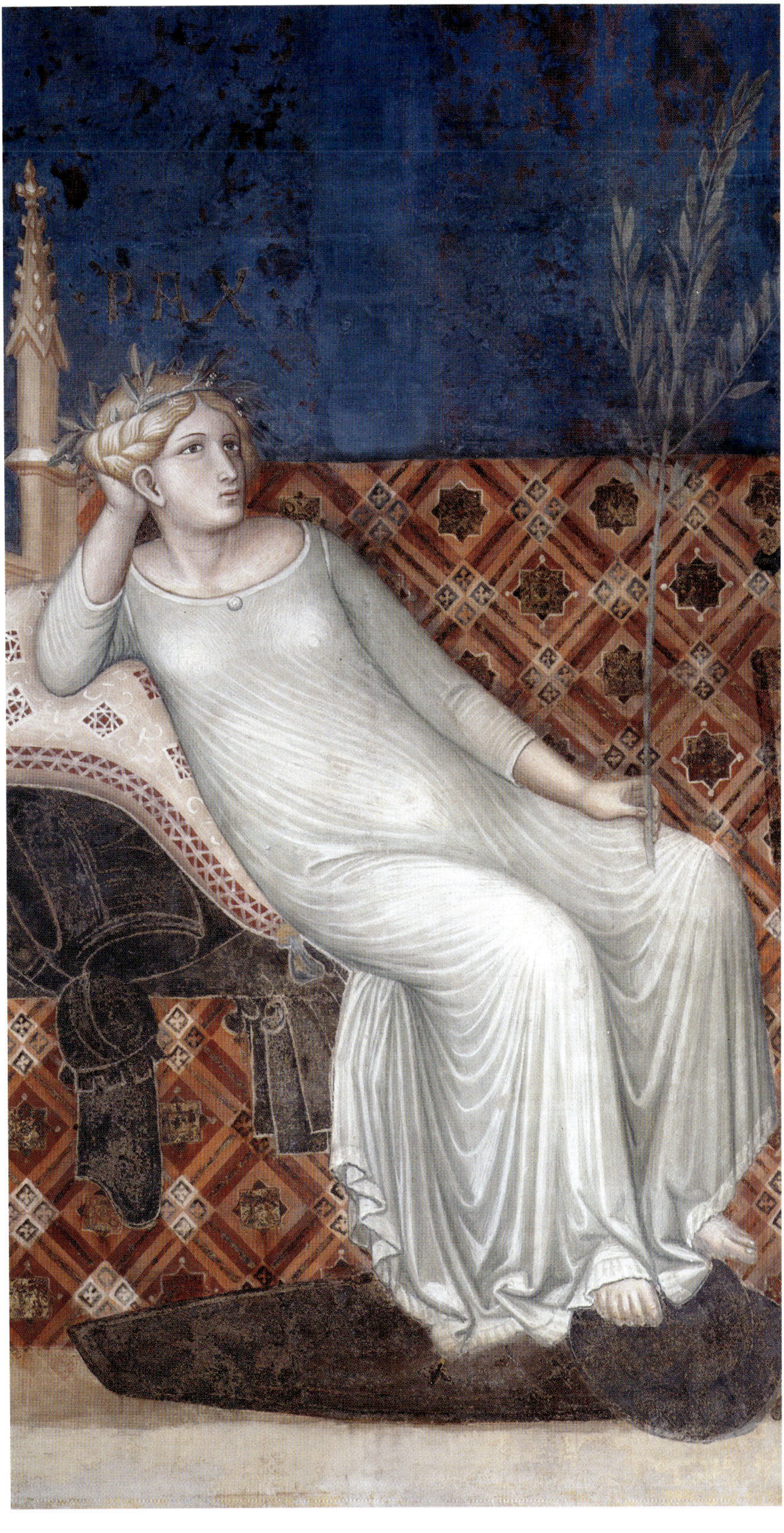
PAX

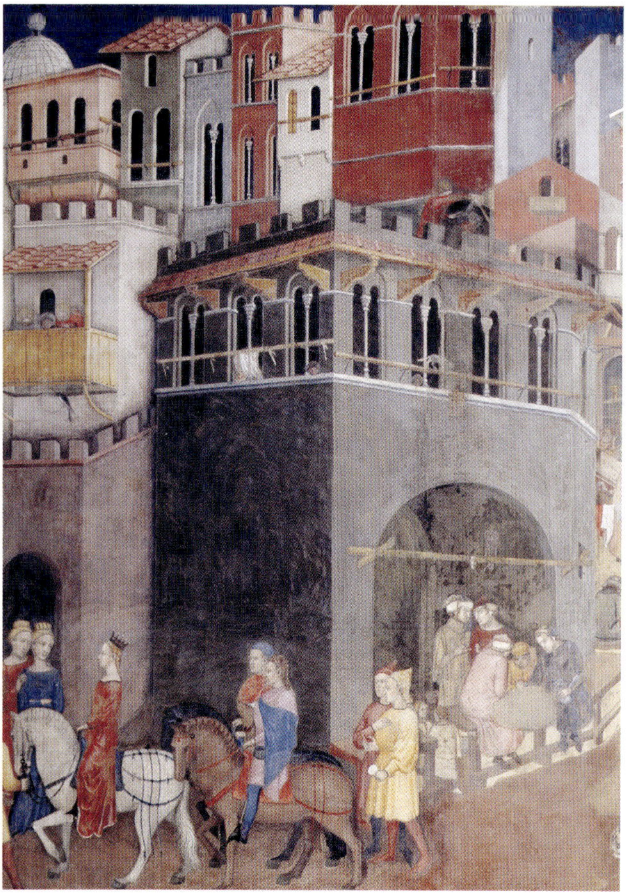

Ambrogio Lorenzetti, *The Effects of Good Government in the City*, detail

wealth of the city, but always with a firm hand, as testified by the presence of soldiers.

The effects of good government are illustrated on the adjoining wall, which faces, and opposes, the Bad Government wall. It presents a plausible picture of Siena, whose cathedral bell tower, with its black and white stripes, and great dome can be seen at upper left, inside the walled city. It is an ideal and a real city at the same time, brightly colored, hard-working, full of people. The backdrop of houses and palaces enclosed within the walls which separate it, like a stage set, from the countryside, is enlivened by stonemasons working diligently so that the already prosperous city can continue to grow, with cloth hanging out the windows and people watching from their balconies.

Even more industrious, animated and active are the streets bustling with trade. People are working as tailors, shoemakers, jewelers, while a teacher addresses a group of schoolboys. Goods are delivered, people meet to talk. On the left of the painting is a wedding procession,

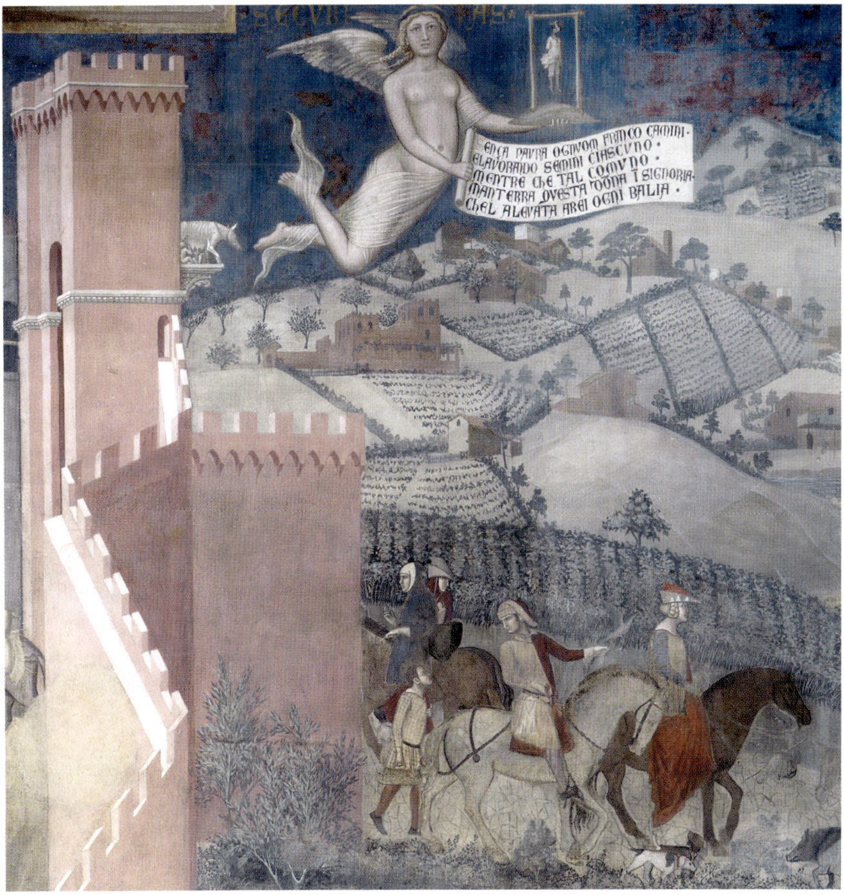

Ambrogio Lorenzetti, *The Effects of Good Government in the Country*, detail

while in the foreground ten elegant young girls cavort happily in the street.

The city gates are open, a sign that this is peacetime and there is no need to close them for defense. The flow of trade and traffic between the city and the countryside is free and constant. Peasants enter with their mules laden with goods to sell, sacks of flour and wool, and hens, firewood, even a pig. A shepherd is walking out with his flock, and a party of well-dressed noblemen on horseback has already gone past the walls, headed for the open country for a picnic or to hunt.

In the countryside, where the air is clear and the atmosphere serene and relaxed, people are working in the fields, planting, harvesting, tending the orderly vineyards next to the farmhouses. The view widens to sweep over the hills to the distant horizon, demonstrating the vastness of the possessions of the Republic of Siena, protected from above by a large winged figure, *Securitas*, under whose vigilant eye "every man" can walk "without fear."

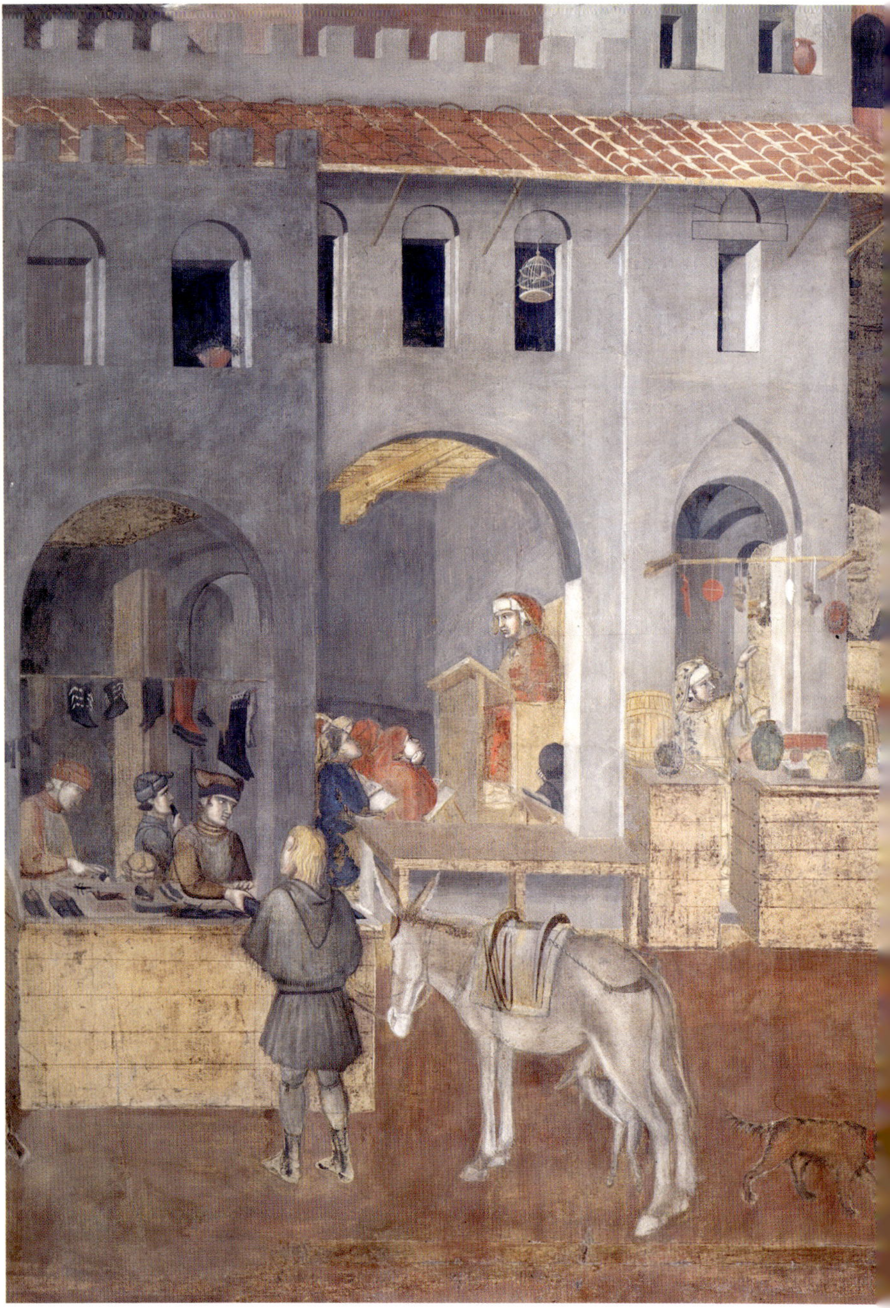

The fresco of Bad Government on the opposite wall has been ruined in certain parts by dampness infiltrating the wall, but also to the "casual attitude" of the occupants of the palace in the eighteenth century (presumably the staff of the Offices of the Court, who were using these rooms) who had the brilliant idea of building a partition wall, attached with beams to the painted surface, to store their files, demonstrating a total lack of

Ambrogio Lorenzetti, *Good Government in the City*, details

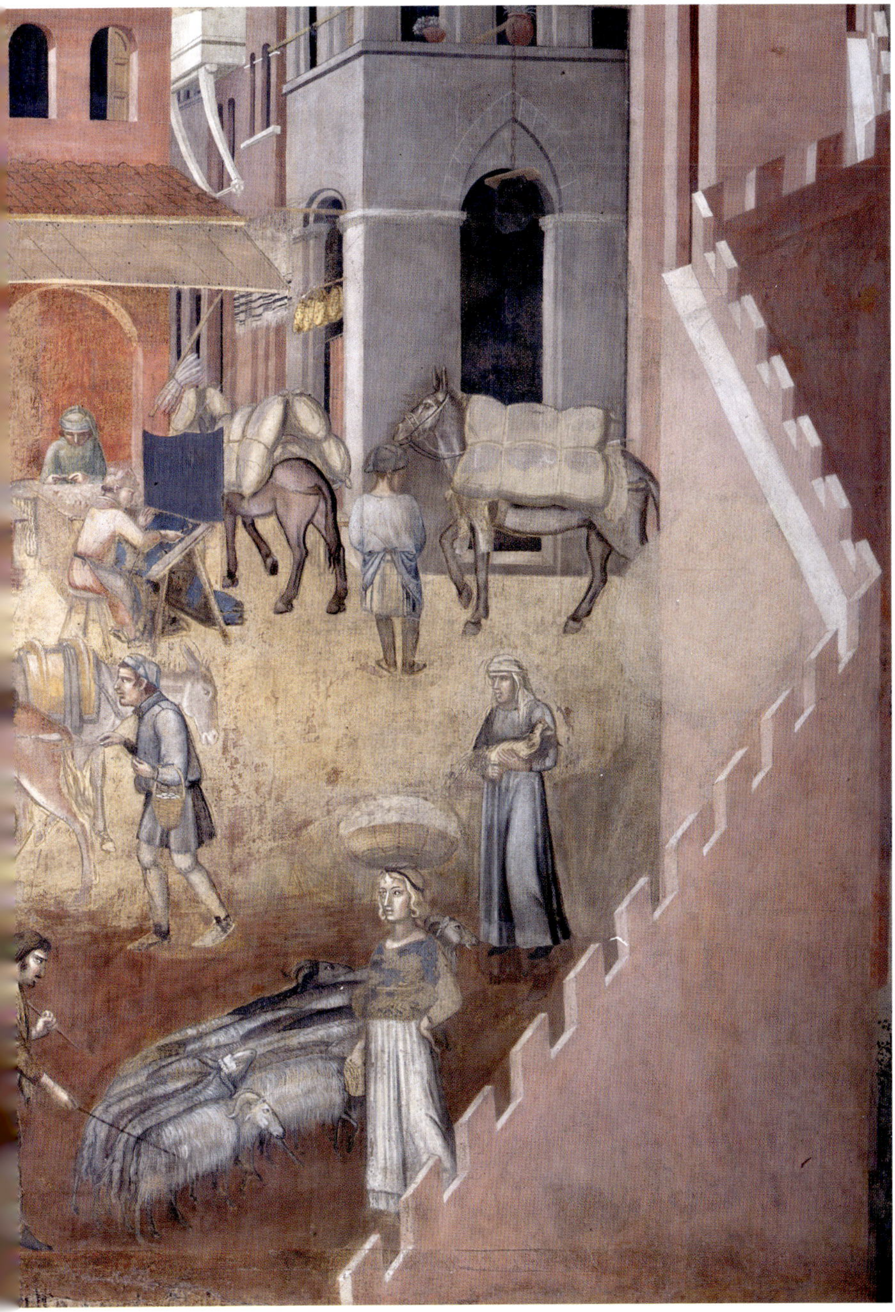

concern for the frescoes, considered primitive and thus barbarous.

Nonetheless, the gaps, even though they deprive the viewer of some undeniably interesting details, give a poetic air, but in a negative sense, to the entire picture, accentuating the sense of abandonment, poverty, decadence, and ruin of the city portrayed there.

Tyranny and vices reign among the crenellated walls.

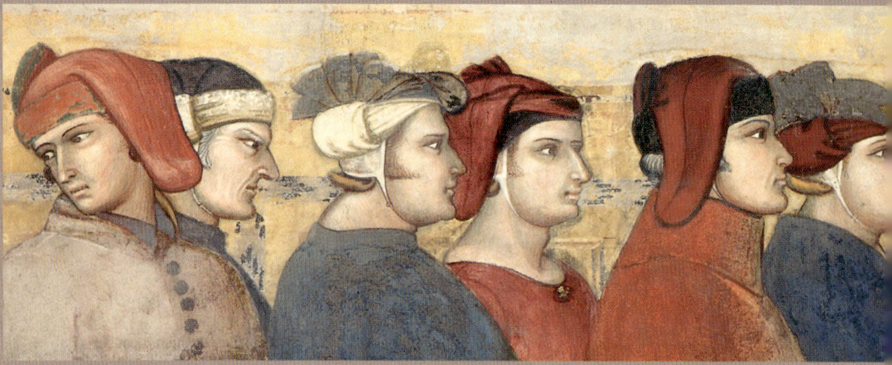

One of the less well-known aspects of the famous big fresco of *Good Government* is the contribution made by the pictures of the people taking part in the life of the city and the countryside to the study of the history of fashion. A frivolous topic, some might say, but an undeniably important one, as has been demonstrated, for the study of a painting, an artist, or a historical period.

It is a well-known fact that in the past, especially in the Gothic and Renaissance periods, artists would commonly reproduce in their works scenes and figures whose setting and physical appearance did not correspond to that of the time when the event took place, but mirrored the contemporary situation when the works were made; in this case, the fresco of Good Government goes even further, making the contemporary nature of the scene its strong point.

Lorenzetti's women are dressed in keeping with early fourteenth-century fashion, with long smooth, floor-length dresses, sometimes cinched by a belt and terminating in a train, covered by cloaks. Their hairstyles feature thick braids wrapped around the head and decorated with ribbons or tiaras.

With regard to women's clothing, the Commune of Siena had issued a group of laws that disciplined, among other aspects of daily life like banquets, parties, weddings and funerals, also the rules of dress and personal aesthetics, such as the appropriate use of jewelry and ornaments. To put a brake on luxury and wastefulness, for example, it forbade the use of pearls and plunging necklines and even regulated the length of the train on dresses. These laws were often not obeyed, and indeed the Good Government, in its display of beauty and wealth, has a value that goes well beyond the merely exterior: the women wear low-cut dresses, their hair is adorned with pearls and jewels, as are Vainglory and other female personifications in the allegory, and some of them wear richly worked fabrics, which were also forbid-

Ambrogio Lorenzetti, *The Allegory of Good Government*, details of the men's headgear

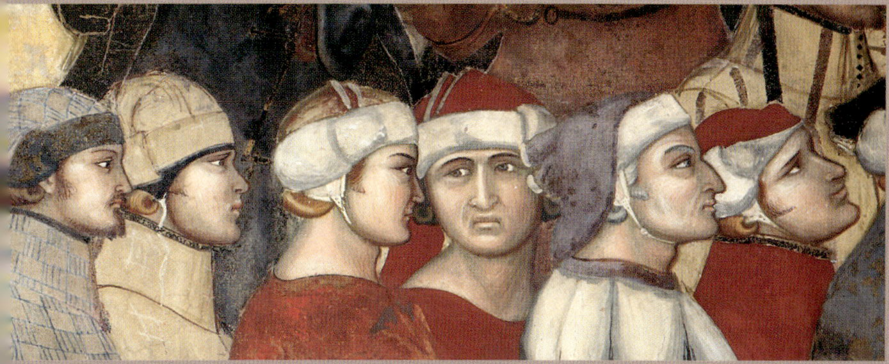

den, like the girls in the foreground with their beautiful dresses decorated with dragonfly, caterpillar, and geometric motifs.

The so-called "dancing girls," who if they really were dancing would be committing another transgression since the laws in force prohibited dancing in public, actually represent a symbolic portrayal of joy, the carefree serenity of youth, and happiness, given that the young women, little more than adolescents, are more probably playing a game called "angels and devils" than dancing.

While Lorenzetti's girls transgress the law in their clothing, they do respect it with regard to their shoes, low flats almost like modern "ballerinas." Honest women, as we suppose these delightful, happy girls to have been, were not allowed to wear "wedges," shoes mounted on platforms made of wood, leather, or cork, which could be worn only by prostitutes, who used them to show off their physical charms and long, rich dresses.

Lorenzetti also offers a broad repertory of men's clothing, especially in the range of headgear, caps and hoods shown off by the wealthy citizens in procession in front of the figure of Good Government, all of them dressed beautifully and in a varied manner, with long tunics and personalized stocking and shoes.

The figure of one young man catches the eye: differently from the others, he wears a short tunic, just below the knee, made of a particularly elaborate fabric, with a sleeve sticking out of a pocket or side slit.

His way of dressing, so different from all the others, shows the signs of a change in taste in men's fashion of the time, and is above all visual, tangible evidence of an intervention in this part of the painting at a distinct moment, soon after mid-century, by a painter who, quite properly, in adding this new character to the picture dressed him according to the trend of that moment.

(L.G.)

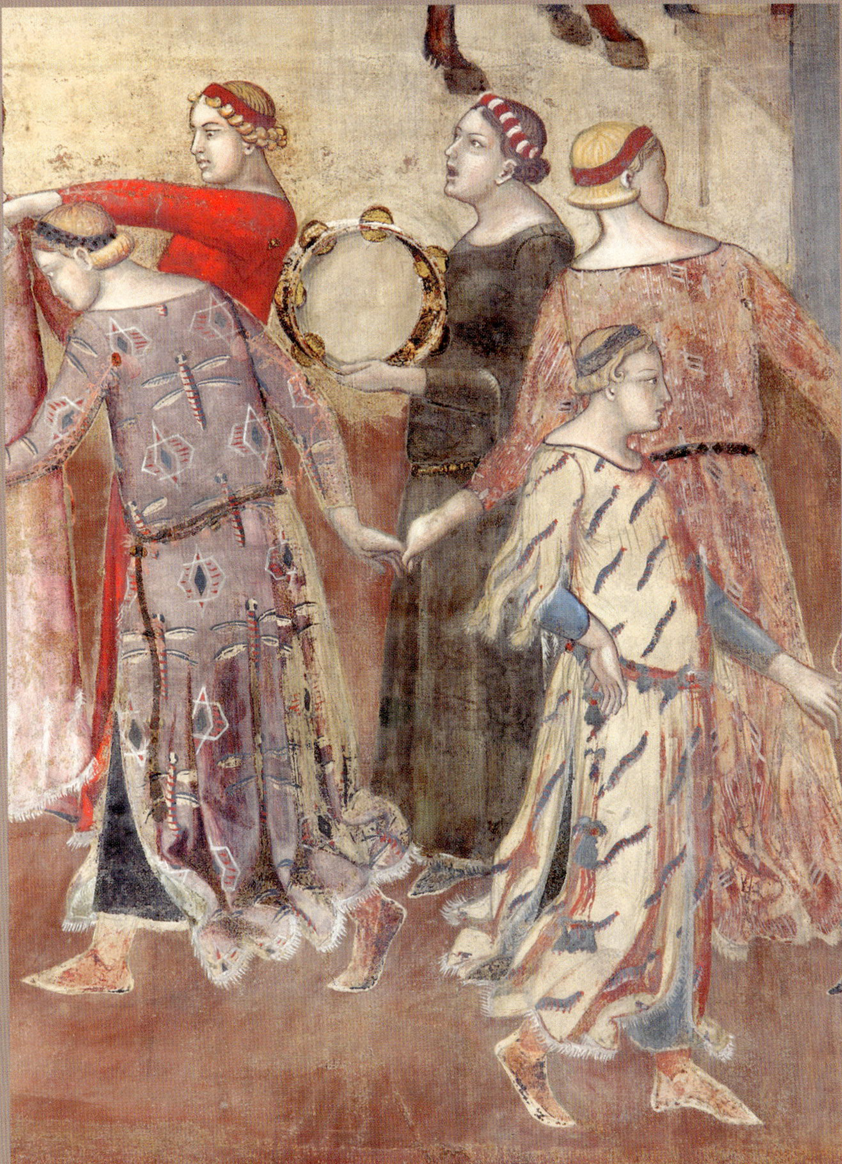

Ambrogio Lorenzetti, *The Effects of Good Government in the City*, details of the girls' dresses and hairdos

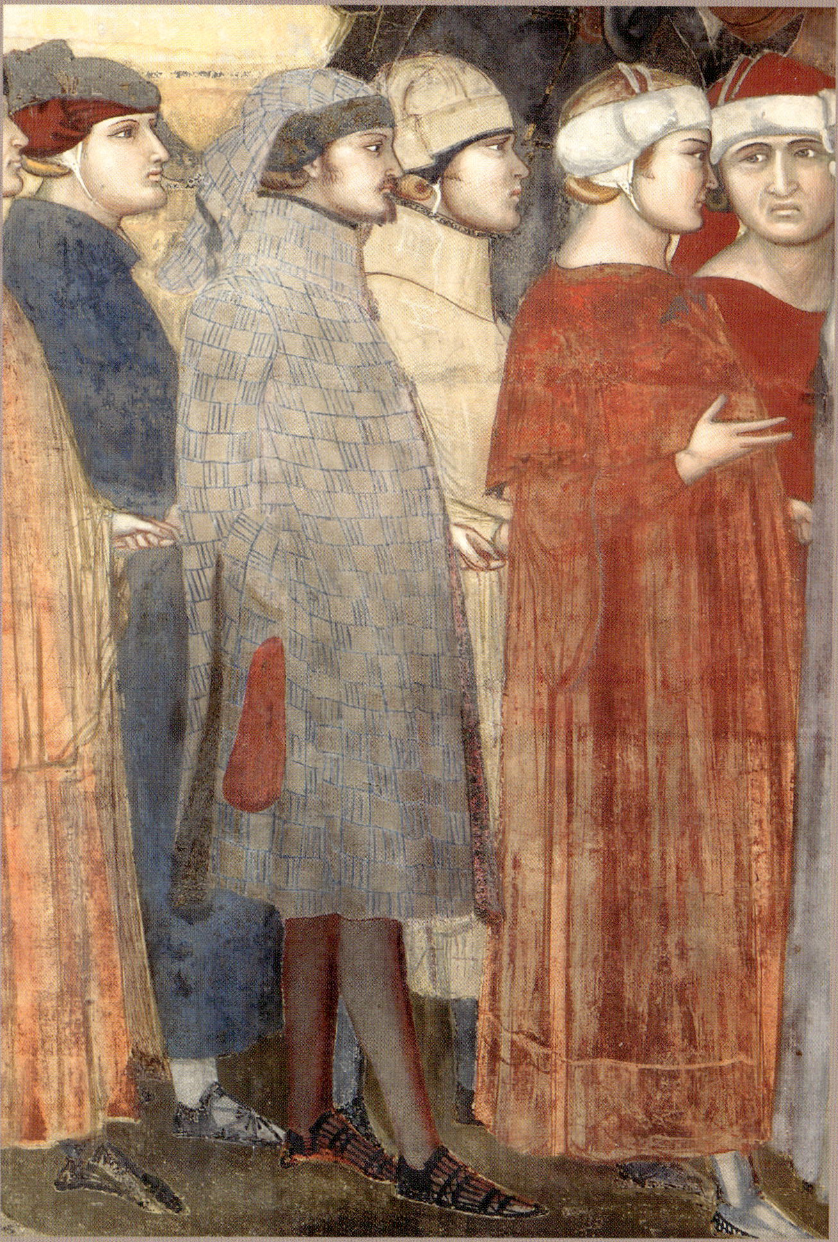

Ambrogio Lorenzetti, *The Allegory of Good Government*, details of the men's clothing

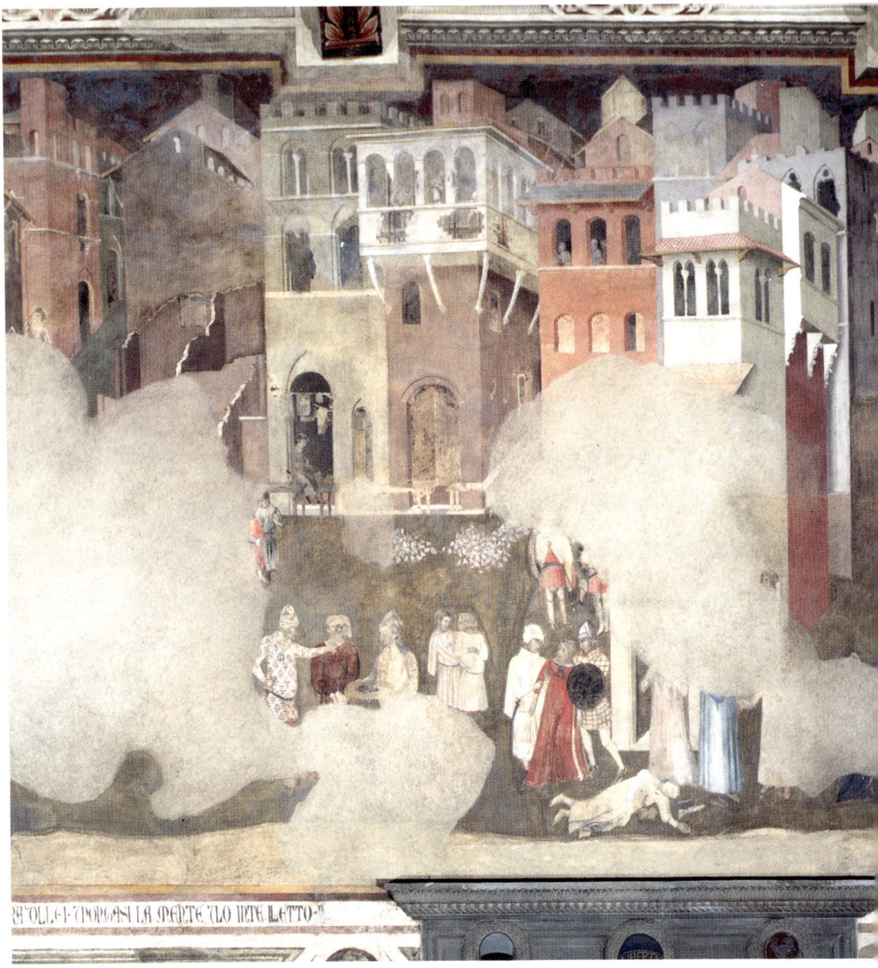

Ambrogio Lorenzetti, *The Effects and Allegory of Bad Government*

Above them are shown Avarice, turning a press from which coins pour out, Pride with a sword and yoke, the symbol of abuse of power, and Vainglory, a young woman admiring herself in a mirror. Tyranny, richly dressed, looks like a devil, with horns and sharp teeth, and has a goat, symbol of lust, at his feet. Around him are the vices: Cruelty, a terrible female figure about to strangle a child; Betrayal, *Proditio*, holding an animal with the head of a lamb and the tail of a scorpion; and Fraud, represented with bat's wings and cloven feet. On Tyranny's right, Furor is depicted as a monster with a human torso and an animal's head and body, holding a knife and some stones, a clear allusion to violent offensive weapons; Division, *Divisio*, the vice which alludes to problems of internal politics in the city, split into factions and torn apart by conflict, is a woman dressed in a white and black dress sawing her own body in two; last is War, a foreboding, heavily armed soldier brandishing his shield.

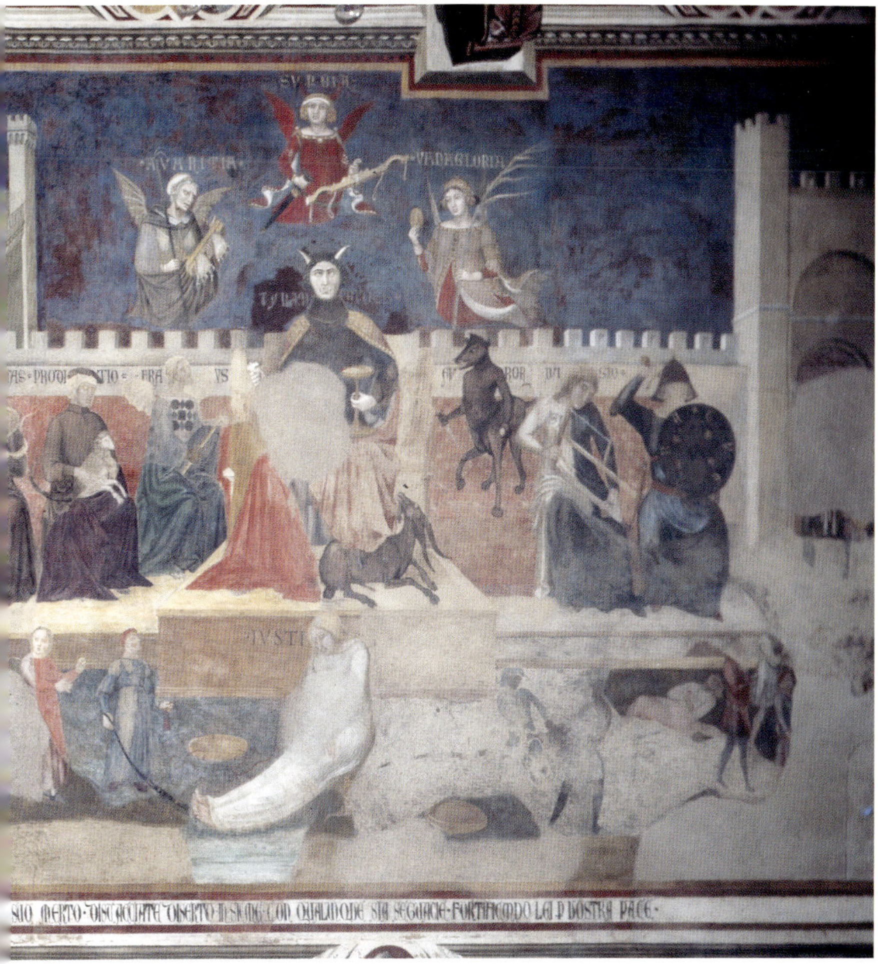

At their feet lies Justice, defeated, a meek young woman clad in a simple white tunic, trussed up as a prisoner, with the pans of the scale, the iconographical attribute of justice, thrown on the ground.
The city, which occupies the entire left part of the wall, is equally dark and gloomy.
The buildings, which in the picture of Good Government are beautiful, colorful, and under construction, here are ruined, blackened by fire, and falling down, and the streets, where the trade, life and harmony of the city pulsated, here are full of soldiers who commit injustice and violence.
Where there the girls were playing, here a young girl lies murdered. The only person who is still working is the blacksmith, but he is making weapons.
The city gate is closed, and only soldiers exit through a small open passageway, going out to wreak more ruin and destruction on the countryside.

A curious note

# The Artistic Iconography of an Elegant Pig

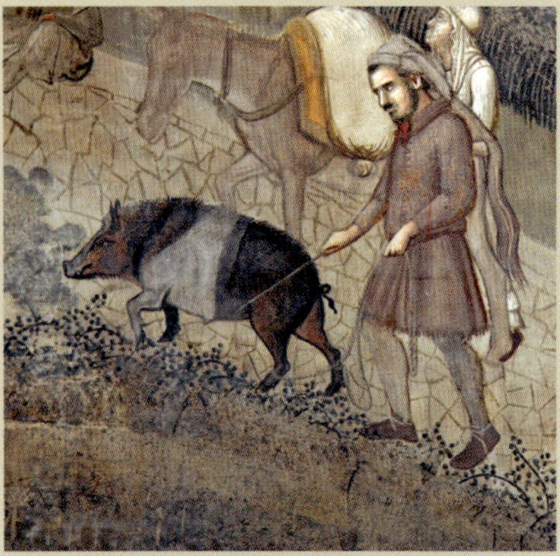

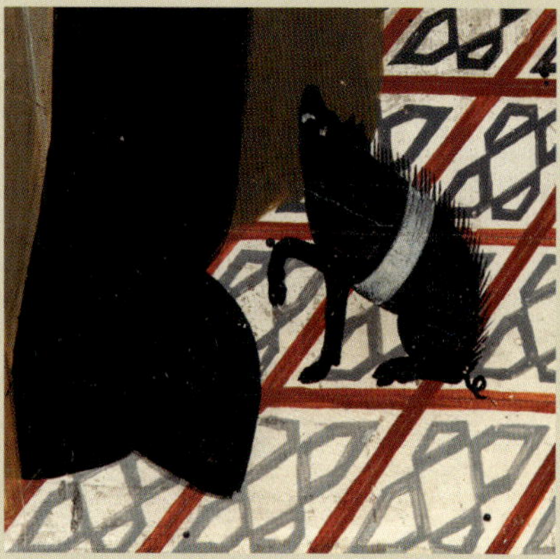

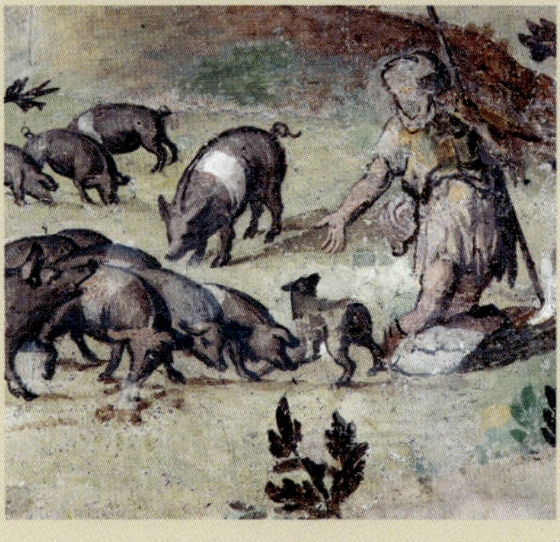

A significant detail in Ambrogio Lorenzetti's *Good Government* fresco is the Sienese belted pig. The peasant in the center of the picture of the countryside is on his way into the city with a pig on a leash – and not just any pig, but an elegant *cinta senese*, with a white "belt"(cinta in the local dialect) running right around the center of its black body. This fresco demonstrates that the *cinta* breed has a very long history; it was almost certainly the result of crossbreeding with breeds from Asia, brought into Italy by barbarians after the fall of the Roman empire. During the Middle Ages the raising of *cinta senese* pigs took on the characteristics similar to today: to obtain meatier animals, the medieval breeders used the feed available to them, the woods rich in acorns, chestnuts, and other resources. The pig's presence throughout the territory is documented by other artistic evidence. A belted pig appears with Saint Anthony Abbot in a panel painting of *Saint Julian with Saints Martin and Anthony Abbot* (1425-27), attributed to the "Master of 1419" now in the Museo Civico of San Gimignano, and Luca Signorelli (16th cen.) depicts a swineherd tending somebelted pigs in one of the *Stories of Saint Benedict* in the cloister of Monte Oliveto Maggiore abbey near Siena. (L.G.)

Ambrogio Lorenzetti, *The Effects of Good Government in the Country*, detail

Luca Signorelli, *Stories from the Life of Saint Benedict*, detail, Abbey of Monteoliveto Maggiore, cloister

"Master of 1419," *Saint Julian between Saints Martin and Anthony Abbot*, detail, San Gimignano, Museo Civico, Pinacoteca

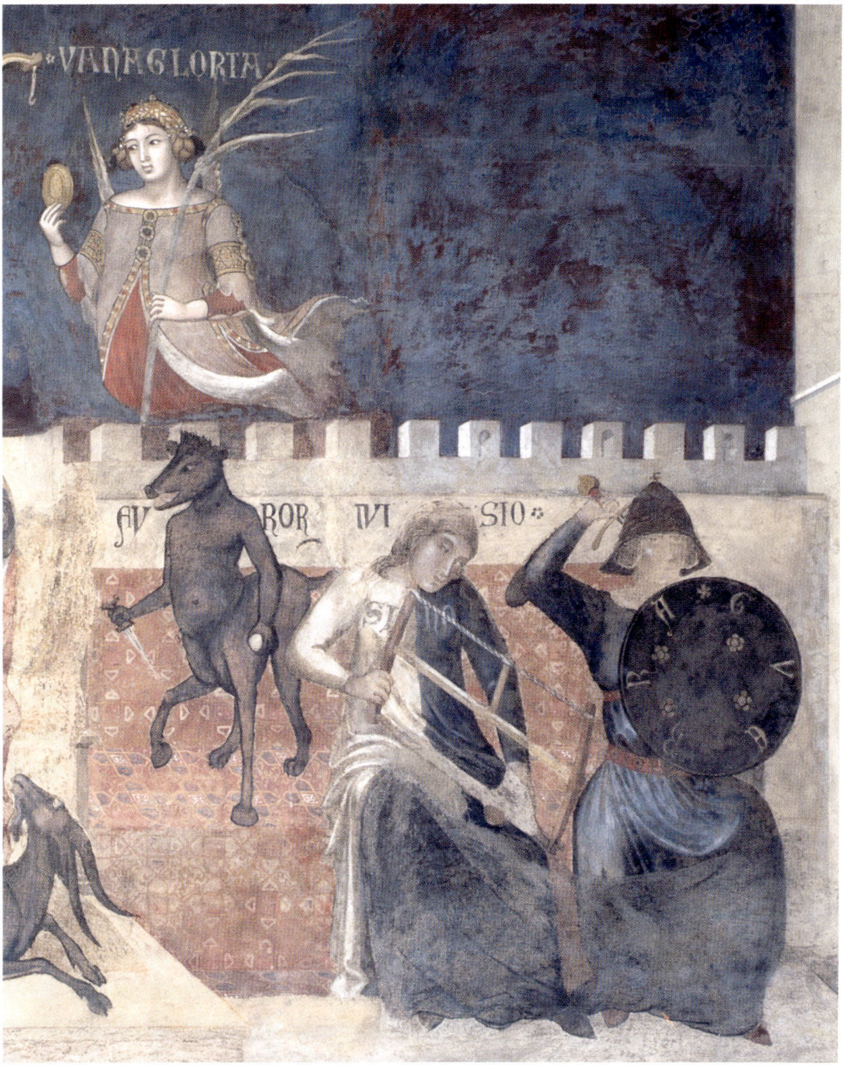


Ambrogio Lorenzetti, *Allegory of Bad Government*, detail of *War*

The idyllic, serene atmosphere of the Good Government's fields does not exist here. The farmhouses are in flames, the trees and crops are dead, the ground bare and full of soldiers. Where on the other wall the farmland hummed with activity and the nobility went hunting undisturbed, here are only desolation and war.

# Portrait of a Landscape

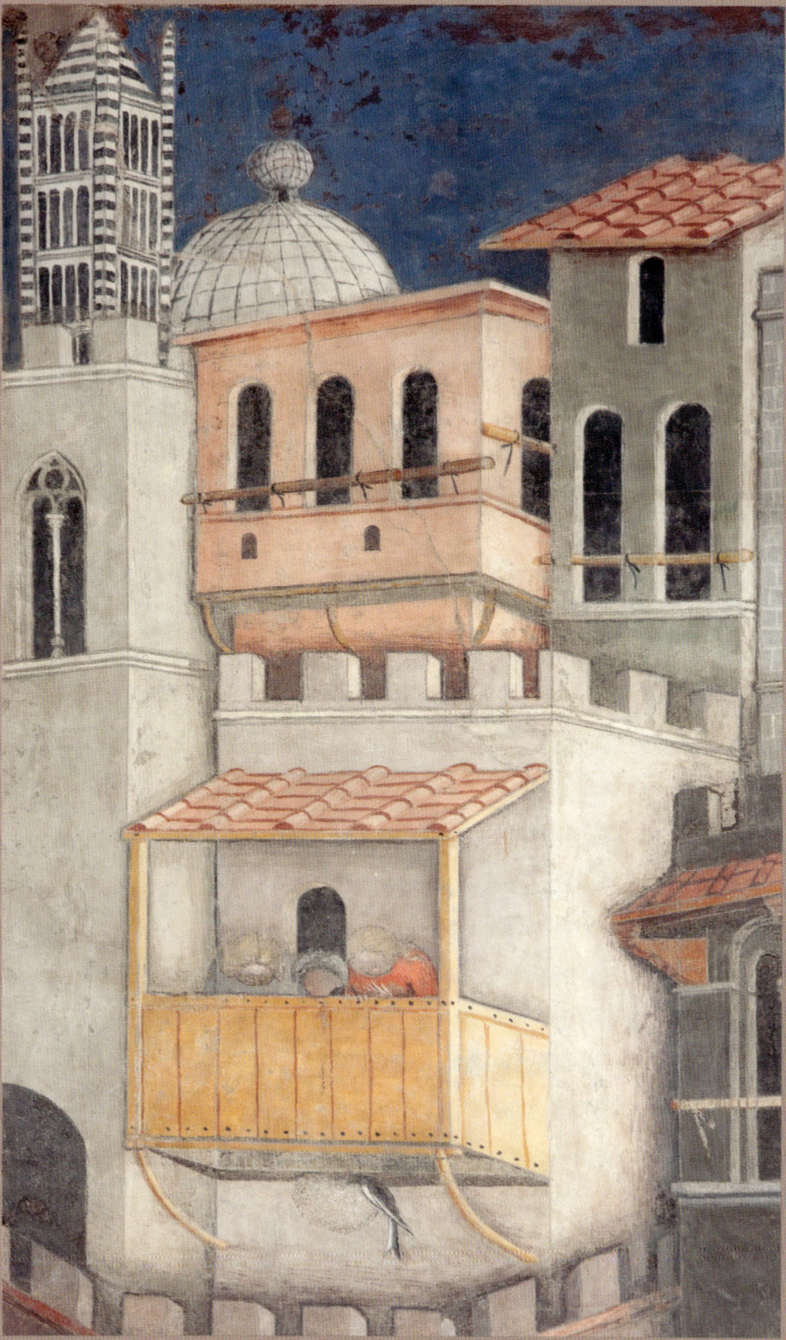

Ambrogio Lorenzetti, *The Effects of Good Government in the City*, detail

The dome and bell tower of Siena Cathedral seen from the Campo

It is a given fact that Lorenzetti's frescoes, commissioned for propaganda and celebratory purposes, describe an imagined, sought-after reality. The images have rightly been called "too beautiful." But it is equally true, as has been reiterated various times, that the references to the contemporary scene are numerous and very important. Thus it happens that the narrowly political, symbolic, and instructional aspect, when actually applied to everyday life, takes on at the same time the tones of narrative, chronicle, and invaluable historical and documentary illustration.

We have already noted that, in the play of identification and recognition, the urban setting, when depicting the actual structures of the city, reduces itself to just a few isolated references to real places, between the cathedral, with its black and white bands, on one side and what is probably Porta Romana on the other.

But when the scene moves out of the city with its towers, streets, shops and buildings, we find ourselves immersed in the colorful, lively open countryside easily recognized as the area around Siena. It is right here in his approach to the description of the rural landscape that Ambrogio shows a totally new sensibility compared to the painters of his time. In the countryside painted by Simone Martini as the background for Guidoriccio da Fogliano, frescoed only ten years earlier (1328), Montemassi Castle is certainly recognizable, but it is placed in an abstract, "symbolic and interchangeable" landscape reminiscent of Giotto and not too different from Duccio's landscapes. This cannot be said about *Good Government*, in which the shape of the land and

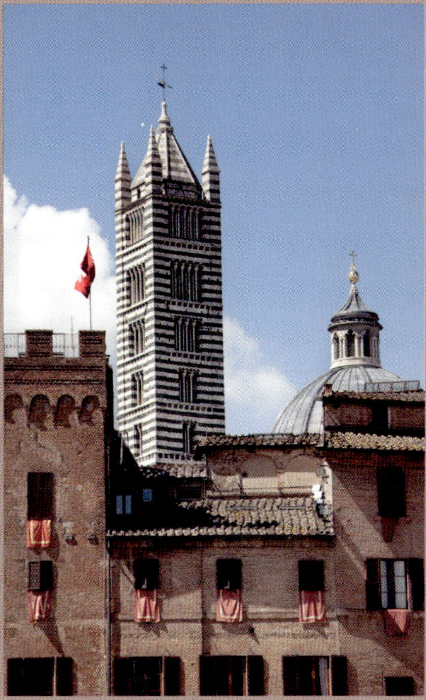

the types of cultivation in the countryside around Siena are real and, all in all, still existent, with the concentration of the planted crops near the city and scattered farmhouses with their little fenced gardens next to them.

Lorenzetti's natural environment corresponds significantly with that of his audience, whether in the fourteenth or fifteenth century or now in the twenty-first. Thank heaven, or perhaps it would be better to say, thanks to those who have lived in and still live, lovingly, in the Sienese countryside, these places do not look too different now than they did when Ambrogio painted them.

Certainly, we do not find now the poetry of peasants at work, of the industrious life that revolved around the farmhouses and the grazing animals.

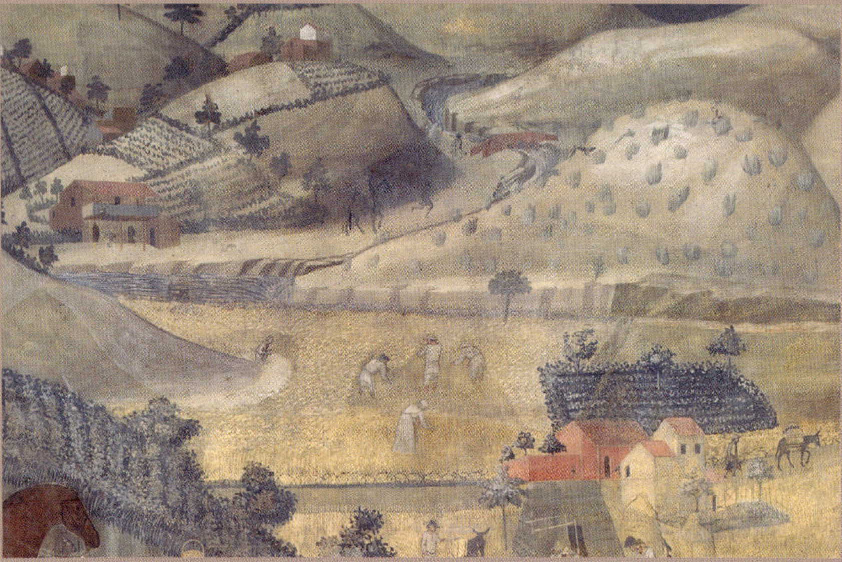

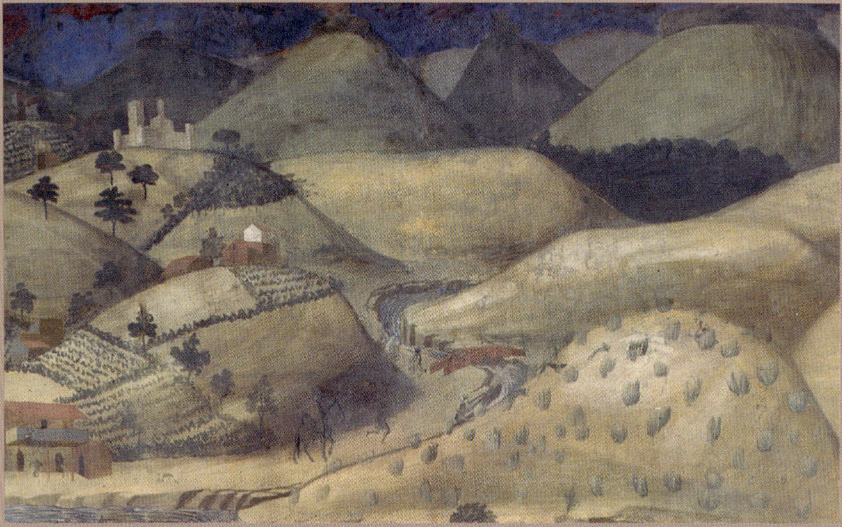

The very valuable, and very costly, "belted" pigs are still there, but well-protected by fences, and no one would dream today of taking one on a leash into the city – at the least he would end up in the newspaper!
But the views are undeniably the same, with the checkerboard of the cultivated fields that mark off the Elsa and Arbia valleys and the bare low hills of the Orcia valley sloping towards the southern part of the territory of Siena, which coincides more or less with the possessions of the ancient Republic. Thus we can still observe, and verify, how the rolling, fertile hills closer to Siena gradually yield to the arid, barren clay fields which thin out, in turn, towards the mountain peaks

Ambrogio Lorenzetti,
*The Effects of Good Government in the Country*, details

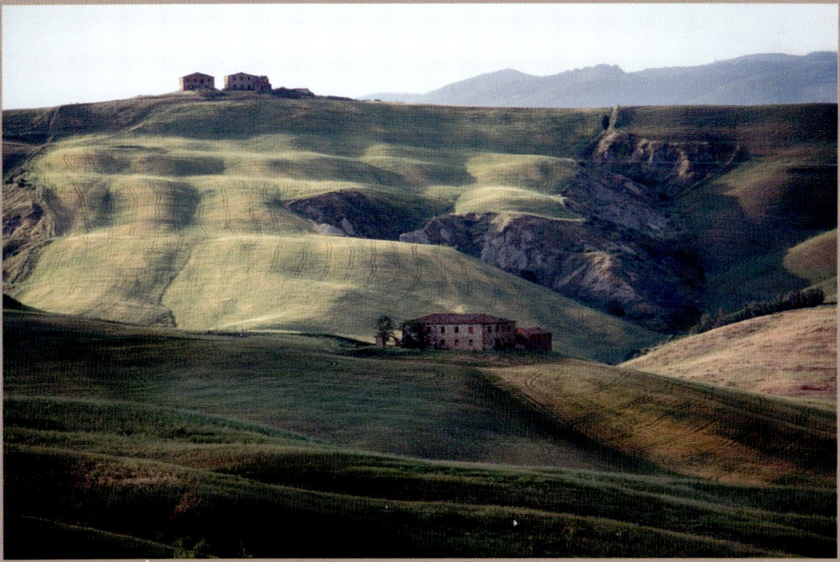

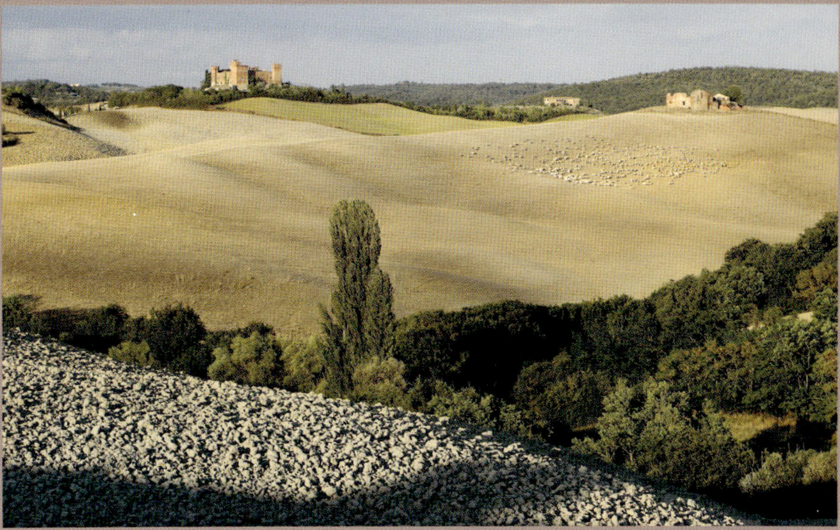

that stretch almost to the sea, towards the legendary port of Talamone, as highly desired in the past as it was hard to reach, passing through the unhealthy and unsafe Maremma area.

And it matters little that, in his need to communicate a complete and immediate visual message, Lorenzetti showed more than one season at the same time, presenting the wheat harvest and the tending of the vines in the same pictorial moment, because the credibility of his message is borne also by these relatively inoffensive simulations that mark off the passage of the months and the fruitful activities of man in a time that is as concrete and real as the places where it unfolds.

(L.G.)

The Sienese countryside

# The Sala dei Pilastri

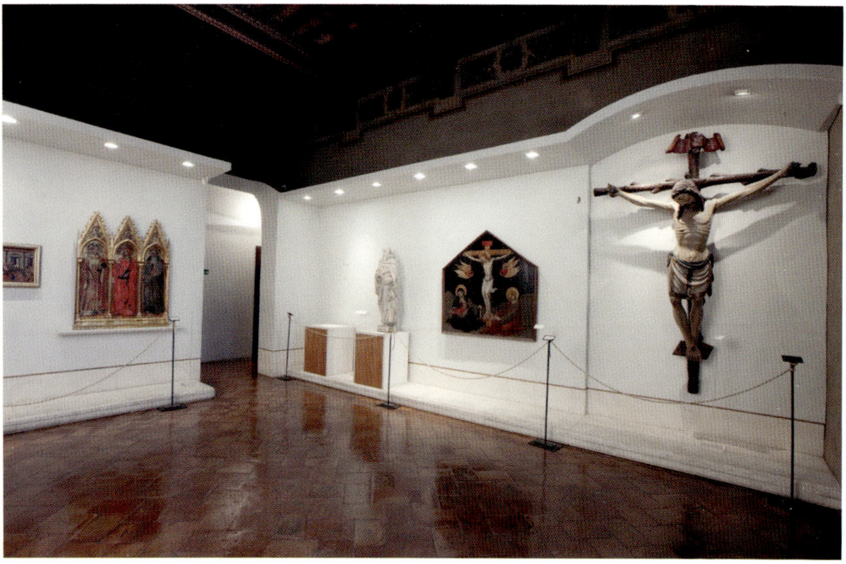

The Sala dei Pilastri

Adjacent to the Sala dei Nove is the Sala dei Pilastri (Room of the Pillars). It contains works from the fourteenth and fifteenth century, some of which are very important to the history of art. Among these are a large painted *Crucifix*, attributed to Massarello di Gilio (documented from 1290 to 1339), small panels by various artists which were once part of larger compositions now dismantled and dispersed, two predella panels by Neroccio di Bartolomeo (1447-1500) showing *Saint Bernardine Preaching in Piazza del Campo* and *A Possessed Woman being Freed during the Saint's Funeral Procession*, and a *Crucifixion* by Sano di Pietro (1406-1481). Among the other works on display, especially noteworthy are:

**Ambrogio Lorenzetti** (doc. 1319-1348), *Saint Michael the Archangel*, stained glass window, ca. 1330
This small window, dated around 1330 and showing Saint Michael the Archangel, is attributed to Ambrogio Lorenzetti.
It comes from the Monteoliveto convent near Porta Tufi. The angel holds a globe in one hand and in the other a sword resting on the defeated dragon.
This is the only remaining example in Siena of a fourteenth-century stained-glass window, after the one by Duccio in the cathedral, dated 1288.

**Andrea di Bartolo** (doc. 1389-1429), *Chest*, painted and gilded wood, gilt over pastille and tempera on wood, ca. 1403-1410.

Various artists and artisans worked on this precious object; they are listed in the ink notation found during restoration in 1982 on the inner surface of the chest, underneath its nineteenth-century covering. The gold-ground paintings can be attributed to Andrea di Bartolo, a Sienese artist still working in the late Gothic style. Taddeo di Francesco (doc. 1389 – *ante* 1428) and Giusa di Frosino (doc. 1389-1440), who were painters of chests, seem to have done the gilding and decorations. The other artisans mentioned are Luca di Giacomo (doc. 1437) for the ironwork and the carpenter Tome di Buonconvento.On the front of the chest, between the city's coats of arms, is the figure of *Saint Peter of Alexandria*, a protector of Siena from 1403 to the end of the century, while on the sides and back appear the four traditional patron saints of Siena, *Crescentius*, *Sabinus*, *Ansanus*, and *Victor*. The *Annunciation* is painted on the lid. The chest, covered with gilded pastille embellished with punched decorations and small colored glass balls, still has its ancient iron handles and clasps. It is thought that this was the chest holding the little containers, "pyxes," for the drawing of the names of the officials of the Republic.

**Francesco di Vannuccio** (ca. 1330/35 – before 1391), *Chest*, tin-plate and tempera on walnut, ca. 1360-1370

On the front is painted the *Annunciation* by Francesco di Vannuccio. The walnut chest is reinforced with tin plate and iron studs along the corners and edges of the lid, five wrought-iron handles, and three clasps lined up across the front.

Andrea di Bartolo, *Chest*

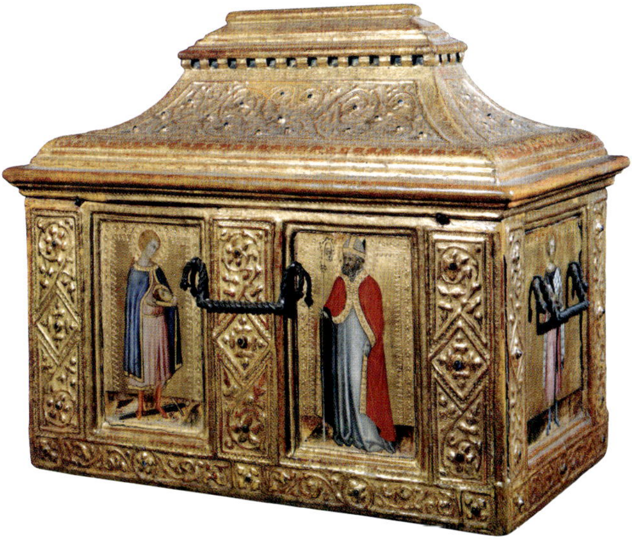

A curious note

## The Papal Golden Rose

Pius II, the Sienese pope Enea Silvio Piccolomini, donated the Golden Rose to his city in 1459, as is written on the nodus of the stem, to mark his first anniversary as pope.

The tradition of the gift of a "golden rose" dates to the eleventh century. This was the beginning of the custom on the part of popes to give this precious object each year to particularly worthy basilicas, sanctuaries, kings, cities, and individuals.

The gift was bestowed personally by the pope in the church of Saint John Lateran in Rome on the fourth Sunday of Lent. The significance of the "golden rose" had a dual meaning, alluding both to the salvation of the Garden of Eden and to the tree of Jesse, which rose from the breast of King David, Jesse's son and the beginning of the line from which the Virgin Mary descended.

The rose given to the city of Siena on 4 March 1459, made of pure embossed, chased and engraved gold and of silver gilt, is 69 centimeters high and, as was the custom, resembles a thorny branch with leaves and five roses.

Siena has another golden rose, kept in the Museo dell'Opera, given it, according to tradition, by its other illustrious pope, Alexander VII, who had it made to a design by Gian Lorenzo Bernini in 1658.

(L.G.)

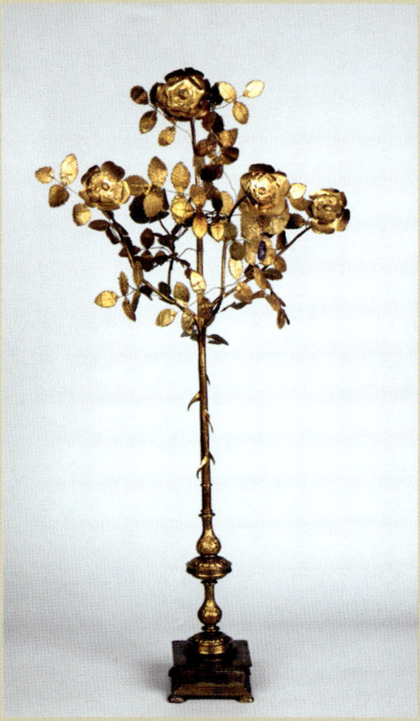

Simone di Giovanni Ghini, *The Golden Rose*

## The Vestibule

Coming back towards the Sala del Mappamondo, on the left, we cross a vestibule which leads to the forechapel and the palace chapel proper.
In this small entranceway is a display case holding some important relics tied to the history of the city and the Palio. Among these are the *gold ring* ($17^{th}$ cen.) and the richly decorated embossed gilt metal *Helmet of the Captain of the People* ($15^{th}$-$17^{th}$ cen.), which has a place of honor in the parade before the two annual races for the Palio, carried by a page on a cushion. The clarions on display, made in Germany in the seventeenth century, play an important part in the ritual of Siena and the Palio because, sounded by the palace trumpeters, they mark the city's important solemn moments. These are special trumpets with a long, thin body, following a typical $17^{th}$-$18^{th}$ century model, and produce the high clear sound which gives them their name.
On the left wall is a detached fresco of *The Virgin and Child*, attributed to Ambrogio Lorenzetti. The painting, dated to 1340, originally graced one side of the large loggia of the palace.
In the center of the wall, a large arch opens onto the atrium which leads to the interior chapel of Palazzo Pubblico, constructed at the beginning of the fifteenth century.

## The Forechapel

This forechapel is an open space covered with frescoes. The cycle's secular and very interesting iconographical theme of *Illustrious Men* derives from the space's former use as the antechamber for the Concistoro, the main governing body of the Republic. The entire cycle, painted by Taddeo di Bartolo in 1415, is devoted to illustrating the political virtues necessary for the proper exercise of power (Justice, Magnanimity, Fortitude, Prudence, and Religion). Their value is reinforced by the portraits of illustrious Romans exemplifying these virtues, chosen from among the most representative historical and political figures who contributed to the great, enduring strength of ancient Rome, such as Julius Caesar, Pompey, Cato, Mucius Scaevola, and Scipio.
The meaning of this choice of iconography, unusual but not completely outmoded in central Italy during this period, should be seen in the framework of the recovery of classical culture which, in Siena too, in an enlightened

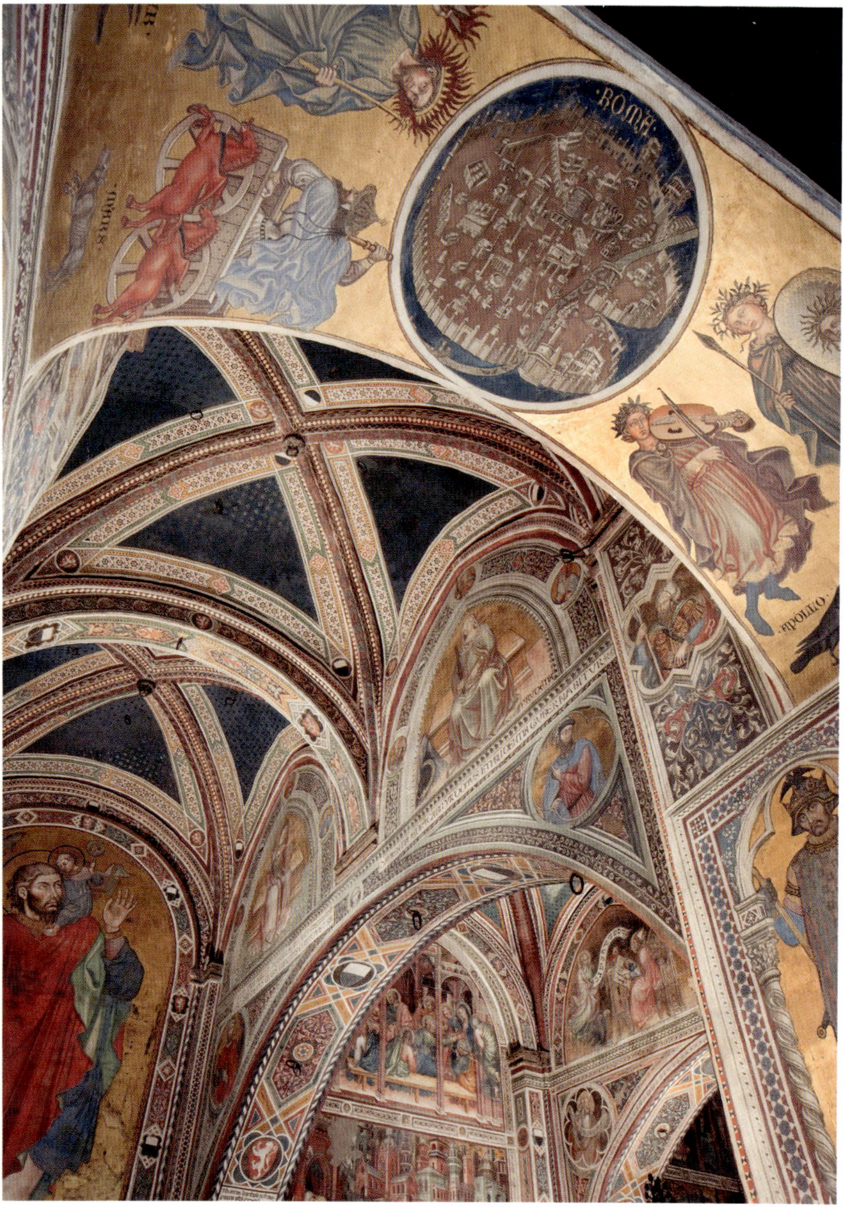

The forechapel

age, had led the city to seek out, or to claim, its quite improbable Roman origins, proposing at the same time the government of ancient times, revisited and repackaged through its most emblematic figures, as the best and only example of "good government" possible.
This message is strengthened by the presence, on the intrados of the arch into the Sala del Mappamondo, of a monochrome map of ancient Rome on a blue background, which should almost certainly be read as a reference to the other, now-lost, map painted by Lorenzetti, establishing in this way another correspondence between the two powers, the two cities, and their history.
Taddeo di Bartolo also painted the monumental *Saint Christopher* on the wall facing the arch opening into the Sala del Mappamondo. Saint Christopher was a wayfarer and is often depicted in cities that are a goal for pilgrims, such as Siena. His presence here, however, should probably be interpreted as a tribute to the titular saint of the church where the public meetings of the Sienese people and the communal government were held before the Palazzo Pubblico was built.
On the same wall are two intricate fifteenth-century wooden inlays, attributed to Mattia di Nanni, known as Bernacchino. These were part of an ancient, elaborate bench which has since been dismantled and show Justice and the Virgin Mary placing Siena in the care of the kneeling *podestà*.
In the showcase containing ancient examples of sacred art from the twelfth and fifteenth centuries, including a refined pax made of embossed copper, silver, and enamel in Siena around 1399-1400, is the Golden Rose donated to the city of Siena by Pope Pius II in 1459, the handiwork of a Florentine silversmith and jeweler who was active in Rome, Simone di Giovanni Ghini.

# The Civic Virtue of "Illustrious Men"

In the second half of the fourteenth century, the iconographic model of "*Viri illustres*" (Famous Men) arose, destined to become a model for the decoration of private and public buildings throughout the fifteenth century.

The portrait as a genre, whether literary or figurative, had fallen from favor centuries before. In the twelfth century, the "Vidas," biographies, of the Provençal troubadours foreshadow in a certain sense the rebirth of the figurative portrait. This trend was expressed in the beginning mainly in tapestries, which were in great demand because they were easy to carry, and engravings.

The *exempla bonorum* of Romance literature gave rise to the most famous medieval secular heroic canon, the *Neuf Preux* (Nine Worthies) – Hector, Alexander the Great, and Julius Caesar, Joshua. David, and Judas Maccabeus, King Arthur, Charlemagne, and Godfrey of Boullion – portrayed as standing full figures in line, often separated by architectural features (real or feigned), and recognizable by the *Tituli*, written captions for the image, and by their coats of arms prominently displayed on shields and banners.

Throughout the fourteenth and fifteenth centuries, these themes were illustrated in painting cycles entrusted to important artists, flanked in the enterprise by men of letters and culture.

Among the monumental cycles of illustrious men are those painted by Giotto at Castelnuovo in Naples before 1334 and

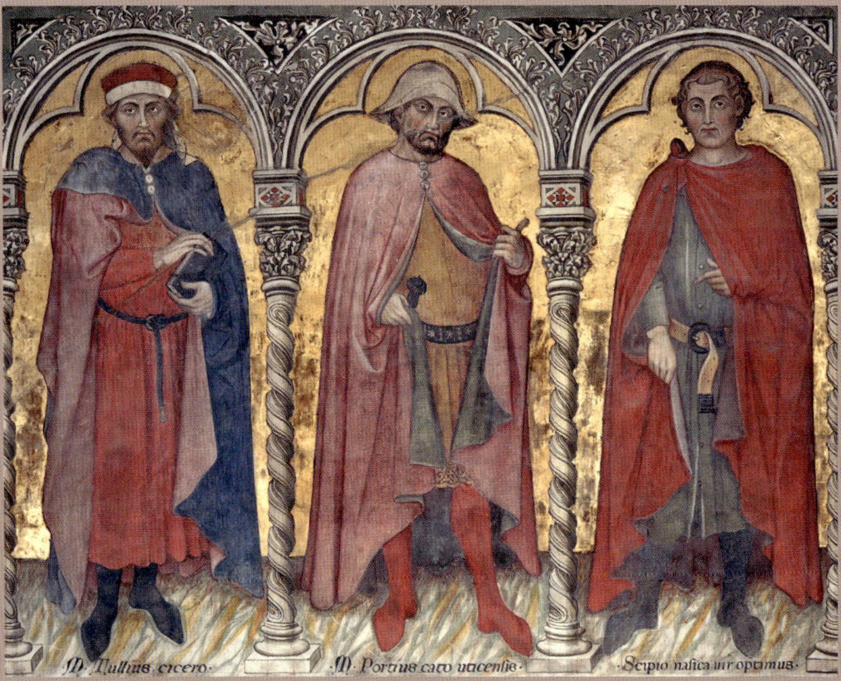

Taddeo di Bartolo, *M. Curius Dentatus, M. Furius Camillus, P. Scipio Africanus*

Taddeo di Bartolo, *Cicero, M. Portius Cato, P. Scipio Nasica*

for Azzone Visconti in Milan (1339). An archetype could be the *Sala Virorum Illustrium* in Francesco del Vecchio di Carrara's palace in Padua, perhaps frescoed by Altichiero between 1368 and 1379. Attention then moves to Florence, with the decoration of the Aula Minor (before 1406) in the Palazzo Vecchio, and Foligno, the Sala degli Imperatori in the Palazzo Trinci (1413-1424), coming finally to the two painted cycles in Siena's Palazzo Pubblico, one in the forechapel, by Taddeo di Bartolo (1413-1414) and the other in the Sala del Concistoro, of 1529-1535, by Domenico Beccafumi. Taddeo's cycle shows the Virtues (*Fortitude, Prudence, Justice, Magnanimity, Religion*), and beneath them the men whose deeds and history exemplify these virtues.

The central idea of the entire composition is based on the ideal of the public good, eternal peace, and love. The fount of inspiration is Republican Rome, which Taddeo depicts on the arch separating the forechapel from the Sala del Mappamondo in a famous map of the city of Rome. In the nearby painting cycle by Beccafumi, the illustrious men are represented by the acts which made them immortal. The scenes are painted on the sides of the vault over the room, the Sala del Concistoro, corresponding to the virtues depicted in the center of the ceiling, glorifying man as a protagonist of his own history through ideals and virtues like patriotism, strictness with himself and others, brotherly love, and justice.

(P.G.)

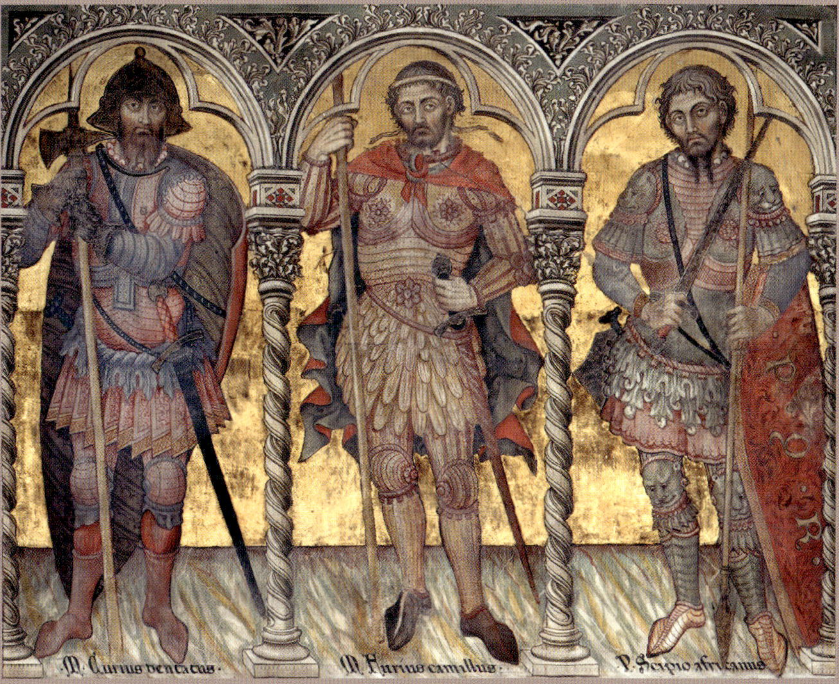

# The Chapel of the Signori

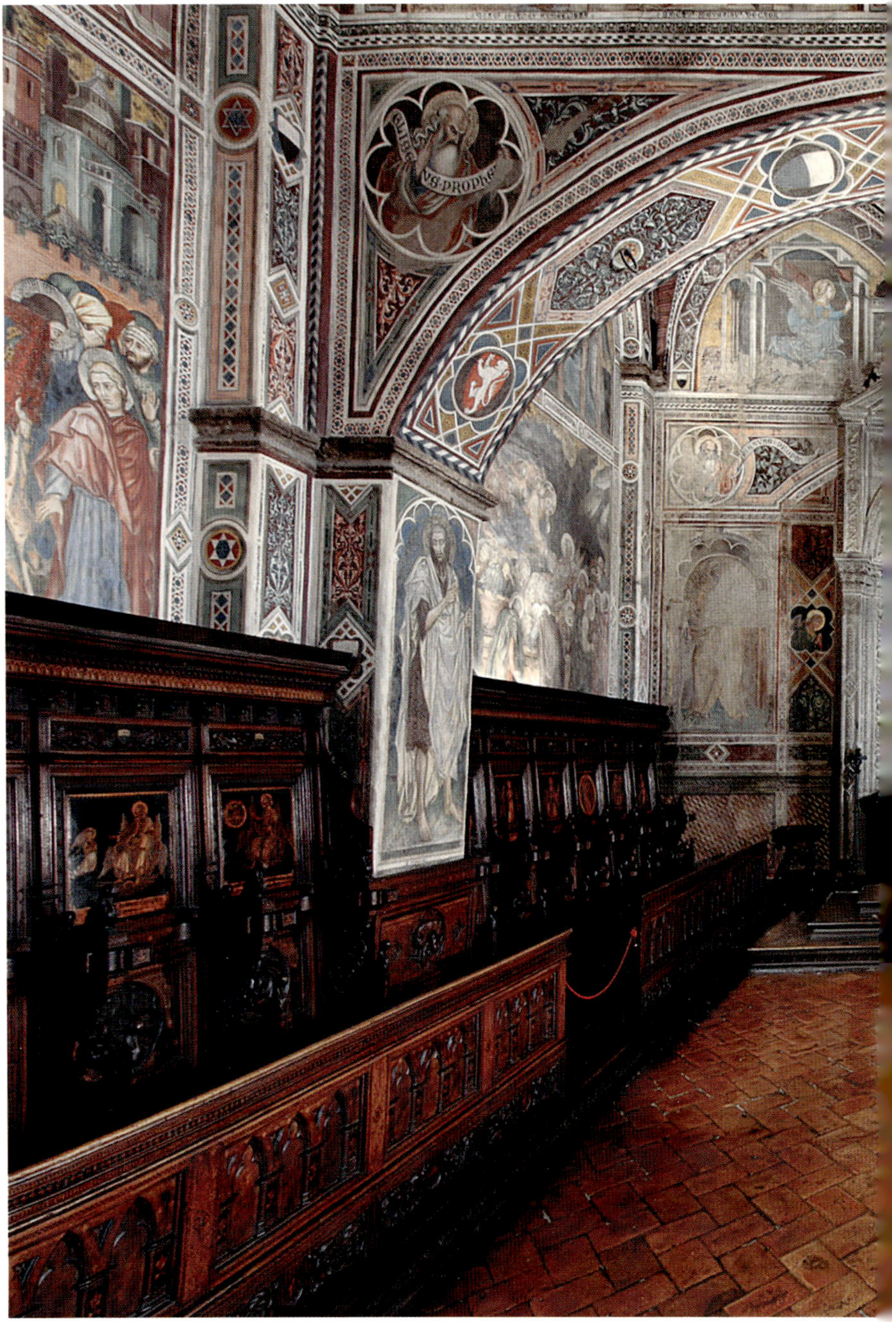

The Chapel of the Signori

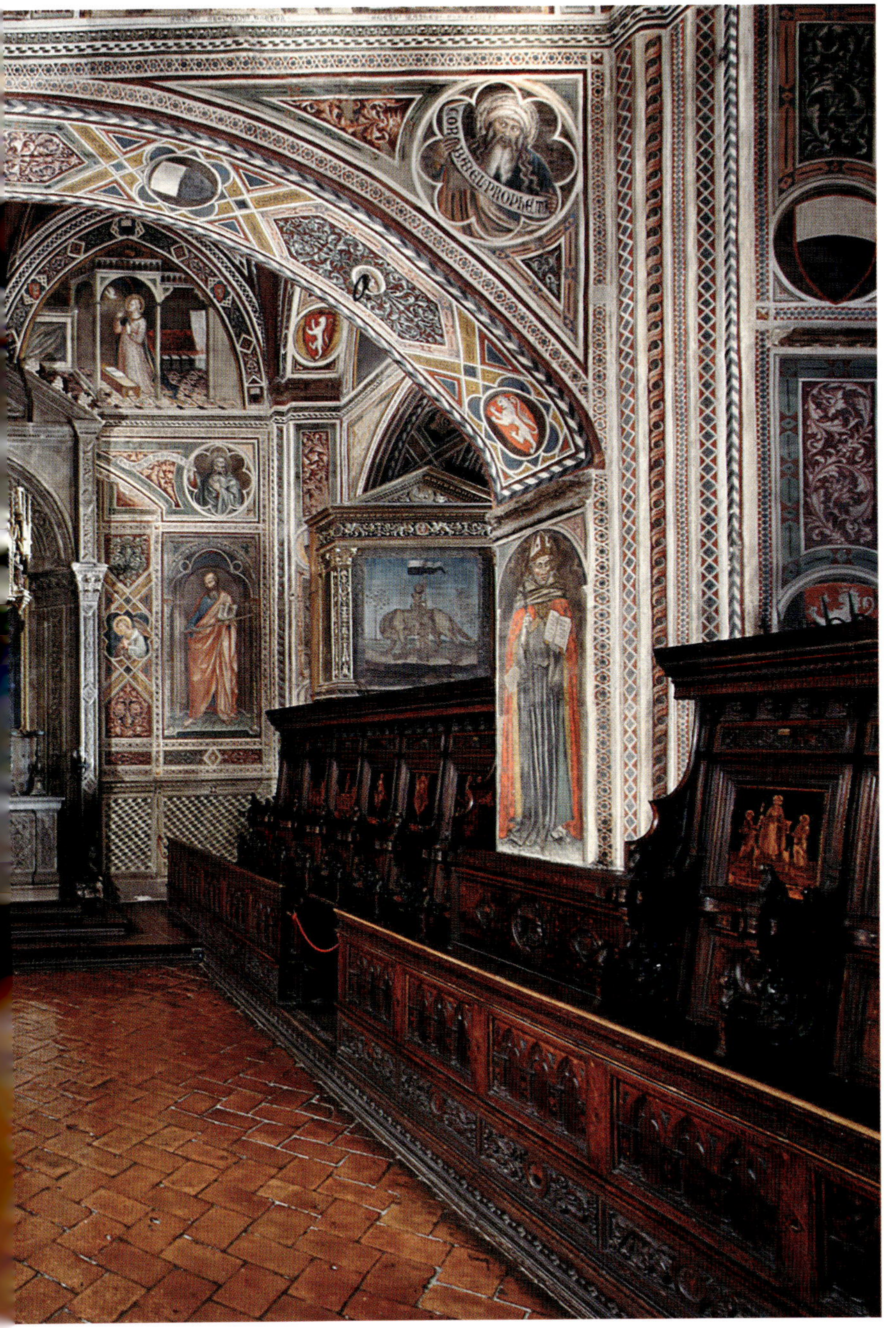

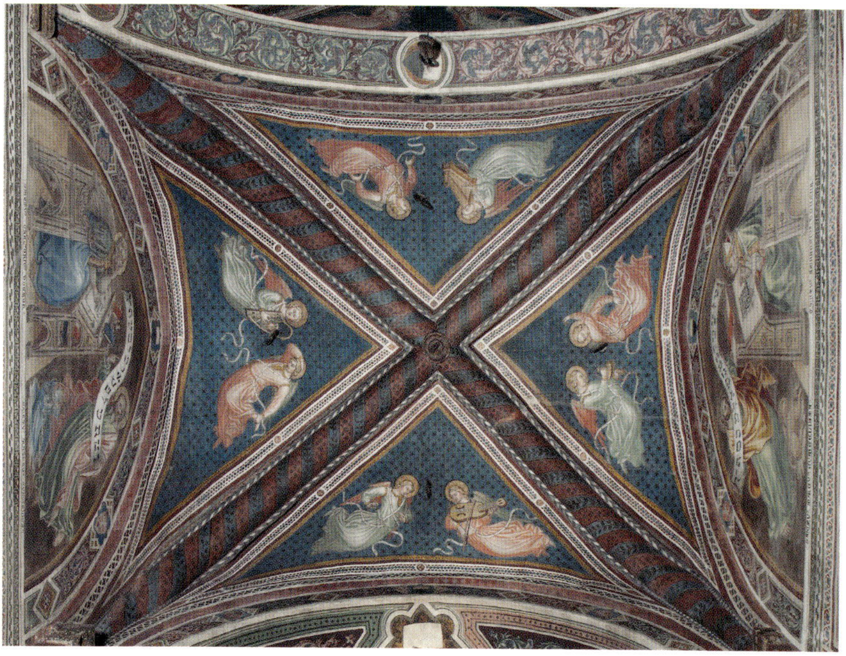

Taddeo di Bartolo, ceiling of the Chapel of the Signori showing *Angel Musicians*

A large wrought-iron grate dated in the 1440s, decorated with quatrefoils and vegetable motifs, leads into the small but rich palace chapel. The commission to decorate it was given in 1407 to Taddeo di Bartolo, the most representative painter of Sienese art around the turn of the fifteenth century, whose style was still very close, in terms of taste and technical skill, to the great school of the first half of the fourteenth century, whose outstanding artistic personalities were Duccio, Simone Martini and the Lorenzetti brothers. Portrayed are episodes from the life of the Virgin Mary, to whom the chapel is dedicated. Above the altar is the *Annunciation*, and the other scenes are on the left wall: *Bidding Farewell to the Apostles*, the *Death of the Virgin*, her *Funeral* and *Assumption*. Painted on the cross vault, still Gothic in style, are thirty-two angel musicians, each playing a different instrument. Some of these are easily recognizable as instruments in use during that period, while others have fallen into disuse, if not totally unknown.

The furnishings in the chapel are also original, and date from the early fourteenth century. Along both side walls are beautiful wooden choir stalls, carved and inlaid between 1415 and 1428 by the Sienese sculptor Domenico di Niccolò, known as "Domenico of the choirs" ("de' Cori") because of this important work for the commune of Siena, which made him famous.

The inlays in the backs of the twenty-one seats illustrate the Apostles' Creed.

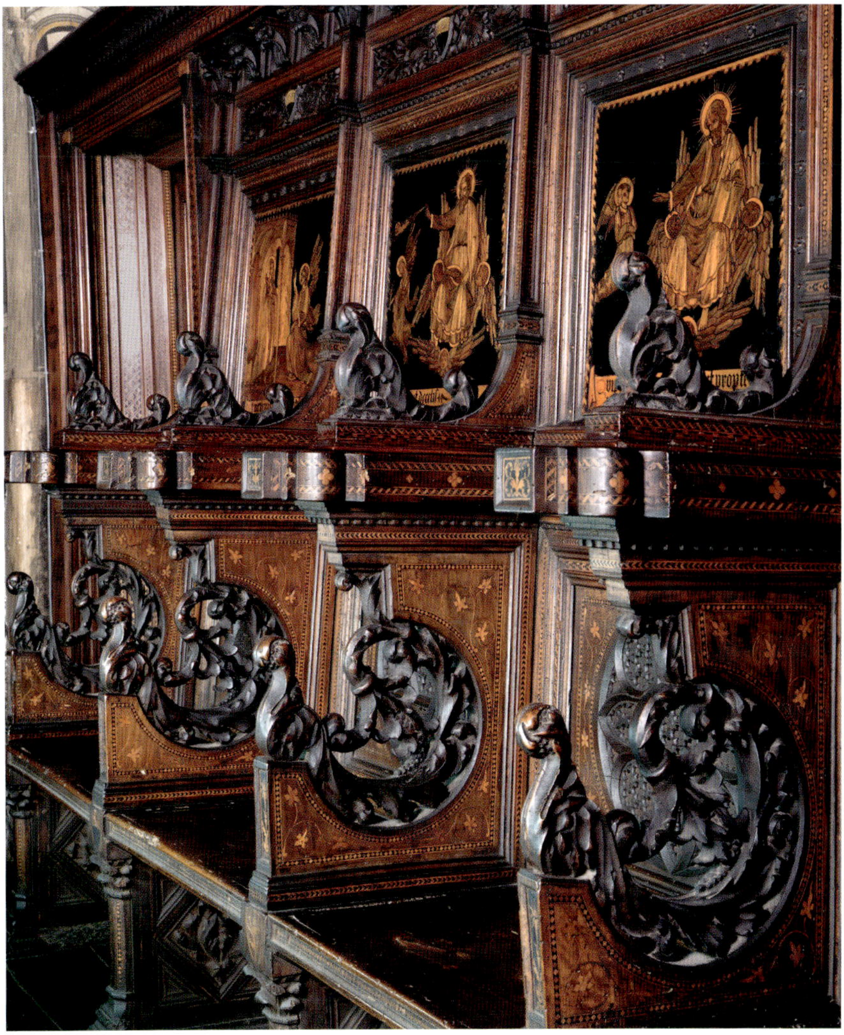

Domenico
di Niccolò dei Cori,
*Inlaid choir stalls*,
detail

Domenico di Niccolò also made the door to the chapel and the intricate central chandelier of carved and gilded wood, a very valuable and unusual light fixture which emulates architectural forms with spires, pinnacles, and statuettes (ca. 1435).

The chapel's altar was made in the sixteenth century by Lorenzo di Mariano, known as Marrina. It comes from the cathedral and was brought here at the end of the seventeenth century, together with the panel painting above it, by Sodoma, of *The Holy Family with Saint Leonard* (ca. 1530). The organ which can be seen to the right of the chapel is also a valuable sixteenth-century piece (ca. 1520), the work of Giovanni d'Antonio Piffaro, one of the best-known and esteemed Italian organ-makers.

Coming out of the chapel, turn right to continue visiting the museum.

A curious note

## The *Costituto* in the Vulgate

At the beginning of the fourteenth century, the Commune of Siena decided to translate into the language of everyday life the aggregation of rules and laws that regulated public life in order to make them comprehensible to the people, in reality the majority, who did not know Latin. The important document in question is the *Costituto*, which had been drawn up in Latin in 1262. This episode in Sienese history is a unique effort at "transparency," unparalleled in the political panorama of that time; it bears witness, yet again, to the high level of democracy achieved by the Republic of Siena. The city government established that the *Costituto* of May 1309, transcribed into the vulgate, had to be "ligatum in Biccherna," that is to say bound and put on display so that all the citizens who so desired and did not know "gramaticum" (Latin grammar), and anyone else who wished, could see, read, and copy everything that was written in it. The office of the Biccherna in the Palazzo Pubblico was made available for this purpose. With this act, the government in office intended to underscore its commitment to safeguarding even the weakest members of society by fostering the spread and the knowledge of the rights and duties of citizens, especially those who did not know Latin, demonstrating a political will never seen before and a broadminded ideological decision. It is no coincidence that the *Costituto* is considered an "unicum" in the history of Italian and European laws and politics; its interest goes beyond national borders to encompass all of western culture. The original document, consisting of two handwritten volumes, is preserved in the Archivio di Stato.

(L.G.)

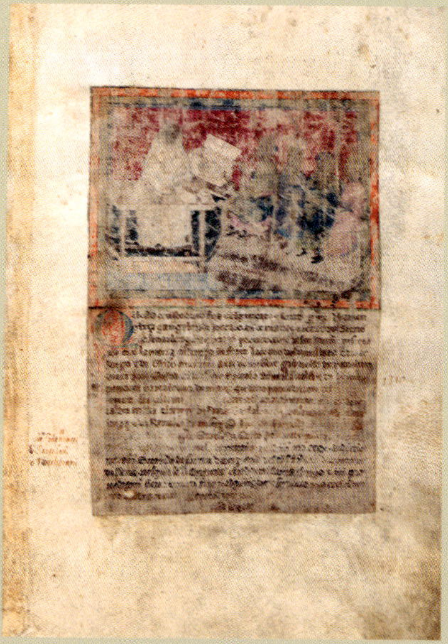

The *Costituto* of the Commune of Siena

# The Anticamera del Concistoro

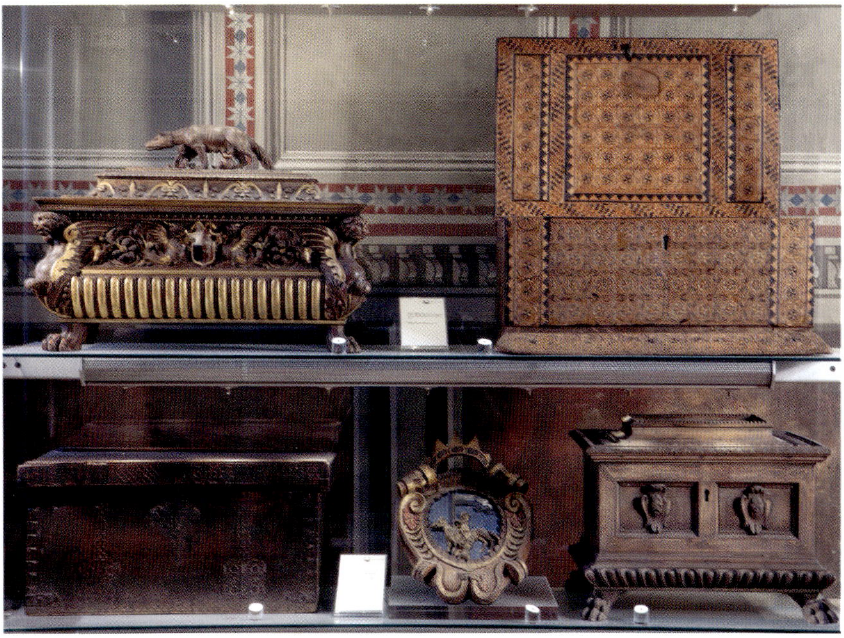

The Anticamera del Concistoro, showcase with wooden boxes

The walls of the large room opening on the left into the Sala del Concistoro and on the right to the Sala della Balìa are hung with detached frescoes from other parts of the palace. This room acquired the function of antechamber in the second half of the seventeenth century, after the adjacent room frescoed by Beccafumi was chosen as the meeting hall for the Concistoro, the most important political institution of the Sienese government in the modern age.

On the entrance wall is a fragment of a fresco attributed to Ambrogio Lorenzetti depicting *Saint Catherine of Alexandria*, *Saint John the Evangelist*, and *Saint Augustine with a Devotee* (first half of the 14th cen.); on the adjacent wall is another fresco with its sinopia preparatory drawing, showing *The Virgin and Child with Saint Catherine of Alexandria, Another Saint and a Donor* (Sienese school, after 1374).

The only fresco originally located in the room is the large *Saint Paul* (ca. 1370), attributed to Martino di Bartolomeo. On the center pillar is a small panel painting of the *Virgin and Child* (ca. 1470), attributed to Matteo di Giovanni.

In one of the two showcases are displayed four carved and inlaid wooden boxes, bearing the arms of the Commune of Siena and the Tribunale della Mercanzia (the court of the merchants guild), made by Sienese

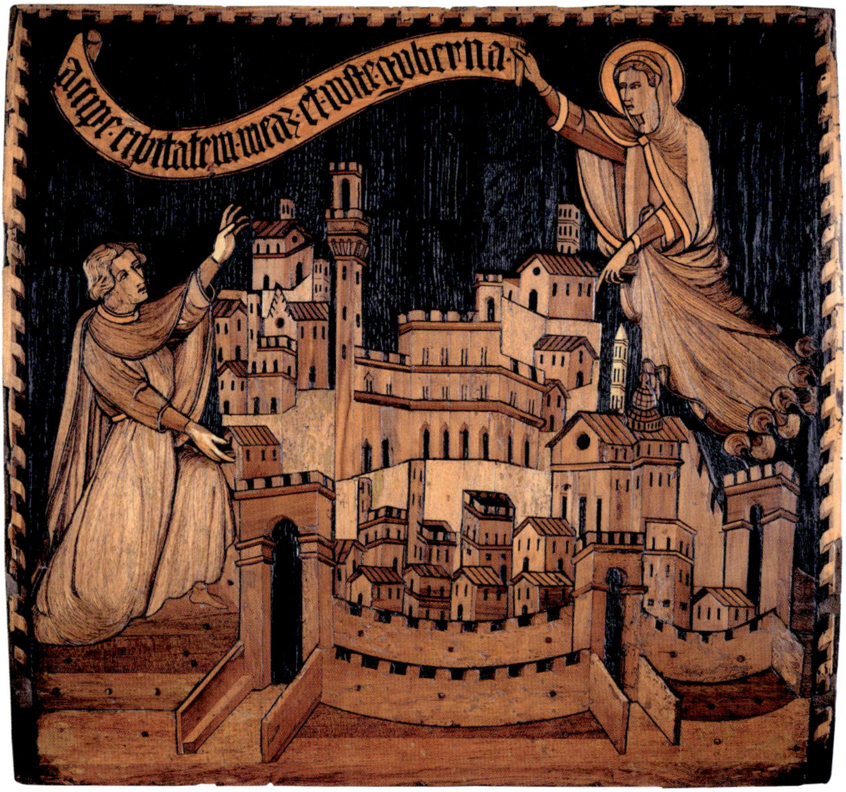

craftsmen between the fifteenth and sixteenth centuries, one of which is attributed to the Sienese sculptor Antonio Barili (1353-1516). The other holds a group of interesting painted wooden boxes dated in the seventeenth century. They are decorated with coats of arms and were used for drawing the names of councilors and officials of the Commune, following an ancient custom used in Siena to guarantee the greatest degree of government turnover and impede the concentration of power. Also on display is a painted wooden "ballot box" for the election of the councilors of the Accademia dei Rinnovati (early nineteenth century) and other objects used for the same purpose.

Mattia di Nanni, known as Bernacchino, inlaid wooden panel (first half of the 15th century), Forechapel

# The Ancient Sienese Magistracies

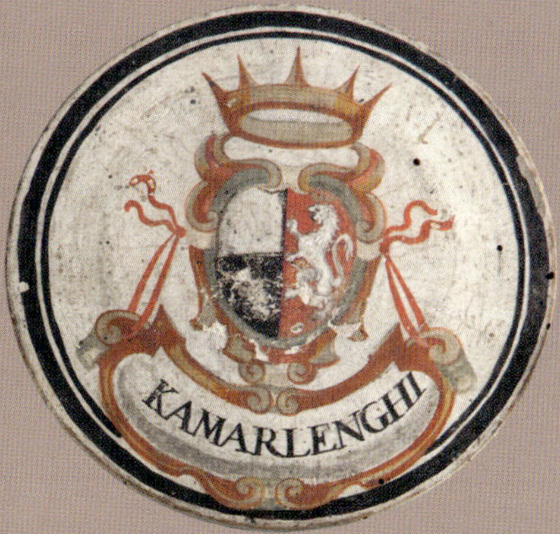

The first documented reference to the existence of the commune of Siena is dated 1125; the commune would take a little more than a century to reach full political and institutional maturity. The Nine, under whose government the city experienced its greatest economic, political, and cultural development, came to power in 1287 and held it until 1355. They were members of a ruling class in the city made up essentially of merchants, bankers, and entrepreneurs, and formed a sort of tight power oligarchy.

The Nine, or "Noveschi" as the members of this sort of 'caste' were called, held a monopoly on government for 67 years, taking advantage of the internal divisions of the city's political and social life and managing to keep in check also the poorer classes of salaried workers and peasants.

Their government took its name from the number (*nove*) of its members, elected each time by secret ballot by the members of the outgoing government. Those elected stayed in office for two months, with the obligation to live in the palace; they were allowed to leave it only for very serious family matters or official engagements of the commune, such as processions or official events tied to city life. This sort of 'imprisonment' was necessary to avoid outside interference, evidently frequent and more harmful than not. The commune provided their lodging on the top floor of the palace, in the wing on the Via Dupré side, corresponding with the large porch, and gave them an allowance for their upkeep, along with a cook, a barber, and messengers to maintain contact with the outside.

In Siena, as in most of the Tuscan communes, the real power, distributed among various institutions in a fluid manner and regulated but often modified to the advantage to one or the other, was vested in the *signoria*, called in Siena the Concistoro (consistory), made up of the Nine, the four Provveditori (superintendents) of the Biccherna (the financial magistracy), the four Consuls of the Mercanzia (members of the merchants guild) and the three Captains representing the three districts, or Terzi (thirds) into which the city is still divided today. In reality, during the period of their rule,

*On preceding page*
Wooden boxes for drawing the names of the councilors and officials of the Commune (17th century)

Wooden cups used for voting (17th century)

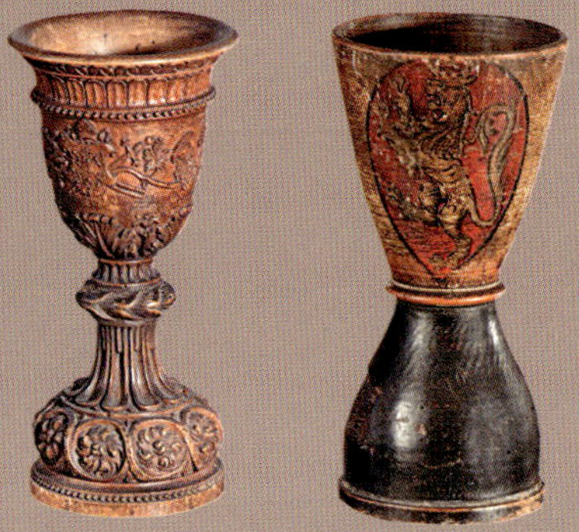

the Nine dominated the other city governing bodies in terms of authority and power, even interfering in some ways with the jurisdiction of the Podestà, the highest magistrate in the city when the commune was founded. He divided his duties with the Captain of the People. The Podestà convoked and presided over meetings of the General Council, the assembly of citizens which was the supreme deliberating and legislative body; among other things, it approved the statutes and building regulations and verified the acts of the *Concistoro*. The Council was composed of about 300 members, chosen among the citizens above the age of 25 who were inscribed in the tax rolls and resident in the city for at least ten years; they stayed in office for one year.

The General Council was also called the Council of the Bell, because they were summoned to meetings by a bell; the building where they met in the first half of the fourteenth century, built for this purpose next to Palazzo Pubblico, was thus known as the Palazzo della Campana ("palace of the bell"). The building was transformed into a theater after the middle of the sixteenth century, when the Medici assumed power over the city; for this reason, from then on, the council went back to meeting in the Sala del Mappamondo.

The *Podestà*, who was called from outside Siena in order to ensure his impartiality and remained in office for one year, was flanked by the Captain of the People. He presided over the Council of the People, which had jurisdiction over some crimes, the protection of the poor and the sick, and the organization of the city militia.

The financial offices of the city were under the jurisdiction of the Biccherna, the principal economic authority of the Republic, which remained active until 1786, even if after the annexation of Siena to the Grand Duchy of Tuscany, its powers, like those of most of the city offices, were very limited, restricted to public works, the water and sewer system, and later, the administrative matters connected with the Palio.

The Archivio di Stato in Siena still holds the so-called "Biccherna panels," from the name of this magistracy. This is a collection of 124 small wooden panels, painted with scenes of civic and religious subjects, used as covers for the bound ledgers of the government's financial records. They cover a span of time from the twelfth to the seventeenth century and were painted by the leading artists in Siena of each period. They are especially interesting because they provide a visual document of the daily life, customs, personages, and major events of five centuries of Sienese history.

(L.G.)

## The Sala del Concistoro

The name of this room, also called in ancient times the "basin" room because of the shape of the ceiling, comes from that of the magistracy of the Republic of Siena which met here until the establishment of the modern form of municipal government in 1786.
A fifteenth-century marble portal leads into the room, attributed to the Florentine sculptor and architect Bernardo Rossellino (1446). The inlaid panels of the door are attributed to the already-mentioned Domenico di Niccolò "of the Choirs" (1414). The fresco cycle on the ceiling, painted by Domenico Beccafumi between 1529 and 1535, marks a milestone in the history of Italian Mannerist art.
The topic chosen for the paintings, the *Public Virtues* of Greek and Roman heroes, follows the themes already developed in Lorenzetti's *Good Government* and Taddeo di Bartolo's *Illustrious Men*, pointing out to those in government and to the citizens the civic and moral examples they should emulate.
The examples they recommend are illustrated by episodes from the lives of famous figures, taken from the writings of the Roman historian Valerius Maximus. The actions of the personages, like those of good governing, must be guided by the three virtues represented in the center of the ceiling: *Justice* (in the middle), *Love of the Fatherland* (on the left) and *Mutual Benevolence* or *Harmony* (on the right). Surrounding the virtues, the historical episodes alternate in square and octagonal frames, joined together in a sort of large frieze which makes room in the corners for figures of Greek and Roman heroes, whose names are inscribed in the cartouches below them.
Starting from the left, the pictures illustrate: *The Tribune Publius Mucius Condemning his Colleagues to be Burned*, *The Beheading of Spurius Cassius*, *Postumius Tiburtius Putting his Son to Death*, *The Reconciliation of Marcus Aemilius Lepidus and Fulvius Flaccus out of Love of the Fatherland* (end wall), *The Killing of Spurius Melius*, *Marcus Manlius being thrown from the Tarpean Rock*, *The Sacrifice of Zaleucus of Locri*, *The Sacrifice of King Codron of Athens*.
The topics of these various episodes all refer to acts of virtue which took place in the political and personal histories of the protagonists, with particular reference to justice, as in the case of Publius Mucius, or justice

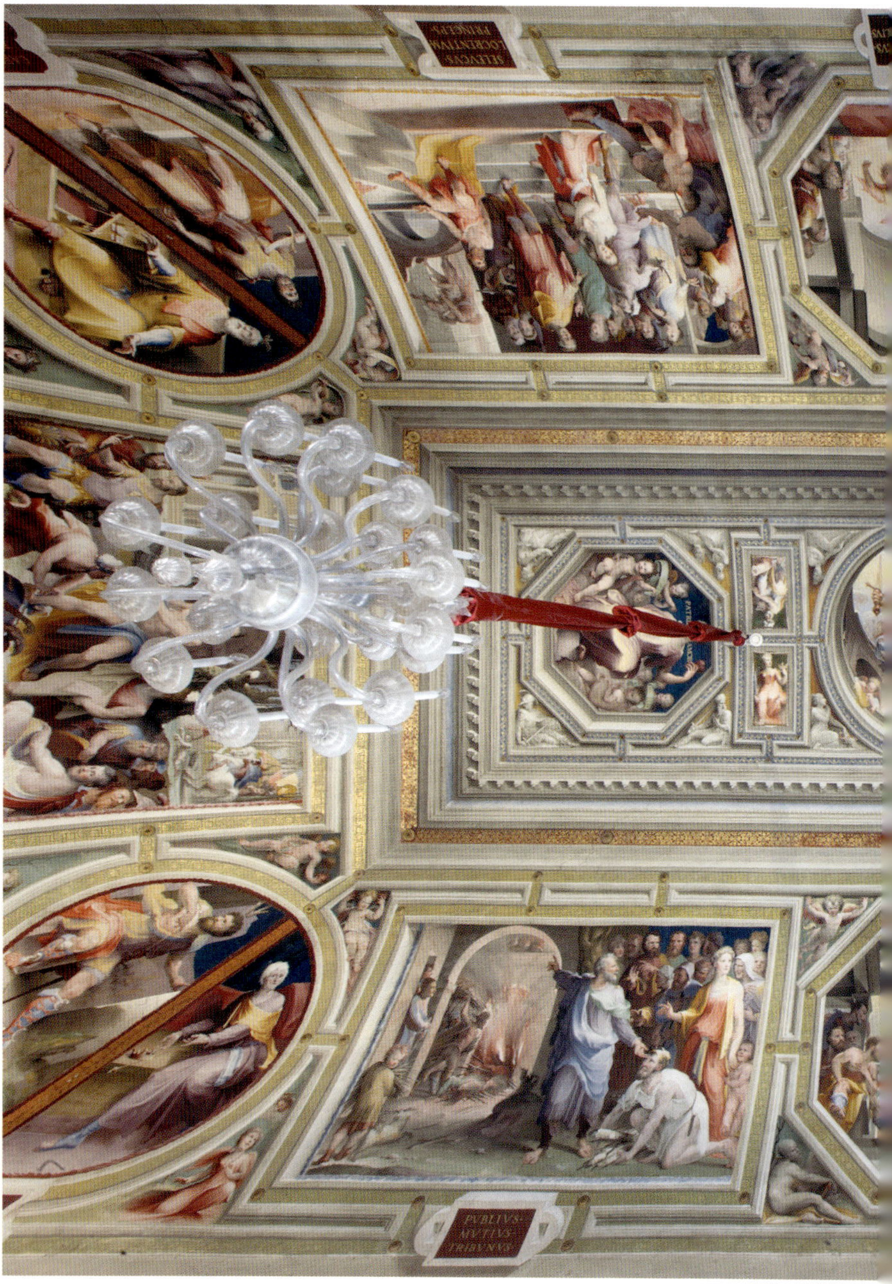


The ceiling of the
Sala del Concistoro

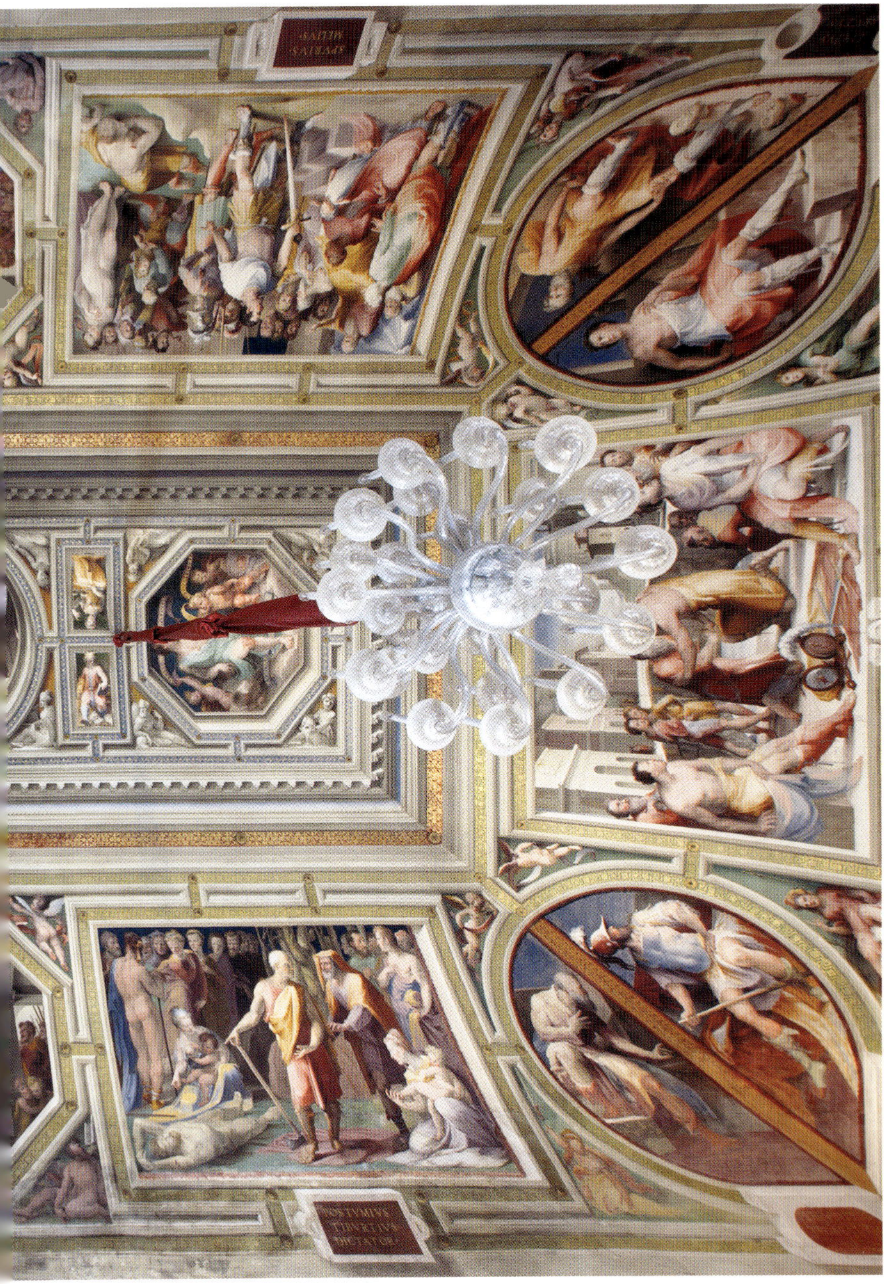

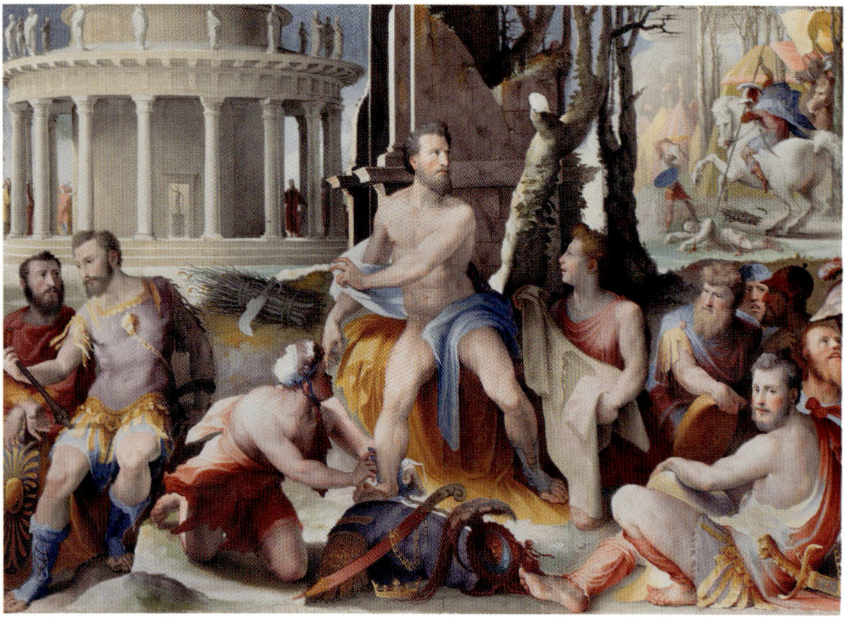

Domenico Beccafumi, *The Sacrifice of King Codron of Athens*

united with filial piety, as with Zaleucus of Locri who, being forced to blind his son for having committed rape, had only one eye of his son put out and one of his own eyes removed in place of his son's other eye. Love of the Fatherland is the theme illustrated by the king of Athens, Codron, who sacrificed his own life in order to fulfill an oracle's prophecy which said that his death was necessary for the victory of his people.

It is certain, however, that above and beyond the meaning of the individual parts and the complex symbolism that binds them together, it is the overall significance of the entire cycle that was especially relevant, not only because it was commissioned by the Sienese government, but also in light of the learned, open cultural environment in Siena at the time. It seems that the city authorities decided to award to Beccafumi the prestigious commission to decorate the room in Palazzo Pubblico after he had frescoed the ceiling of a drawing room in the palace of Marcello Agostini, a short distance from the Piazza del Campo, with episodes from ancient history and mythological and allegorical topics.

The layout of the ceiling in the Sala del Concistoro, which owes much to Beccafumi's experiences in Rome,

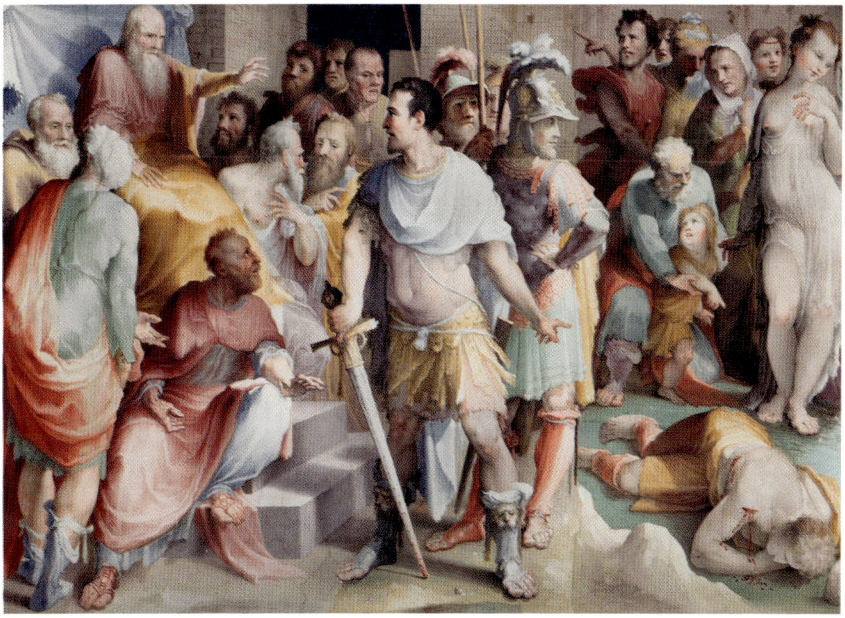

Domenico Beccafumi, *The Killing of Spurius Mellius*

presents a modern illusionistic approach, alternating daring foreshortening with patches of sky and landscape in the midst of complex architectural settings, all presented with rigorous perspective and great compositional skill.

Even given the severity of the dramatic, magniloquent topics presented, Beccafumi expresses himself with greater freedom and inventiveness in the details of the events collateral to the main stories and in the presentation of a gallery of supporting actors, a category congenial to him, such as the young women wearing turbans or floating veils, lively, curly-haired children, and pensive old men.

The entire cycle is pervaded by a soft luminousness, heightened by a chromatic freshness which bursts out in the iridescence of some of the clothes, where the painter, in one of his signature touches, dissolves colors and fabrics under powerful jets of light, or blurs and mixes them as gusts of wind wrap them around powerful, muscular bodies.

Above the entrance door is a large canvas of *The Judgment of Solomon* (ca. 1675-1680) by Luca Giordano, a late seventeenth-century Neapolitan painter.

# The Protagonists
# Domenico Beccafumi

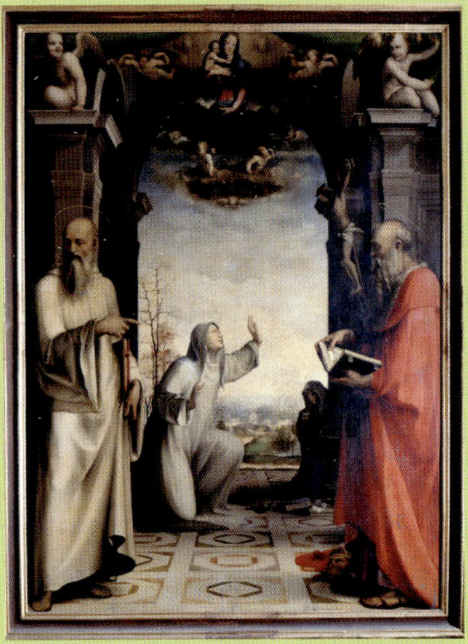

The first mention of Domenico di Giacomo Pace, better known by his nicknames Mecarino or Beccafumi (from the surname of his protector Lorenzo Beccafumi), can be found in a deed for a plot of woodland dated 1507, which mentions him as being of age and a painter, giving credence to the hypothesis that he is one Domenico di Giacomo, baptized in 1484. Scholars maintain that the artist, who would go on to become one of the emerging figures in Italian mannerism, was trained in Siena in the workshop of the eccentric painter from Urbino Girolamo Genga. Among his earliest works, in the vein of reworking themes from classical antiquity which was much in vogue in Siena at the time, are *Lucretia* at Oberlin College (Ohio) and *Penelope* in the Seminario Patriarcale in Venice. This antiquarian climate is evident also in the information furnished by Giorgio Vasari, who says that in 1512 Beccafumi frescoed the façade of Palazzo Borghesi alla Postierla, in competition with Sodoma who was decorating Agostino Bardi's house. Beccafumi's decoration is now lost, but a preparatory drawing survives, showing war trophies, battles scenes, and personages from Roman history. In 1513 the artist was involved in the renovations of the Cappella del Manto (Chapel of the Cloak) inside Santa Maria della Scala hospital, and that same year received payment for the triptych of the *Holy Trinity*, now in the Pinacoteca in Siena, the prototypes for which can be found in works by the Florentines Fra Bartolomeo and Mariotto Albertinelli. Beccafumi drew from their research on light being done in those same years for his altarpiece of *Saint Catherine Receiving the Stigmata*, painted for the since-destroyed monastery of San Benedetto outside Porta Tufi in Siena around 1514-1515; however the definition of some of the landscape details seems to force the heavy classicism of the scene, foreshadowing the harsher, more strident tones that would be a strong characteristic a few years later (around 1518) of the frescoed lunette of *The Meeting at the Golden Gate*, still visible in the Cappella del Manto. Considered by this point to be one of the best artists in Siena in the early sixteenth century Beccafumi worked (before 1518) with Sodoma and Girolamo del Pacchia on the frescoes in the Oratory of San Bernardino, headquarters of the Compagnia di Santa Maria degli Angeli della Veste Nera, where his daring, eccentric anticlassical perspective visions are in close affinity with the *Saint Paul Enthroned* painted in that same period for the Saint Paul Chapel in the Tribunal of the Mercanzia

Domenico Beccafumi, *Saint Catherine Receiving the Stigmata*

and now in the Museo dell'Opera in Siena. Around 1519, scholars hypothesize that Beccafumi went to Rome, drawing from Raphael's mature painting a strong impulse towards further evolution of his style. The immediate repercussions can be seen in the now dismantled decorative complex for Francesco Petrucci's bedchamber, which included the panels of *The Cult of Vesta* and the *Lupercals*, both in the Martelli collection in Florence, *Marcia* and *Tanaquil* in the National Gallery in London, and in all probability, *Venus* in the Barber Institute of Fine Art in Birmingham. Still in keeping with the revival of themes from Roman history, the artist painted for the drawing room of the home in Siena of the Venturi family, connected with Petrucci through marriage, a ceiling frescoed with topics taken from a famous text by the Roman writer Valerius Maximus, most likely commissioned for the wedding between Alessandro Venturi and Bartolomea Luti celebrated in 1519. In the course of the following decade, Beccafumi produced masterpieces like the marble inlays in the pavement of Siena cathedral, the altarpiece of *The Nativity* for the church of San Martino, and the panel painting of *Saint Michael Driving out the Rebellious Angels*, in the two versions in the Pinacoteca and the church of the Carmine in Siena. Between the end of the 1520s and the beginning of the 1530s, Beccafumi was once again involved in the marble inlay decoration of the floor of Siena Cathedral, executing *Stories of Moses on Mount Sinai*, the marvelous cartoons for which are now on display in the Pinacoteca. In those same years, he also worked on the frescoes for the ceiling of the Sala del Concistoro in the Palazzo Pubblico, finished between 1534 and 1535 and depicting complex episodes of civic virtue connected with Greek and Roman history. In 1533-1534, Beccafumi was in Genoa in the service of Andrea Doria, for whom he painted several works that are now lost, and between 1537 and 1539 he is documented in Pisa in connection with paintings in the cathedral apse. By this point the head of a flourishing workshop which enabled him to fulfill his numerous commissions, the artist was active again in Siena Cathedral from 1535, painting the frescoes on the walls of the chancel, designing the marble inlay in the floor, and, at the very end of his career, sculpting two bronze candle-bearing angels. Among his last works are the monochrome fresco of *Saint Christopher* for the former monastery of Monna Agnese, and the *Annunciation* in the church of Sarteano.

(V.R.)

# The Sala di Balìa

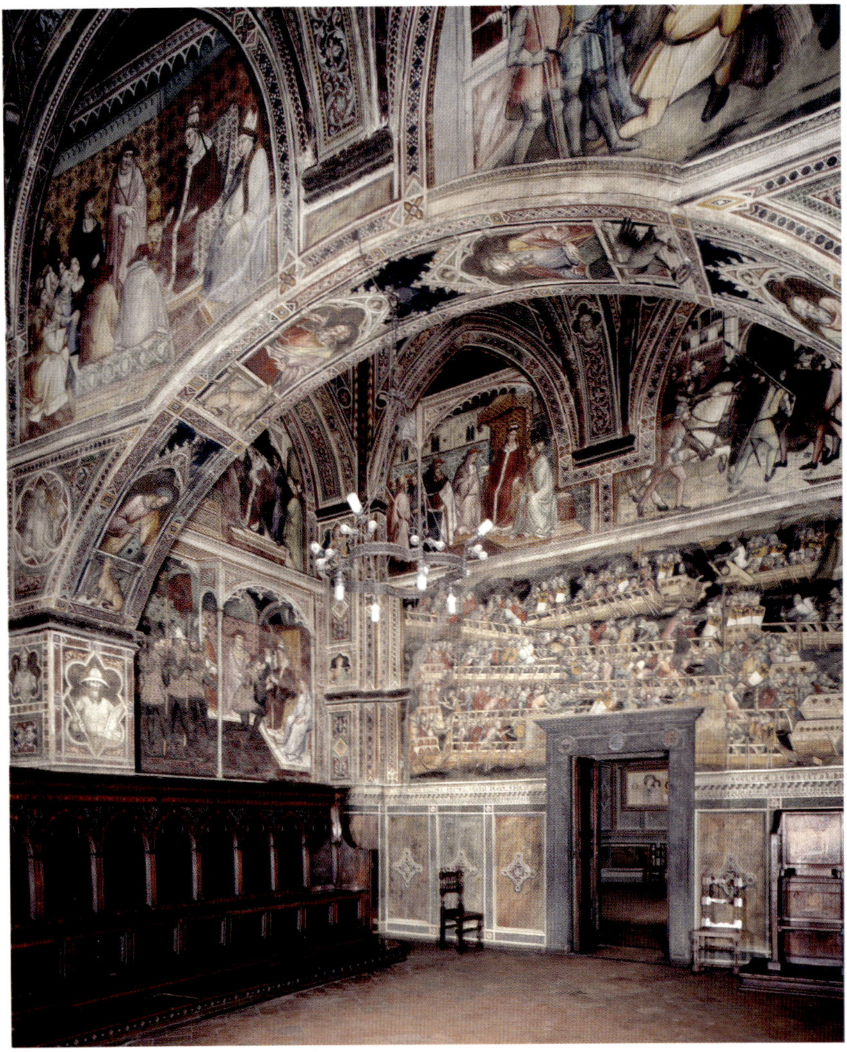

The Sala di Balìa

Coming out of the Sala del Concistoro, cross the antechamber again and go into the Sala di Balìa. This room, also called "Sala Nova" ("New Room"), was used for meetings of the Balìa, the executive body of the Sienese government. It was decorated in the early fifteenth century as part of the work on the palace that led also to the construction of the adjacent palace chapel, with which it communicates through an elegant inlaid wooden door (1426), attributed to Domenico di Niccolò de' Cori, who made the inlaid choir stalls in the chapel.

On the ceiling, painted by the late Gothic artist Martino di Bartolomeo, are the *Virtues* (in the webs of the ceiling and on the pillars); the four *Evangelists* are pictured on the underside of the central arch.

In 1408, the painter Spinello Aretino, from Arezzo but Florentine in style, was commissioned to fresco the walls of the room with episodes from the life of a great figure from the past, Pope Alexander III, born Rolando Bandinelli Paparoni into a noble Sienese family, who became pope in 1159 and served until his death in 1181. The scenes celebrating the life of this important pontiff, remembered for his fight alongside the communes against Emperor Frederick I Barbarossa, are a bit of an anomaly in the iconography of the palace since they do not report episodes strictly tied to Sienese life as do the other painting cycles. Nonetheless, the iconographical program fits into that particular historical moment, when Siena, during the period of the Western Schism, was engaged alongside Pope Gregory XII in the struggle against the two antipopes. The glorification of the deeds of a pope like Alexander II thus appears as a tribute and proof of loyalty to papal power at a difficult time.

Entering the antechamber of the Concistoro, the scenes illustrated in the first part of the room (from right, on top) show: *The Coronation of Pope Alexander III*, *The Pope Giving the Blessed Sword to Doge Ziani of Venice*; (wall above the door) *The Meeting between the Pope and King Louis VII of France*, *The Pope Disguised as a Carthusian Monk Fleeing from Rome Occupied by Frederick Barbarossa*, *The Naval Battle at Punta Salvatore between Venetian and Imperial Forces*; (above the window) *Frederick Barbarossa Sending a Message to the Pope in Anagni*; (above the central arch) *The Consecration of the Antipope Victor IV*, *The True Pope Alexander III Recognized in Ninfa in the Guise of a Monk*. On the back of the arch: *The Lateran Synod*, *The Legendary Burning of the Four Antipopes who Hindered Alexander's Actions*; (above the window) *Pope Alexander III Pardoning Frederick Barbarossa*; (above the door) *The Congress of Venice*, *Pope Alexander III Canonizing Saint Canute, King of Denmark, and Saint Thomas, Archbishop of Canterbury*, *The Pope's Return to Rome Accompanied By Frederick Barbarossa and the Doge of Venice*; (to the right in front of the window) *The Founding of Alessandria*, and *Barbarossa Submitting to Alexander III*.

The inlaid wooden bench running along the walls of the room was made in the early fifteenth century (1410).

Coming out of the Sala di Balìa, we encounter a steep stone staircase. Climbing to the top, we come out on the beautiful porch called the Loggione, while if we continue straight ahead on that same floor, we enter the Sala del Risorgimento.

A curious note

# Engraved Memories

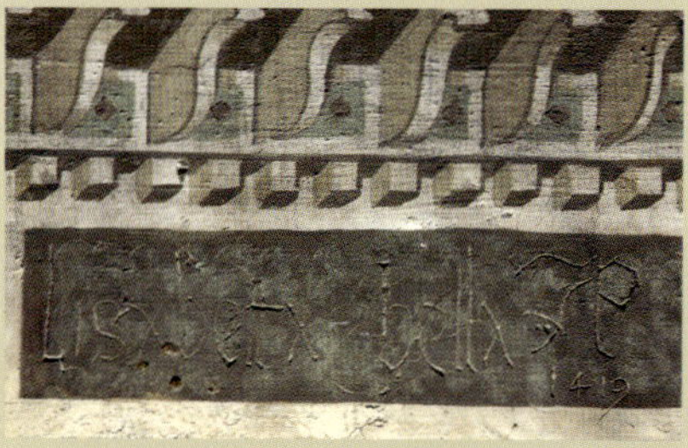

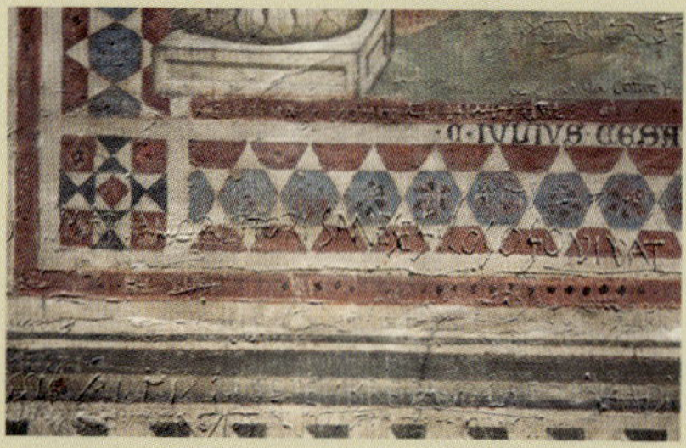

Passionate observers and lovers of architecture, monuments and works of art will, unfortunately, certainly not have missed seeing the numerous instances of the nefarious custom of writing or inscribing names, dates, declarations of love or of soccer loyalties, even political symbols when not outright vulgarities, on statues, walls, furniture, and surfaces that are certainly not appropriate for this use. This is the result of bad upbringing and the boorishness of the present time, one might say. An observation with which everyone can agree, if it were not for the fact that leaving strictly personal mementos on the walls is an ancient custom. Suffice it to remember the well known graffiti found on some buildings in Pompeii, which certainly have to be earlier than the famous date of the eruption in AD 59 and have become valuable evidence of civic life and customs in the city that was destroyed. Not even the Palazzo Pubblico, so rich in history and works of art, has been spared this execrable habit.

Looking closely, for example, at a wall in the Sala della Balìa, on the bottom edge of *The Naval Battle between Imperial and Venetian Forces*, one can find cursive inscriptions, some of them very old. Not all are completely legible – many have been mutilated or damaged – but on the right we can distinctly read these words scratched into the wall: "Adì VI Settembre in Sabbato ad hore XXI… morto in questo loco el traditore" (on Saturday, 6 September, at 9 p.m… the traitor died on this spot). The message is disquieting: who wrote it and when, given that the year is not recorded, who was the traitor, and above all, how did he die and why?

It seems that this refers to an episode that really happened and is narrated in ancient chronicles of the city. In the year 1456, Gisberto da Correggio, a captain of the Sienese army during the war in Maremma against the Count of Pitigliano, was summoned by the Balìa to answer to the charge of treason. He did not succeed in proving his innocence, and the sentence was carried out immediately. Stabbed to death, Gisberto was then thrown out the window, while the people, "hearing a commotion in the palace," came running into the square. A completely different tone is struck in another inscription not far from this one. "Lisabetta bella 1419" (Beautiful Elizabeth 1419) is clearly legible in what certainly looks like an open and enthusiastic declaration of love. Other more or less comprehensible inscriptions with coats of arms, names, dates, and drawings can be distinguished.

Other writings of this kind can be found near the holy water font in the forechapel. Here too some dates can be read: 1510, 1414, 1563, and the name of "Mariano Bettori sanese filosofo" (Mariano Bettori

Sala di Balìa, wall graffiti, 1419

Graffiti on the arch of the Forechapel

Palace Loggia, graffiti, 1874

a Sienese philosopher), but it is practically impossible to understand who wrote these and why, since they appear put there by chance and unquestionably private. It is easier to interpret the ones on the pillars and stone parapet of the palace loggia. Mixed in with those left by modern visitors, among the inscriptions made using markers, ballpoint pens or pencils, can be fairly easily deciphered some inscriptions flanked by strange signs and designs. These are ancient, some even dated in the fifteenth century, which someone long ago left here, who knows how and on what occasion, just like today's disrespectful visitors. For the most part these are names, combined with dates, some of which even specify the day, month, and year, or coats of arms. In one of the oldest inscriptions, scratched into the brick of a pillar, we read "14 di s[ettembr]e 1494" (14 September 1494), and the heraldic emblem of a mountain of five hills surmounted by three plinths; this can be identified as the arms of the Landucci family,. Among the many signs that can no longer be deciphered, many coats of arms can be connected with old Sienese families like the Azzoni, Venturi, Zondadari, Salimbeni, and Silvestri. These same emblems are reproduced in paintings in the rooms inside the palace, decorated with historical and heraldic mementos by the various government officials in the seventeenth and eighteenth centuries. One could hypothesize that during the period when the government officials lived in the palace, someone who was waiting to be received may have recorded the date of the day or year and his family's coat of arms, sort of like a signature, just as people doodle today on a piece of paper during a phone call or

while waiting to see someone. Or these could be the signs of boredom left by someone who, in forced residence here, whiled away the time looking at the view, leaning on the parapet of the terrace. A different, and more credible, kind of attribution can be given to the writings dated in the second half of the nineteenth century. During this period, we know that the Loggia was part of the prison and was used only be prisoners who came here for their "hour of air." The written testimony from this period is extensive: "1874 ARNALDO BECCI," "SARTORI 1879," "LOCATTI 1879." Among these, the most heartrending is one written by a young boy 14 years old, condemned to 31 months in jail, as can be deduced from the inscription, worn away by time and scratched with a hand still inexperienced in penmanship: "ORAZIO DI SINNA CONDANNATO A 31 M[ESI] D[I] A[NNI] 14 1874" (Orazio, of Siena [?], condemned to 31 months, 14 years old, 1874).

(L.G.)

## The Loggia

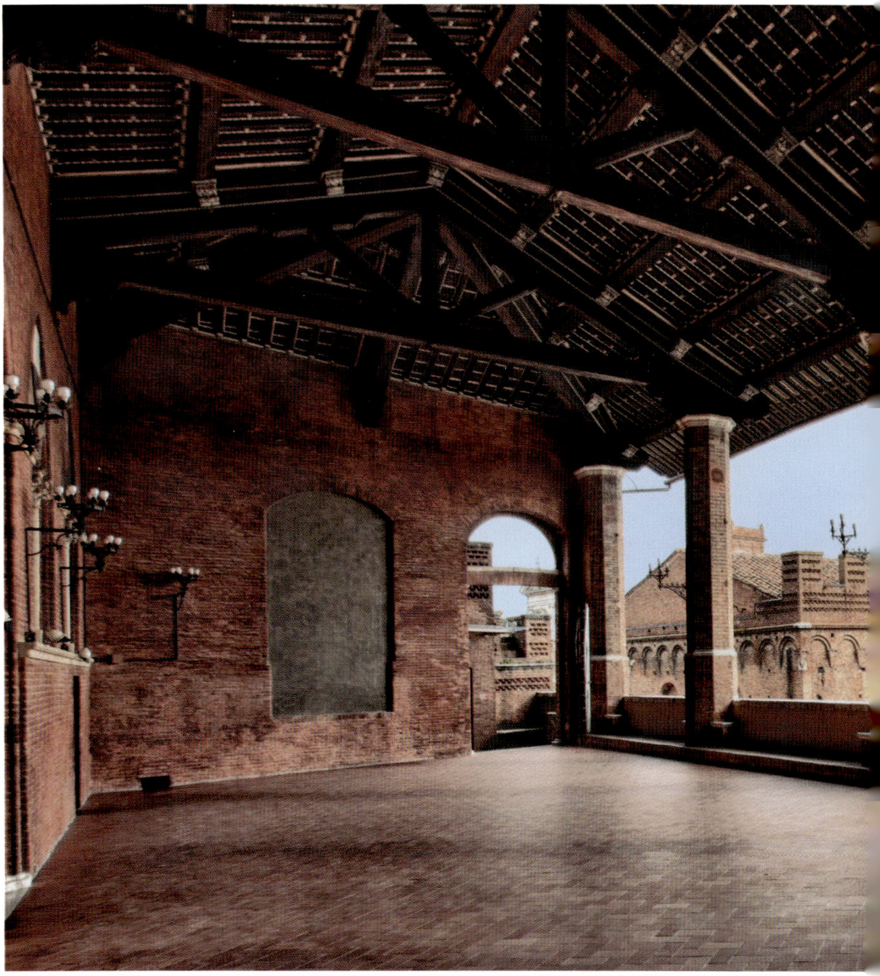

The Loggia seen from the palace interior

The spacious porch which opens on the back of the palace is worth the climb because of the beautiful view it offers. From this terrace on clear days you can see a much of the southern part of the province of Siena, which stretches to the slopes of Mount Amiata, the mountain that stands out solitary against the horizon; the eye sweeps all the way to the high plain where the fortress of Radicofani rises on a curious promontory whose top seems lopped off, marking the historical boundary between the Republic of Siena and the Papal States.
The Loggia was built around the middle of the fourteenth century, in the final phase of construction of the Palazzo Pubblico, for the purpose of giving the members of the government of the Nine a place to walk

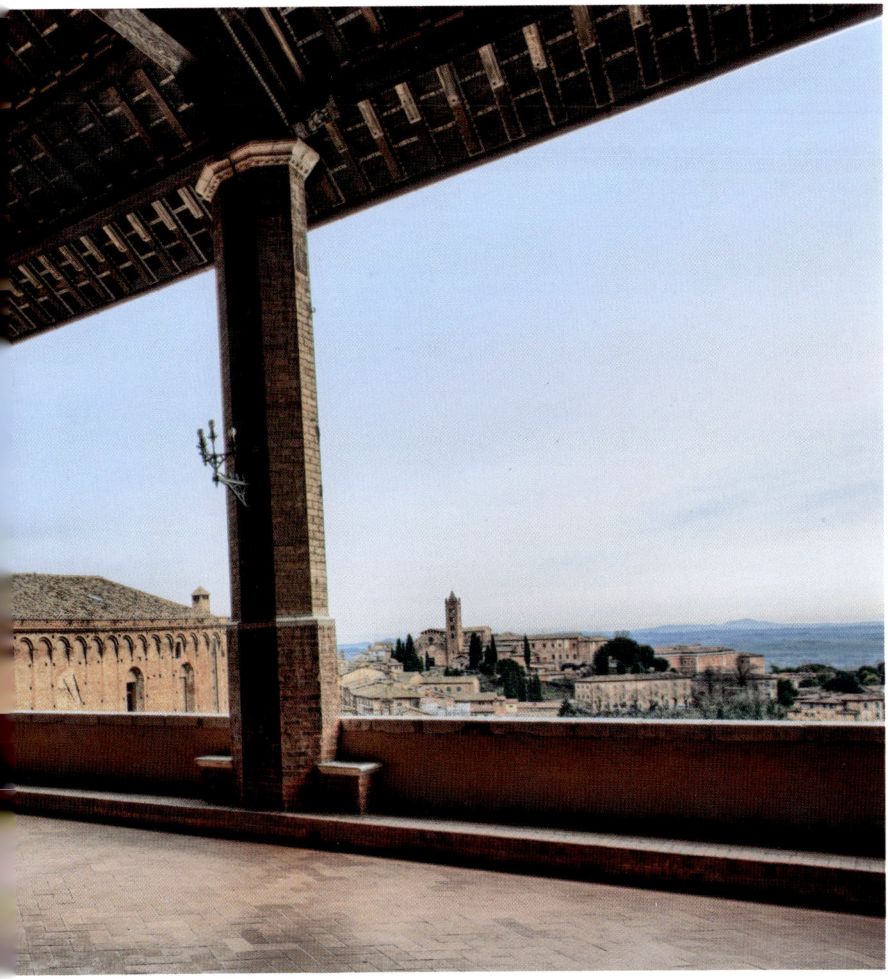

around in the open air, since the laws forbade them to leave the palace for the entire duration of their mandate, except for special occasions like public holidays or grave family reasons.

The Loggia also affords an unusual foreshortened view from below of the Mangia tower. On the left can be admired the majestic bulk of what is now the Teatro dei Rinnovati but was once the grand meeting chambers of the General Council of the Republic.

The church visible on the left is Santa Maria dei Servi, at the end of the street that defines the Salicotto neighborhood. On the right of the broad green area inside the city walls, the street running uphill is Via Dupré, with the convent church of Sant'Agostino at its summit.

## The Sala del Risorgimento

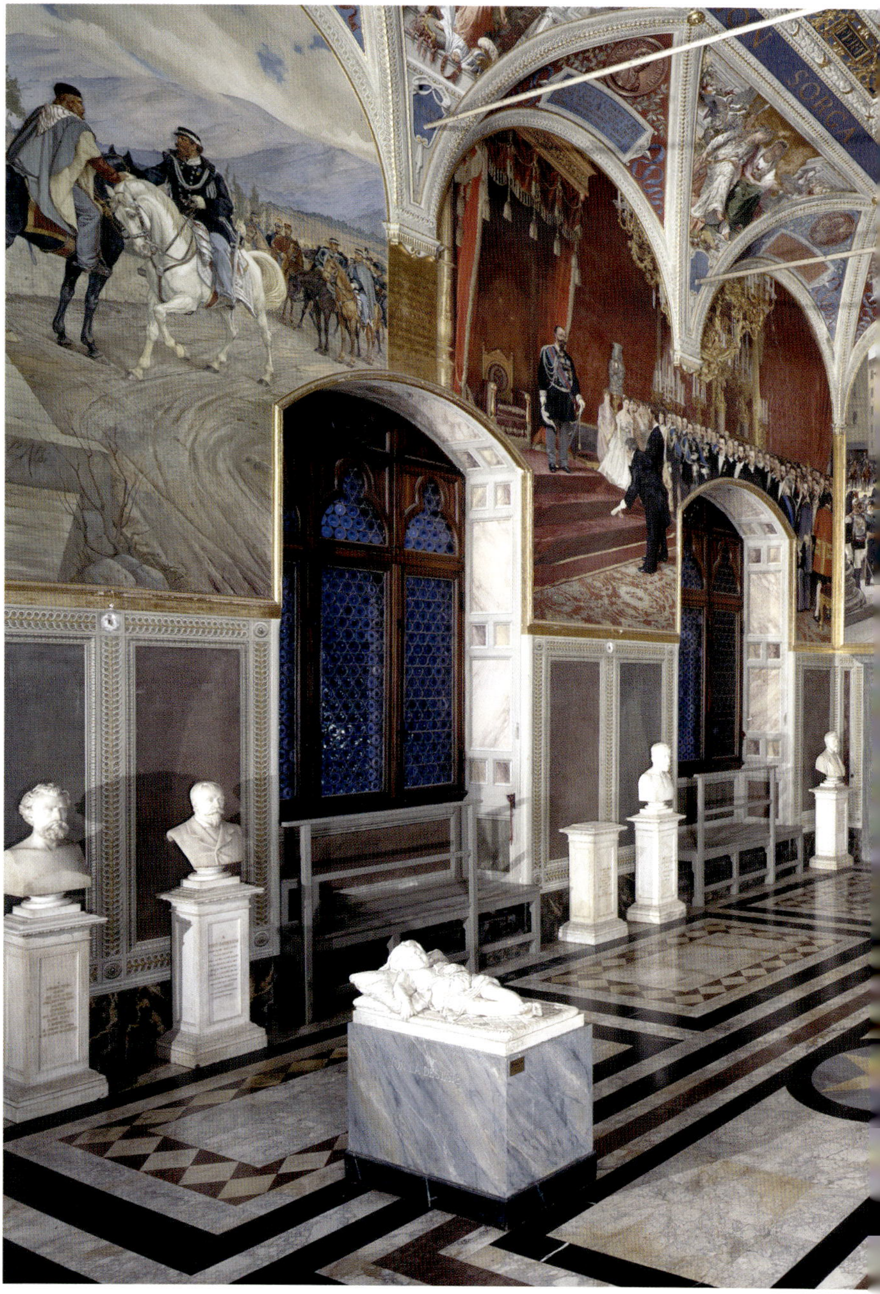

The Sala del Risorgimento

The Risorgimento Room is the most "modern" in the museum, created in a space earlier divided into two floors, where the Podestà had his audience chamber. Returning to the ancient custom of celebrating important civic or political events on the walls of the Palazzo Pubblico which had more or less died out in the seventeenth and eighteenth centuries, it was decided in 1881 to commemorate

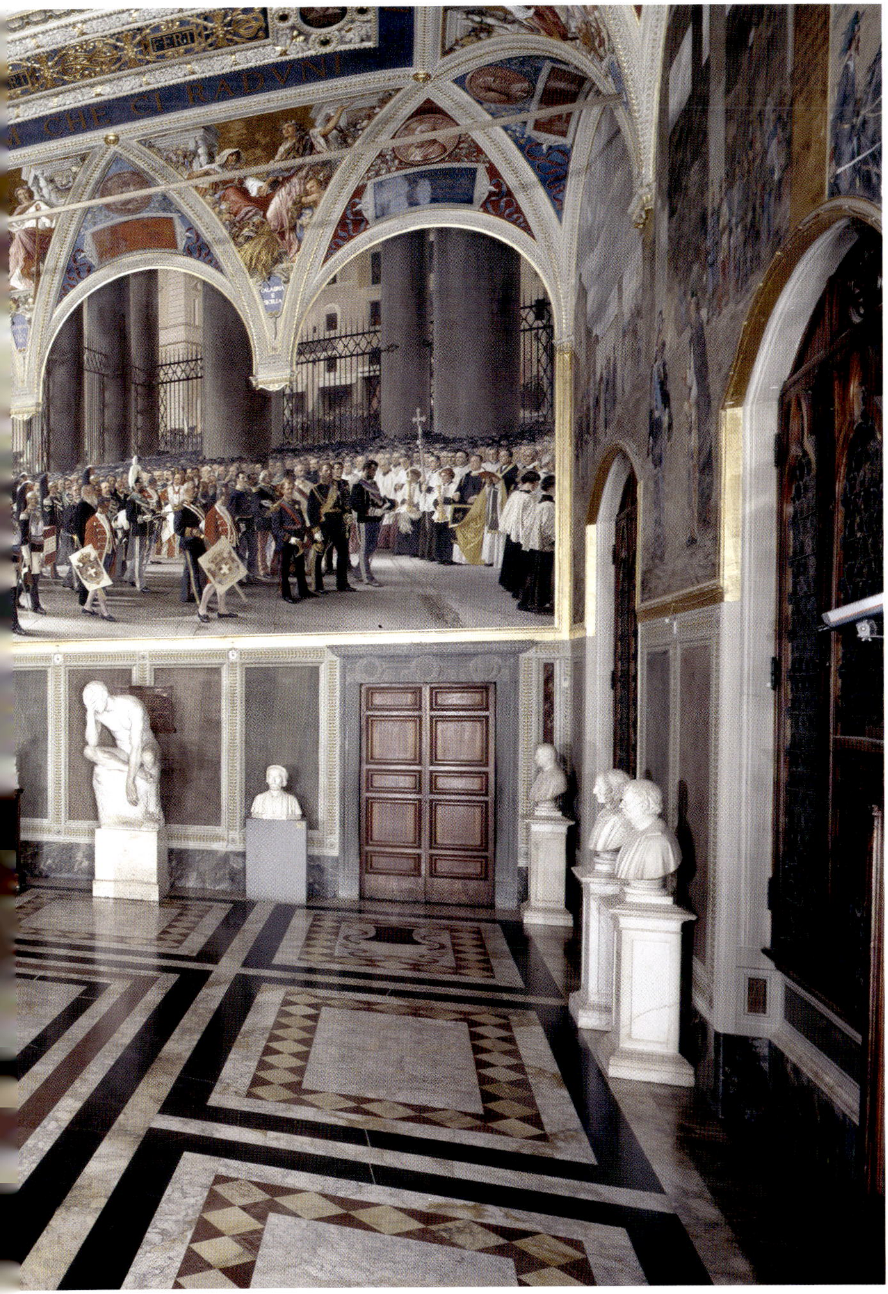

the death of Vittorio Emanuele II, the first king of united Italy, by illustrating the main events of his life.
In reality, the project had another purpose as well; besides paying tribute to the Risorgimento and the unification of Italy, it also had the declared intent to celebrate the modern school of Sienese painting created by Luigi Mussini, who was charged with coordinating the undertaking.

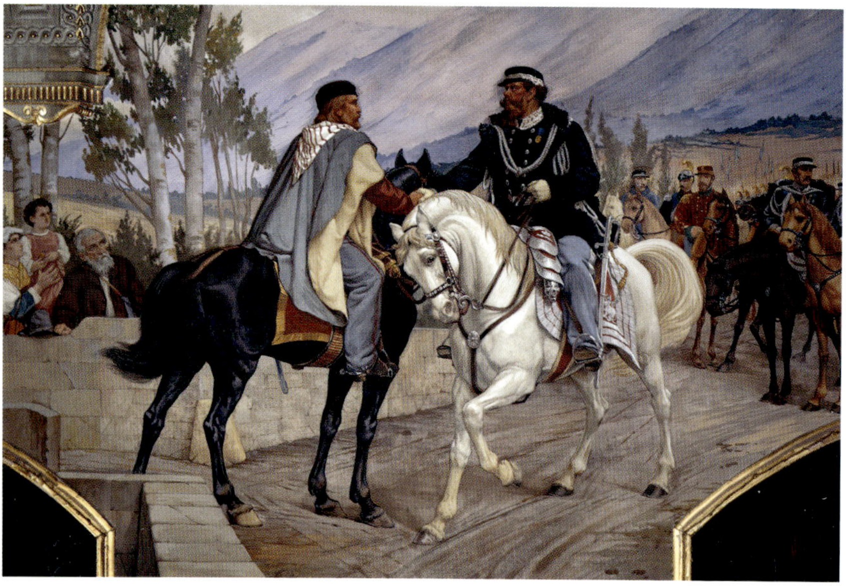

Pietro Aldi, *Vittorio Emanuele II Meeting Giuseppe Garibaldi at Teano*
Cesare Maccari, *Vittorio Emanuele in Florence Receiving News of the Plebiscite in Rome*, detail

He called his closest collaborators and students to execute the paintings (1886-1888).
The grand scenes, illustrated in the upper section of the walls, present episodes from the Risorgimento in which the king was directly involved: *Vittorio Emanuele Meeting General Radetsky at Vignale* and *Vittorio Emanuele II Meeting Giuseppe Garibaldi at Teano* were painted by Pietro Aldi; *The Battle of San Martino* and *The Battle of Palestro*, both crucial for the outcome of the second war of independence, were painted by Amos Cassioli; and Cesare Maccari painted *Vittorio Emanuele in Florence Receiving News of the Plebiscite in Rome*, set in the throne room of the Palazzo Pitti, and *The Funeral of Vittorio Emanuele II in the Pantheon*.
On the ceiling, as though to raise the instructional and historical tone of the wall frescoes to an emotional level, were painted allegorical subjects alluding to the unification of Italy. In the center, inside a large round medallion, is the *Allegory of Free Italy* by Alessandro Franchi. The neo-Renaissance decorations, a clear allusion to Raphael, were done by Giorgio Bandini; on the pendentives are allegorical figures representing all the regions which made up the newly formed country, painted by Franchi, Ricciardo Meacci, Antonio Luigi Ridolfi, and Gaetano Marinelli.
The room also holds two display cases with Risorgimento mementoes, including the uniform worn by the king in the Battle of San Martino, which he personally gave to Luigi Mussini in thanks for the portrait painted by the

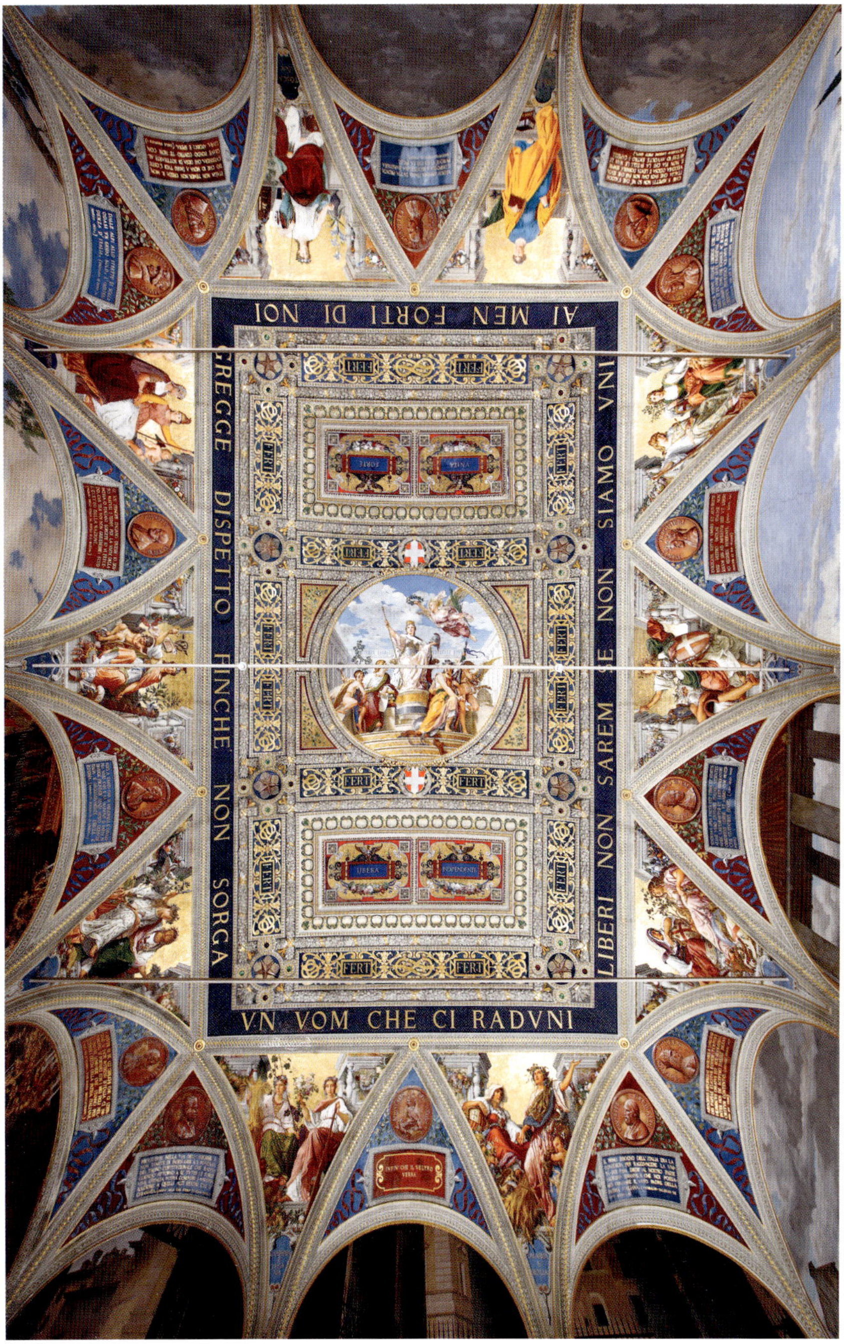


The ceiling of the Risorgimento Room

artist. The carved wooden case containing the uniform was made specifically for this purpose by Pietro Giusti. The large marble statue depicting *Grief* is a twentieth-century work by Emilio Gallori. Noteworthy, too, is the sculpture of *Luisa Mussini Asleep*, the daughter of the famous artist, made by a student at the Academy of Fine Arts in Siena.

# The Nineteenth Century in Siena and the Academy of Fine Arts

Founded in the late eighteenth century, Siena's Academy of Art, while illustrious from its birth, progressively gained fame and esteem in the following century not only in Tuscany but also internationally, thanks to the great masters who directed it and, consequently, the excellent students it was able to train, who in turn infused new life and vigor into the institute.
After the Risorgimento battles ended, in which the Sienese had fought as volunteers first in the university battalions and then with the many followers who swelled Garibaldi's army, Siena found itself in a new position. No longer thought of as a beautiful, sought-after place but one outside the path of history, now it was once again considered one of the noblest cities in Italy, thanks to its never-waning desire for independence and its illustrious status as the capital of an ancient state. This new situation gave a boost to all the activities that took place in the city and especially to those that were able

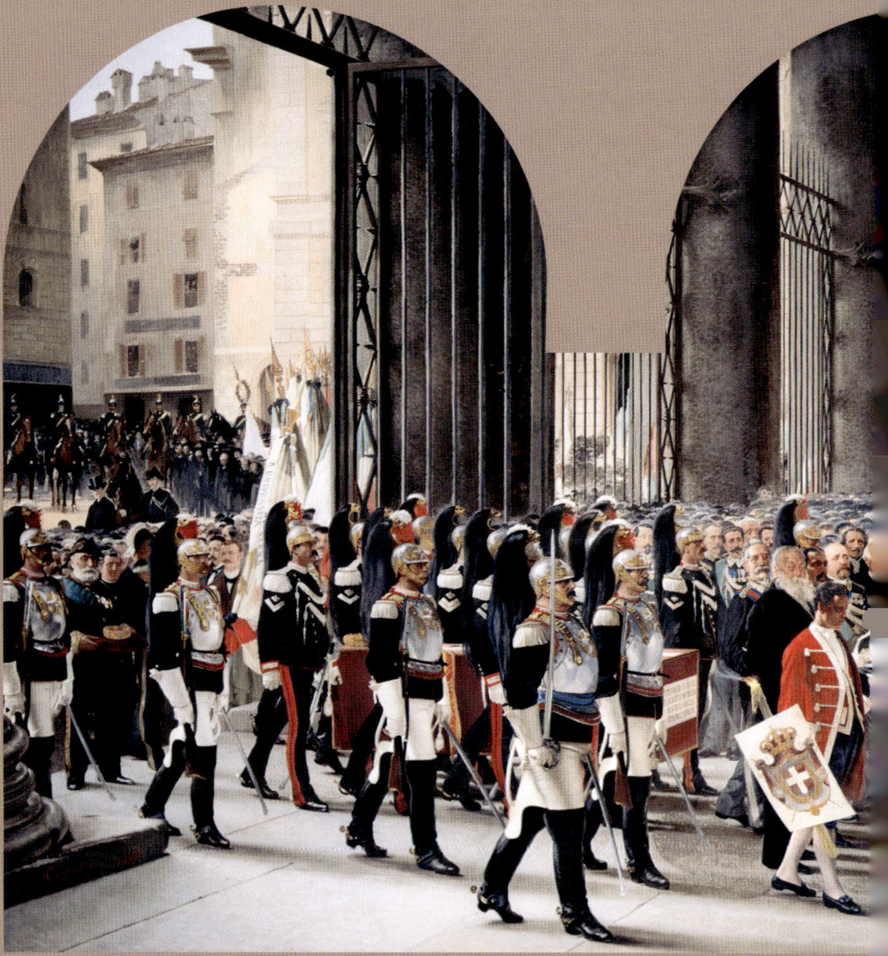

Cesare Maccari, *The Funeral of Vittorio Emanuele II*

to bear witness to so much past glory and to present it once more. Under the long directorship of Luigi Mussini, the leader of the Purist movement in art, and with the support of several charity institutions created to sustain young artists such as the Biringucci Fellowship, the Academy became a real forge of figures and endeavors which narrated the greatness of Italy through the outstanding episodes drawn from its vast history, from the splendor of the Roman Empire to the great season of the Risorgimento. Mussini's most successful students were Amos Cassioli, Pietro Aldi and Cesare Maccari, even if figures of the caliber of Angiolo Visconti, Gaetano Marinelli and others who later turned towards popular realism, such as Paride Pascucci, should not be ignored. Even though Cassioli was not permitted to pursue more innovative paths because of Mussini's constant calls to order, and Aldi was not able to develop his fresh naturalist vein due to his untimely death, Maccari did have

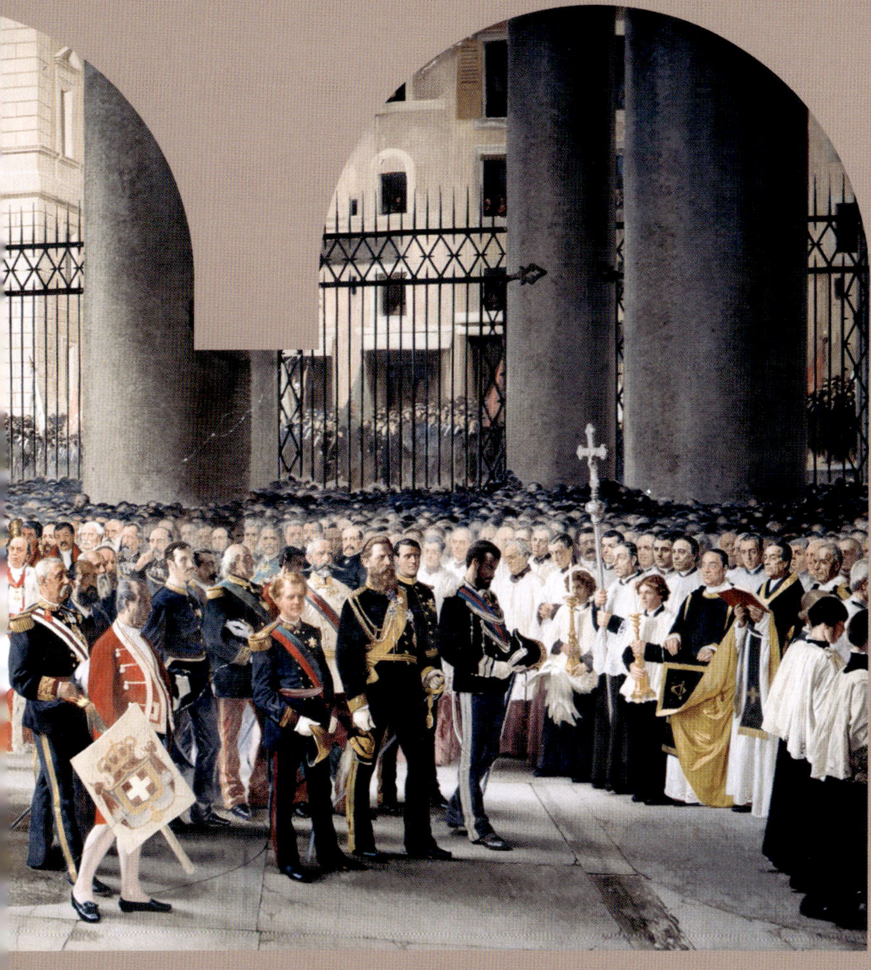

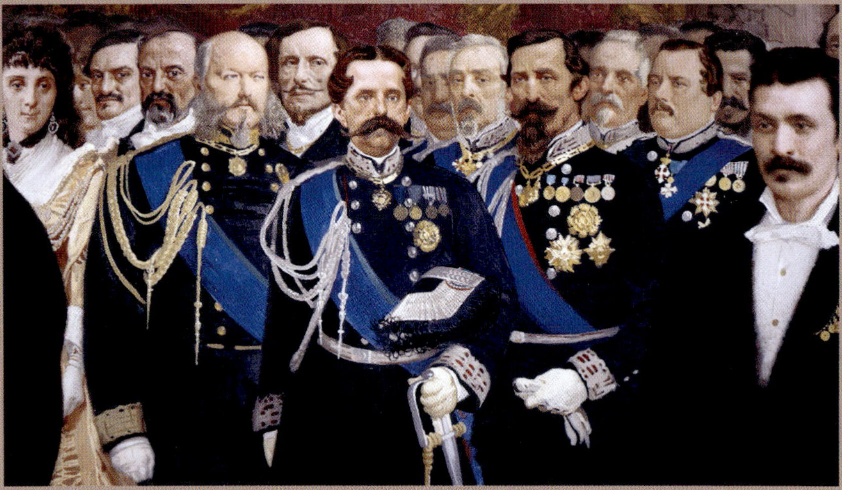

the skill and good fortune to be involved in the greatest painting undertakings of his time, like the Marian sanctuary in Loreto, the new Senate of the Kingdom of Italy, and the Palazzaccio, seat of the court of Rome, just to mention the most highly-praised.
It was these three painters who concluded the project to decorate the Sala del Risorgimento in the Palazzo Pubblico, the concrete tribute that Siena, with true originality, chose to offer the first king of Italy: a fresco cycle which, following the example of the medieval series already present in the Palazzo, was meant to "narrate" to those entering the room the tangible evidence of the events that had made Sienese owe remembrance and gratitude to a given event or historical figure.
Moreover, along with a meticulous narration of fundamental historical events for the realization of national unity, the painting cycle presents a real pantheon of personages illustrated in the context of their deeds with the meticulous attention of a biographer, making it one of the most celebrated icons of the Risorgimento period.
In the twentieth century, the Academy continued its commitment to training a vast host of artists, a task that in this new millennium it is trying to fulfill as it should, teaching the techniques and topics that have made the Sienese school of art great but at the same time curious and open to all the suggestions and many problems that were appearing on the world scene.

(M.C.)

Cesare Maccari, *Vittorio Emanuele II Receiving News of the Plebiscite*, detail

## The Picture Gallery

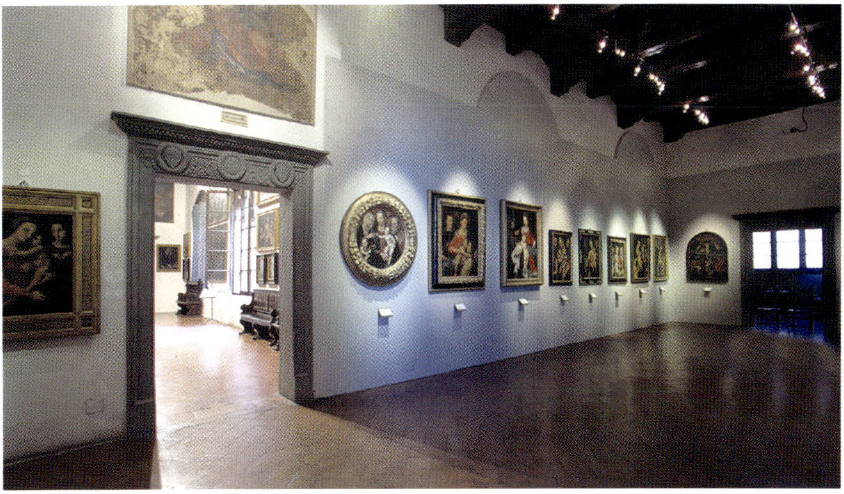

The rooms of the Picture Gallery

Coming out of the Sala del Risorgimento, walk past the Bookshop, to where the Picture Gallery begins.
This is a collection of paintings datable between the late sixteenth and the eighteenth centuries, coming from various collections. It also contains some pieces that were originally in other parts of the building. The arrangement of these rooms – which is particularly interesting because it manifests the evolution of Sienese painting from the sixteenth to the eighteenth century by displaying paintings by the greatest painters of the period – is constantly changing, so we shall limit ourselves here to pointing out some of the most important and meaningful works.

*First room*

**Giovanni Antonio Bazzi, known as Sodoma** (1477-1549), *The Virgin and Child with Saints*, sinopia; *Saint Sebastian*, sinopia and fresco; *God the Father*, fresco, 1537-39

On 6 March 1537 the Signoria commissioned Sodoma to paint the large fresco for the Cappella di Piazza, the chapel built at the foot of the Torre del Mangia as an *ex voto* after the plague of 1348. The work was supposed to be finished within that same year, but engagements outside Siena kept him from finishing it until 1539. As a result of its original location, essentially outdoors, the painting was frequently subjected to restoration at least until the end of the nineteenth century, but it seems that, at the end of the century, it was "barely visible" and was truly "in a deteriorated state." In 1971-72 the deci-

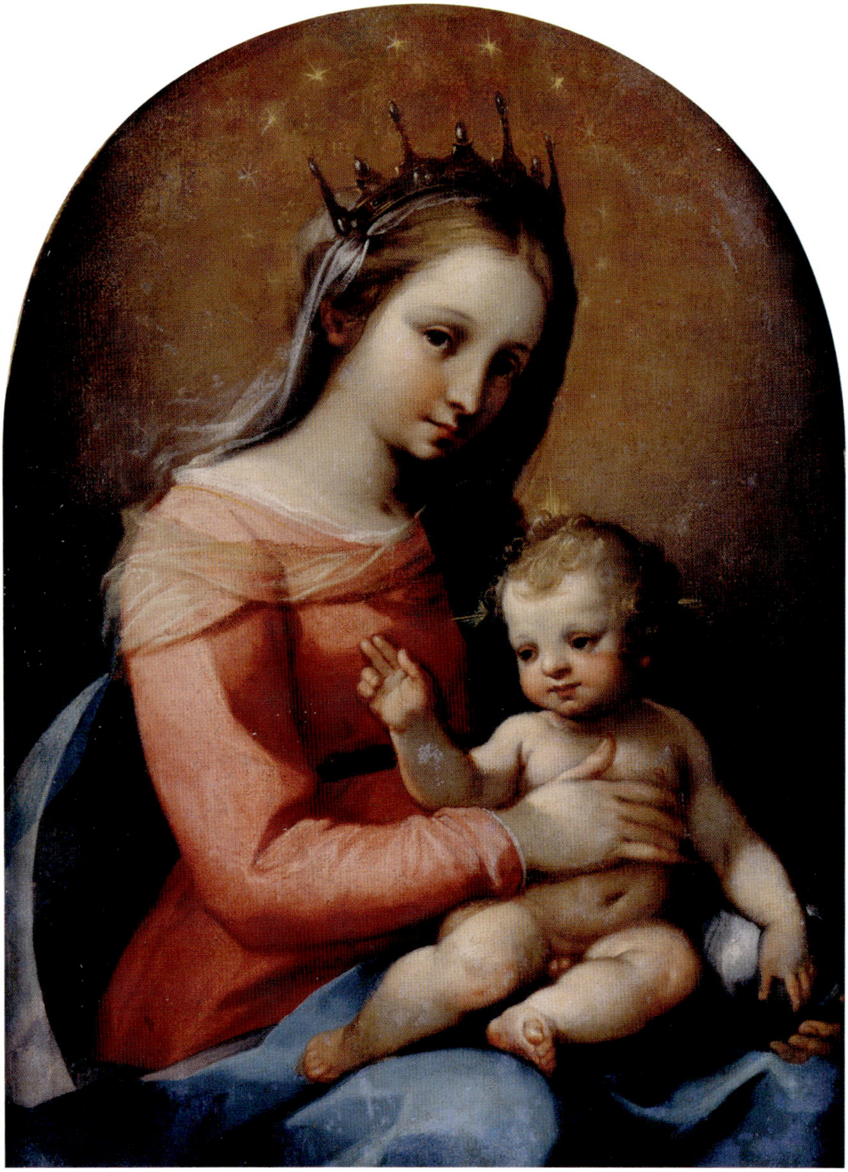

Ventura Salimbeni, Coffin stand of the Compagnia di Santo Stefano ai Pispini, *The Virgin and Child*

sion was made to detach it and to try to recover at least the sinopia underdrawing, that is to say, the preliminary sketch made with red clay immediately after the spreading of the wet plaster.

**Bartolomeo di David** (1482-1545/46), *Saint Onuphrius, The Virgin and Child with the Young Saint John the Baptist, The Man of Sorrows with Two Angels, Saint Andrew*, oil on wood, ca. 1532.
The four paintings have been identified as parts of a coffin stand belonging to the Compagnia di Sant'Onofrio, from which they came into the museum. These coffin

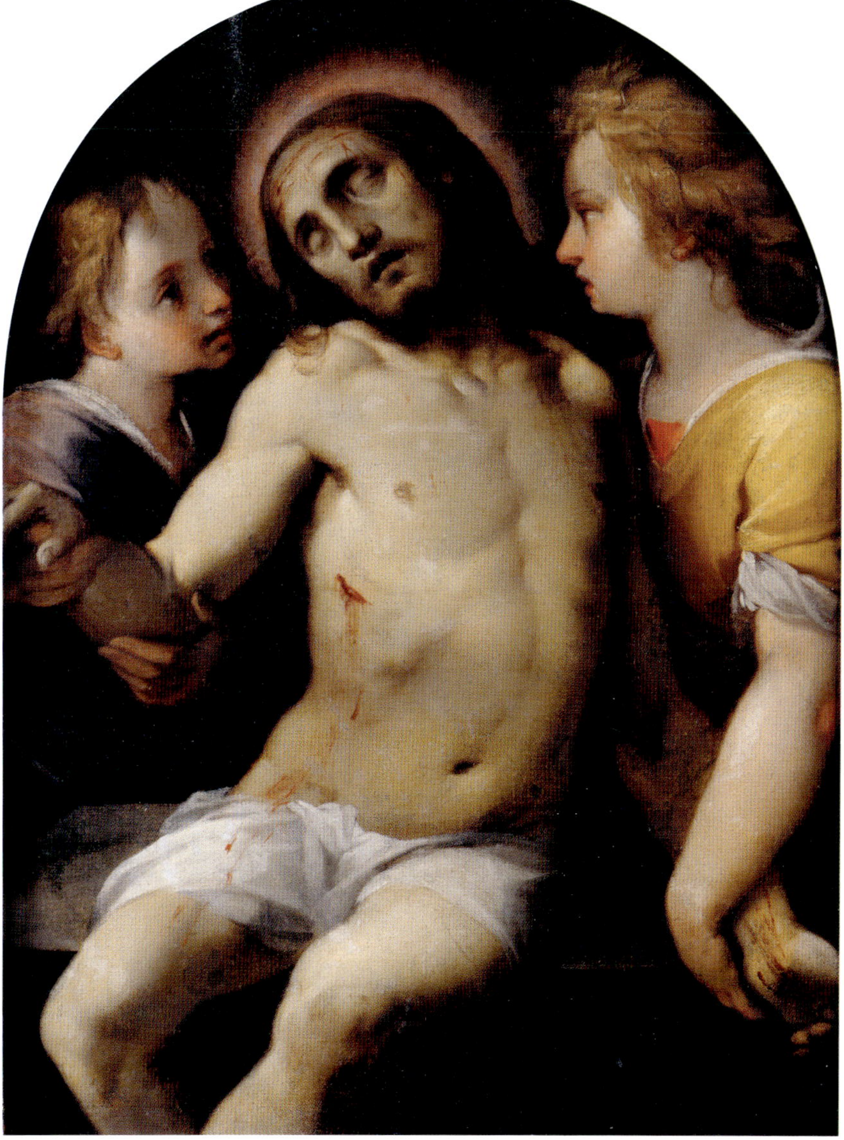

Ventura Salimbeni, Coffin stand of the Compagnia di Santo Stefano ai Pispini, *The Man of Sorrows*

stands were wooden frames used to support the casket for carrying or during the wake. In the past, they had painted or decorated panels at either end, often with sacred images on both sides, thus each stand had four pictures. Bartolomeo di David is a painter from the circle of Domenico Beccafumi, whose manner he emulates closely. If anything, one can note an evolution toward a more realistic and classical style in his mature phase, when these paintings were most probably made.

**Ventura Salimbeni** (1568-1613), *Saint Stephen, The Virgin and Child, Christ in the Tomb, Saint Lawrence*, oil

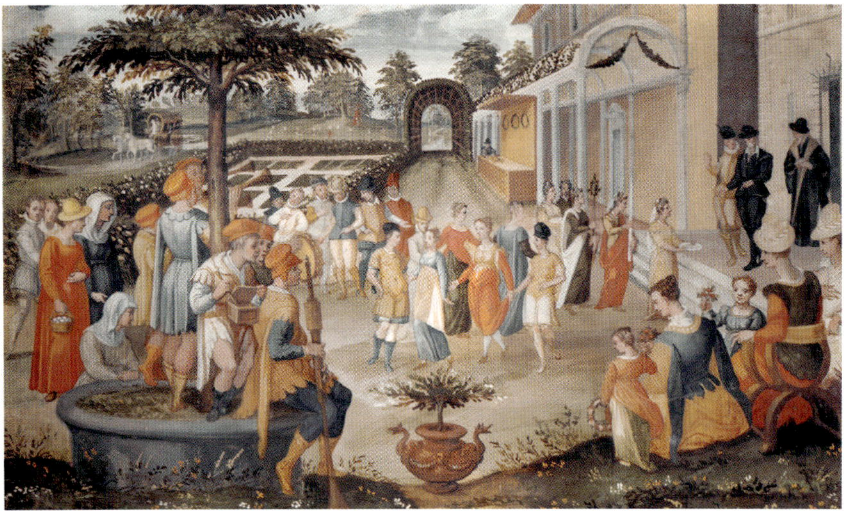

Cristofano Rustici, *Six months of the year, May*

on canvas with a rounded top, 1604.
The paintings were part of a coffin stand and were commissioned from Ventura Salimbeni by the Compagnia di Santo Stefano in 1604. In these paintings the artist shows a special grace and gentleness, which are a main characteristic of his style, accompanied always by refined color chords, as seen here in the complex folds of cloth rendered with touches of the brush.

**Cristofano Rustici** (1560-1640), *Six months of the year: January, May, June, September, October, November*, oil on canvas, third or fourth decade of the seventeenth century. These six small canvases reproduce the activities that distinguish the months illustrated. *January* is represented by scenes of family life in a patrician home: an old man warms himself at a brazier, a woman is spinning, and the servants are busy with housework, while in the background is a glimpse of a snowy street. *May* presents a carefree party in a luxurious garden, with fine ladies and their elegant escorts, and in the background other guests arriving in a coach. *June* shows harvest time, with peasants first toiling in the fields and then resting in the shade of an ilex tree, and people fishing beside a lake. *September* presents a rich man's pastime, hunting for partridges at night, with the men setting out for the countryside with their hunting gear. A lively scene is the grape harvest in *October*: the grapes are picked and put in baskets and tubs and brought to a porch, where nude children press the grapes under the owner's watchful eye. In *November*, finally, the peasants give their lords seasonal game.

Giacomo Cozzarelli,
*Hitching ring*

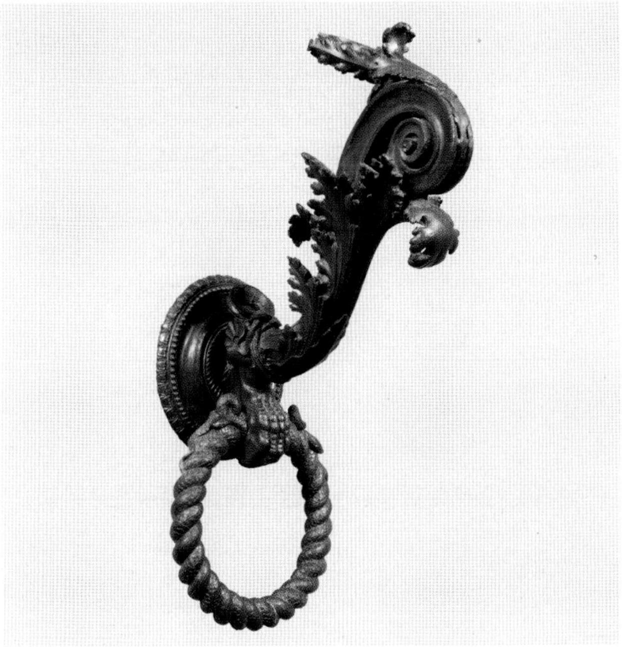

Described in meticulous detail, these delightful genre scenes and settings owe a great debt, both in terms of iconography and style, to a series of Medici tapestries that arrived in Siena around 1630 and are preserved in the Palazzo della Provincia.*Second room*

**Sienese sculptor** (Neroccio di Bartolomeo de' Landi), *The Sienese She-wolf*, marble, 1487
This group in Montagnola marble reproducing the she-wolf and twins, the symbol of Siena which alludes to the mythological Roman origins of the city, comes from the column in Piazza della Postierla which still today marks the Terzo di Città. In ancient times, Siena was administratively divided into thirds (Terzi); each third was marked by the presence of a column with a she-wolf on top. On the column now, in place of the ancient she-wolf, is a marble wolf by the contemporary sculptor Giuliano Vangi.

**Giacomo Cozzarelli** (1453-1515), *Hitching ring and Torch-holder*, bronze, 1509-1512.
These two objects were once part of a complex of seven pieces, three torch-holders and four hitching rings, which were once on the façade of the Palazzo del Magnifico Pandolfo Petrucci on Via dei Pellegrini (the others are in the Pinacoteca Nazionale). The hitching rings have a complex design, with the large ring formed by

entwined snakes, hooked by an eagle's beak, to which acanthus leaves are attached, terminating in a curl. The traditional attribution to Cozzarelli is confirmed by precise stylistic similarities with other works by the artist, such as the two angel candleholders on either side of the high altar in Siena Cathedral, made in collaboration with Francesco di Giorgio Martini.

*Third room*

**Rutilio Manetti** (1571-1639), *Saint Paul*, oil on canvas, ca. 1636

The painting has the artist's signature, "Rutil Manet. F.," on the edge of the book and comes from a private collection (Del Taia) in Siena. It is a late work, produced in a moment when Manetti's interest, influenced by suggestions from Caravaggio, was oriented towards genre scenes, attracted by their more grotesque or naturalistic aspects. In portraying Saint Paul, Manetti captures the more human essence of the saint, using a strong light that hits the old man's hand and lined, gaunt face.

**Giovanni Paolo Pisani** (1574-1637), *Saint Galganus*, oil on canvas, 1610.

The painting was commissioned by the Commune of Siena as a "historical memento" of the governing officials, whose arms were painted on the now-lost frame. *Saint Galganus* reveals some weakness of style in the slender, melancholy figure of the saint with his languid eyes, but strengthens in the landscape background which shows depth, and in the competently painted episode of the angel with the cherubs.

**Bernardino Mei** (1612-1676), *Saint Bernardine of Siena and Donor*, oil on canvas, ca. 1653-54.

The painting comes from the Compagnia di Sant'Onofrio, whose rector is probably the person shown as the donor. It was painted in an intermediate phase of the interesting development of Mei's style, in which he showed a certain "eclecticism." The composition manifests an interest in light borrowed from Caravaggio, but by now merely superficial and devoid of content, along with an attempt at pathos suggested by the mystical, inspired pose of the saint.

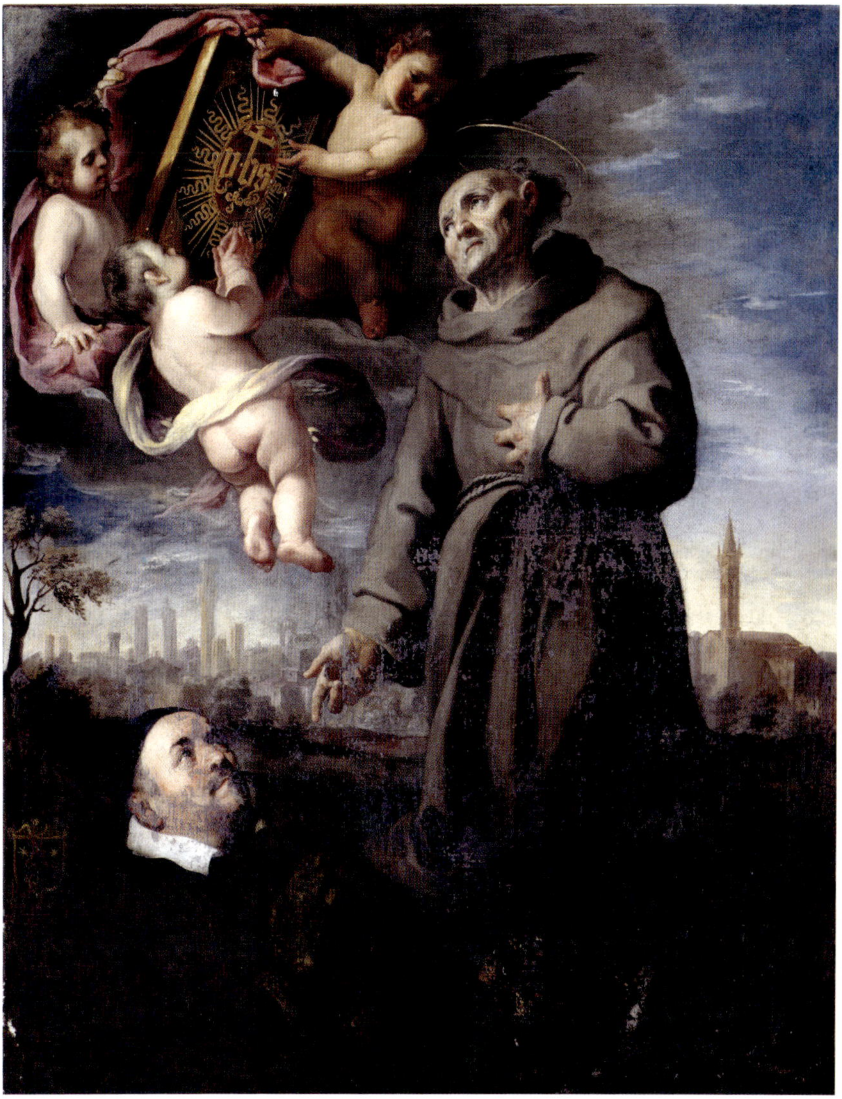

Bernardino Mei, *Saint Bernardine of Siena and Donor*

The interesting echo of the baroque in the three cherubs holding the monogram of Christ is perhaps the most attractive part of the painting.
The showcases in the center of the room hold examples of Sienese pottery from the fifteenth to the eighteenth centuries, as well as sacred objects like chalices, cruets, candlesticks and reliquaries once used in the palace chapel.
The tour of the picture gallery ends by retracing your steps or by passing once again through the Risorgimento Room, heading back to the bookshop.

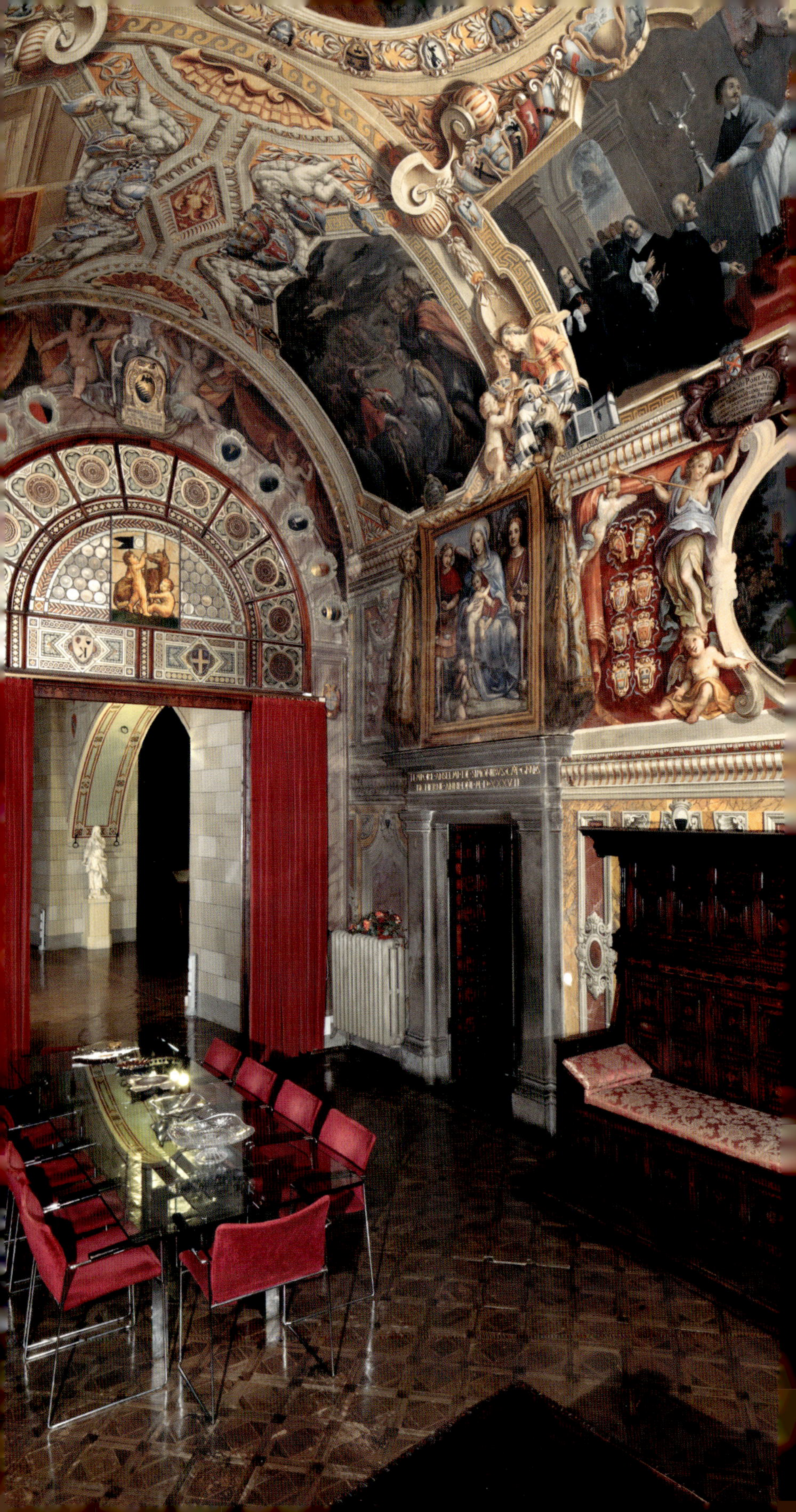

# Art in the Palace
# Memories of an Ancient Republic

*Letizia Galli*

The Accounts Room of the Biccherna magistracy, decorated in the seventeenth century with frescoes by Deifebo Burbarini, is now the Mayor's office

The Hall of the She-wolves

Palazzo Pubblico continues still today to be Siena's seat of city government, just as it has been since the early fourteenth century. It houses the offices of the mayor and municipal departments, the council meeting chambers, and some city services. Over the centuries, the art works and civic memories have built up, layer after layer, marking the history of the palace and its rooms.

Only the *piano nobile* ("noble floor," the first floor European style), where the Civic Museum is located, can be visited by the public, since the ground floor and second floor are reserved for offices.

The ground floor is entered directly from Piazza del Campo through the portal on the right, on the opposite side from the main entrance called the *Entrone*. The other doors, which were numerous, as can be observed by looking closely at the façade, have been converted to windows in the course of various renovations over the centuries. The large entrance, where the seventeenth-century staircase leading to the upper floors begins, opens onto the so-called Sala delle Lupe (Hall of the She-wolves), a spacious area off which the inner rooms

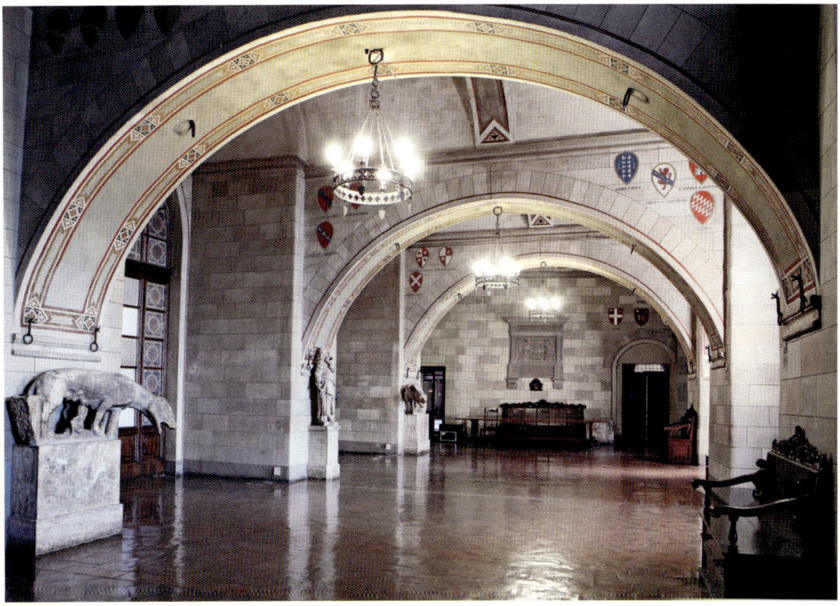

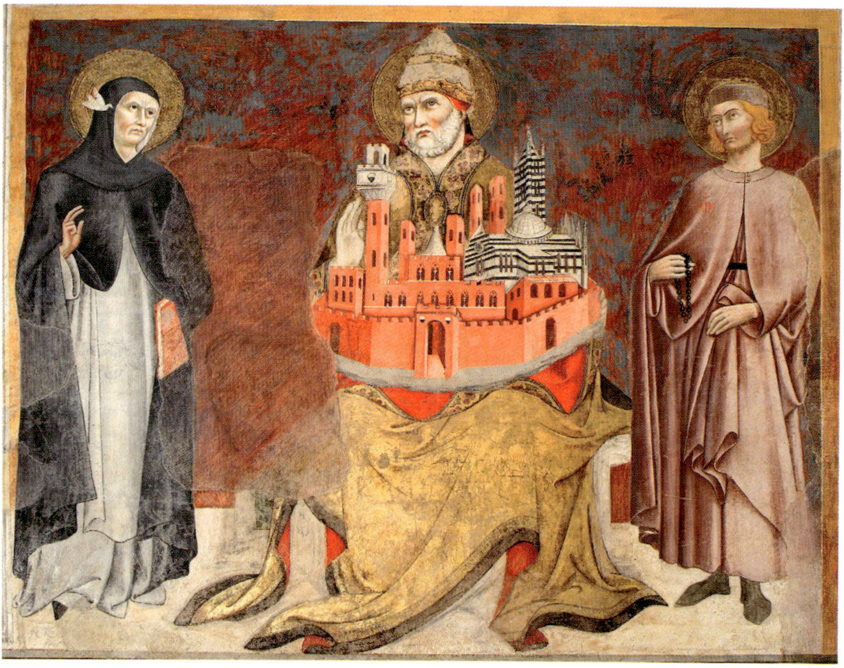

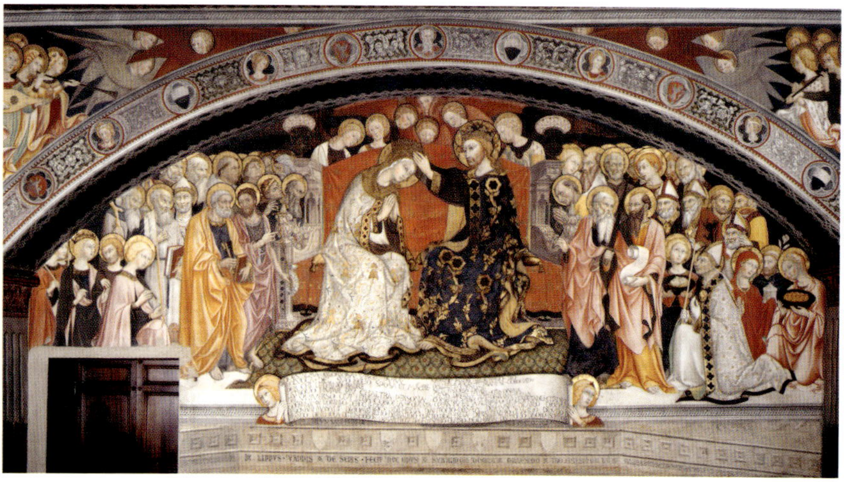

open. The hall takes its name from the presence of two fourteenth-century marble she-wolves, which once functioned as rainspouts on the palace exterior.

On the right, the rooms overlooking Piazza del Mercato, where the mayor and department heads now have their offices, were once the offices of the Biccherna, the important magistracy that handled the city's finances. We know from documents that the interior was decorated as early as 1293, but the art that now covers the walls of these rooms dates from the fifteenth to the seventeenth century. All the paintings are by Sienese artists and illustrate various sacred and secular subjects: patron

Sano di Pietro, *The Coronation of the Virgin*, 1445, Chancellery of the Biccherna (now part of the mayor's offices)

Sano di Pietro, *Saint Peter of Alexandria between Blessed Andrea Gallerani and Ambrogio Sansedoni*, detail, 1446, Hall of the She-wolves

# Arms of the Nobility and Governors

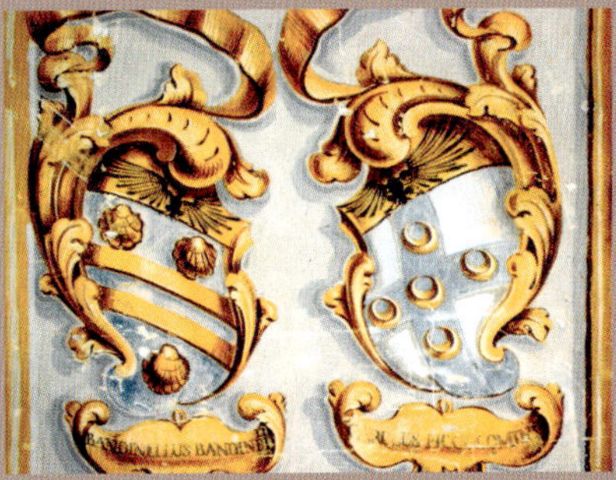

Aristocratic coats of arms frescoed in the rooms on the top floor of the Palazzo Pubblico

Siena's Palazzo Pubblico, like all the town halls which traverse the history of the cities whose symbols they have become, is rich in coats of arms, emblems, and heraldic depictions of the men who over the centuries have been connected with it as they performed their government duties, when not actually living there. Men for the most part belonging to noble families, who left evidence of their office, or in any case of their passage, through their families' coats of arms.

Starting in the late twelfth century, during tournaments the "heralds" had the job of shouting out the description of the insignia of the horsemen as they presented themselves for the fight, and they collected their information in manuscripts describing the colors of the arms and the helmets of the competing horsemen. With the disappearance of the figure of the herald and the change in function and nature of these collections, which were up to then the prerogative of the feudal nobility, the custom spread of painting the aristocratic coats of arms of the governing class on town halls.

We can say that there were two periods in the history of Sienese heraldry: in the first, the time of the republic, only families of feudal origin were considered noble, while in the second, under Medici rule, all the citizens who had resided in the Consistory and their descendants were considered noble.

Many of the frescoed arms decorating the interior of the Palazzo Pubblico include the emblems of the current Captain of the People and the residents of the Consistory, for the most part Suebese aristocrats, even if during a close study it emerged that some noble families whose arms appear in Palazzo Pubblico are not of Sienese origin. Some members of these families had asked to be admitted or aggregated to the Sienese nobility; and too, many families have the same surname, but different arms and histories.

Many of these arms, painted for the most part in the seventeenth century, are in what is now the mayor's office on the ground floor of the palace, while others are on the second floor, on the ceiling of the council chambers.

Another substantial group of coats of arms, made of stone and marble, is located in the Cortile del Podestà, and the most recent group of all was painted around 1920 by the Sienese artist Umberto Giunti as part of the decoration of the Sala delle Lupe.

(P.G.)

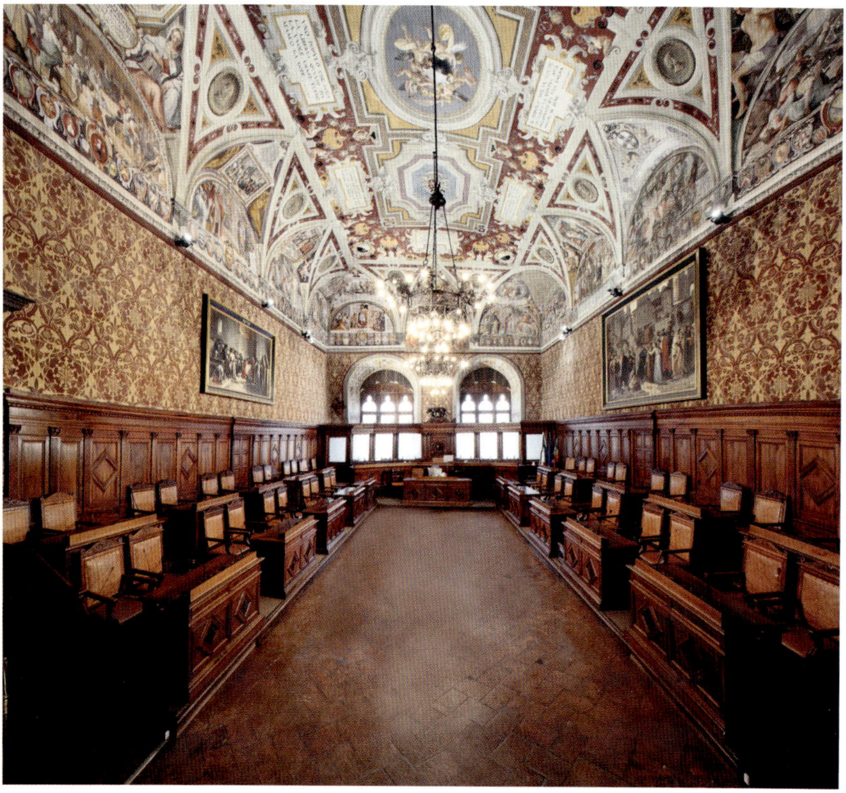

The ancient Hall of the Captain of the People is now the City Council Chamber

saints, scenes from the life of important Sienese personages, historic events in the city, and heraldic and allegorical decorations.

The second floor is reached from the Loggia overlooking Piazza del Mercato.

The top floor of the building was composed essentially of a large apartment, made up of various rooms, where the Nine magistrates resided; from the fifteenth century onwards, it was assigned to the Captain of the People and his counselors.

The large central room is now used for meetings of the City Council. The ceiling of this room, illustrating episodes from the civic and religious life of Siena, is divided into lunettes and sections painted between 1592 and 1600 by the leading Sienese artists of the period.

The same style and type of subject matter continues in the somewhat later (seventeenth century) decoration of a small adjacent room, probably used as a dining room by the governing authorities during the winter months.

# The Sienese She-Wolf between Legend and Iconography

The legend of the birth of Siena handed down by the fifteenth-century *Aldobrandini Chronicle*, compiled by an anonymous author concealing his identity behind the pseudonym Tisbo Colonnese, establishes a close connection between the founding of this city and the mythological origins of Rome.* The chronicle tells that the oldest core of Siena was founded by Senius and Ascanius, the sons of Remus who, fleeing Rome after their father was killed by their uncle Romulus, brought with them the Roman emblem of the she-wolf nursing the twins, stolen from the Temple of Apollo, adopting it as the symbol of the city they founded. When they finally reached the Tuscan hills, on the spot where Siena would later rise, the two brothers decided to make a sacrifice to Diana; seeing two clouds of smoke rising from the pyre, one white and the other black, they took this to be a sign of the emblem of the new city, the black-and-white shield known as the Balzana.

While recent studies have shown that this evocative tale reported by the anonymous writer was only a humanist invention created to lend nobility to Siena's origins on the basis of existing traditions and folk narratives whose origins are obscure, it is equally true that, together with the Balzana, the emblem of the she-wolf nursing the twins was adopted as early as the Middle Ages by the cultural and artistic elite of Siena as the symbol of civic identity.

Starting at least as early as the late thirteenth century, we find a progressive proliferation of sculptures of the she-wolf and twins, many of which have survived to our day, placed on columns or near doors or gates to mark the points of greatest interest in the urban context. Among the earliest examples of the she-wolf and twins still known to us are a bas-relief produced by Giovanni Pisano's workshop, set inside one of the scrolling acanthus tendrils on the column of the left portal of the cathedral, and the sculpture now in the Museo dell'Opera but originally on one of the two columns in front of the cathedral. The eighteenth-century men of letters Girolamo Gigli and Girolamo Macchi report, besides the columns surmounted by sculpted images of the she-wolf nursing the twins standing in front of the churches of San Cristoforo, San Domenico, and San

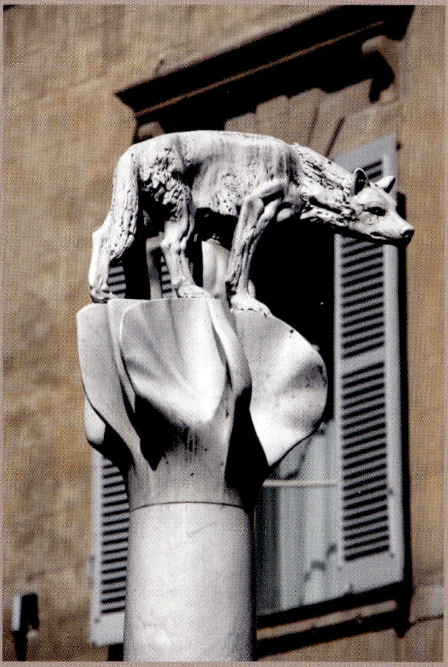

Giuliano Vangi,
*She-wolf*, 1996,
Siena, Piazza Postierla

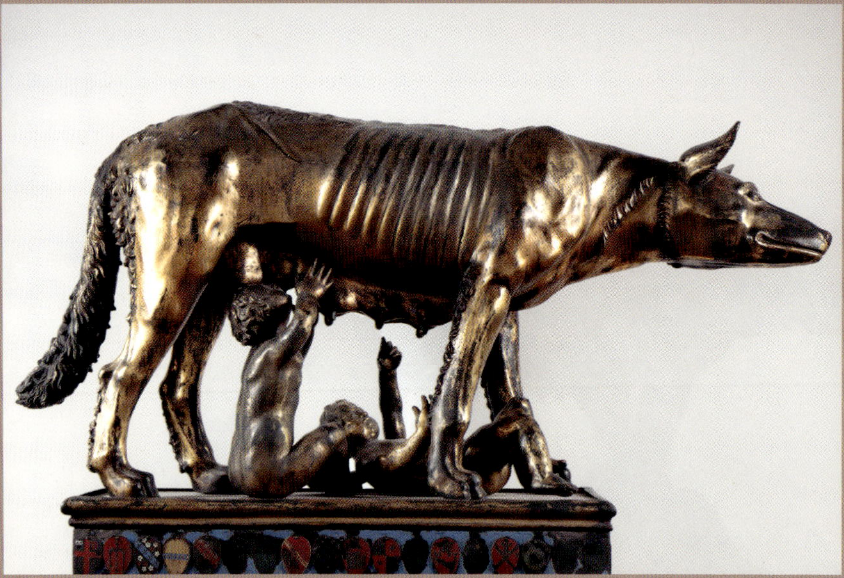

Pellegrino alla Sapienza in the past, numerous examples made in various eras and still today visible throughout the city or replaced by copies, with the originals preserved inside the city's various museums.
The close union between Siena and its heraldic device seems to reach its peak in the decoration of the Town Hall, by definition the emblematic building of civic identity. But beyond the intriguing idea handed down to us by Gigli and Macchi of a she-wolf that used to wander around inside the Sala del Mappamondo in Palazzo Pubblico, or the custom, testified by Sano di Pietro's painting of *Saint Bernardine Preaching in Piazza del Campo* (now preserved in the Museo dell'Opera), of keeping a live she-wolf in a little fenced-in area in front of the building, the palace still today has a significant number of sculptures, paintings, and works of the applied arts, both exterior and interior, that present as their main or secondary subject the she-wolf nursing the twins, used with decorative or symbolic intent.
Besides the oldest examples, two rainspouts originally placed on the sides of the elevated central section of the façade, replaced by copies in the nineteenth century, with the originals now on display inside the large entrance atrium of the municipal offices (called the Hall of the She-wolves), others worthy of mention are the eight spouts arranged in two rows on the top of the Torre del Mangia, the two bas-reliefs by Agostino di Giovanni facing the emblem of the Captain of the People on the lunette over the right portal, and the bronze she-wolf by Giovanni and Lorenzo di Turino, formerly on the column in front of the building and currently preserved in the Civic Museum. While this heraldic beast acts as a recurrent motif in the exterior decoration of the building, it is possible to discern its unmistakable silhouette, albeit in a less prominent position, also in the painted and ornamental additions to the interior. Besides the large nineteenth-century fresco in the vestibule, attentive visitors can find the oldest depictions of the she-wolf nursing the twins in one of the roundels on the frescoed band running around Simone Martini's wall painting of *The Virgin and Child Enthroned in Majesty* in the Sala del Mappamondo and at the feet of the personification of Good Government in Ambrogio Lorenzetti's famous fresco in the Sala della Pace, as well as on the front of the famous sixteenth-century organ in the chapel.

(V.R.)

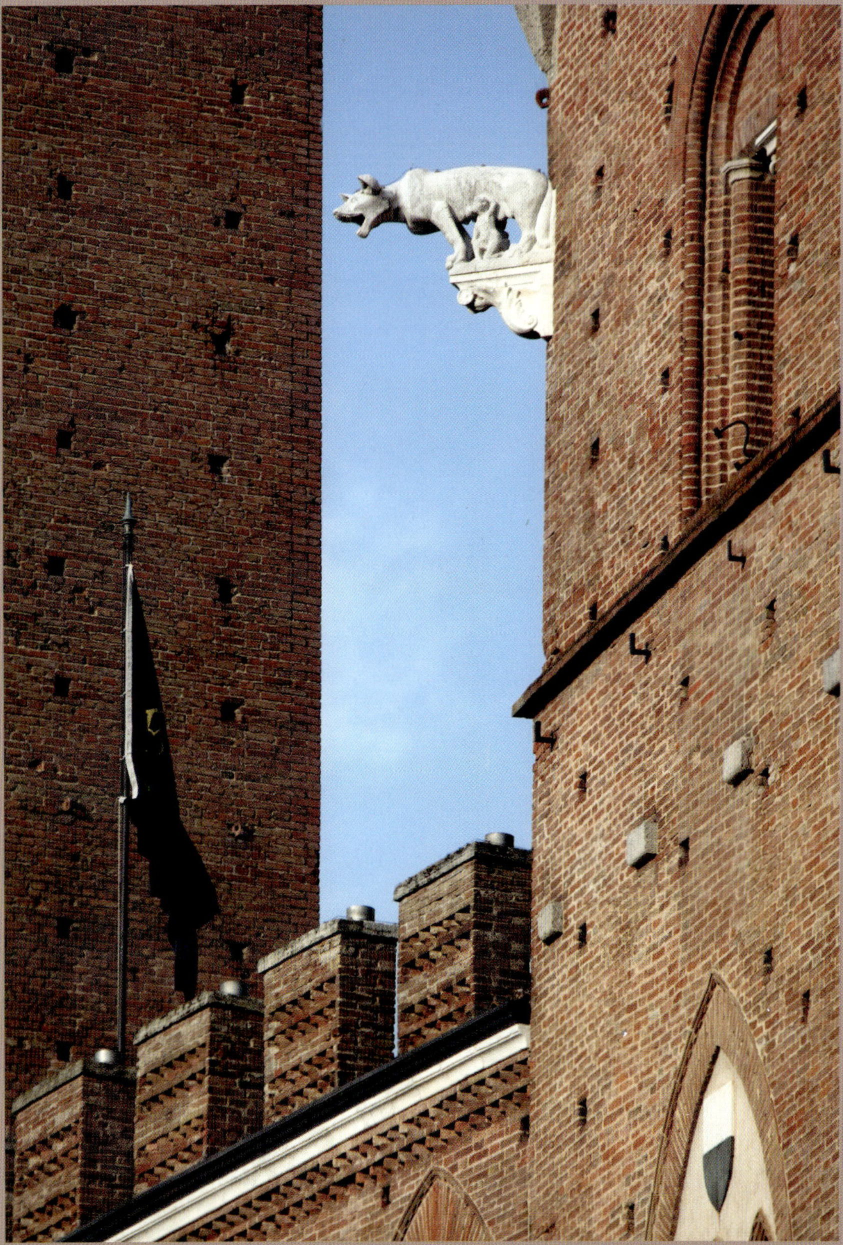

A monumental marble she-wolf, once used as a rainspout, on the side of the central tower of the Palazzo

Giovanni and Lorenzo di Turino, *She-wolf and Twins*, ca. 1429, formerly on a column in front of the palace entrance

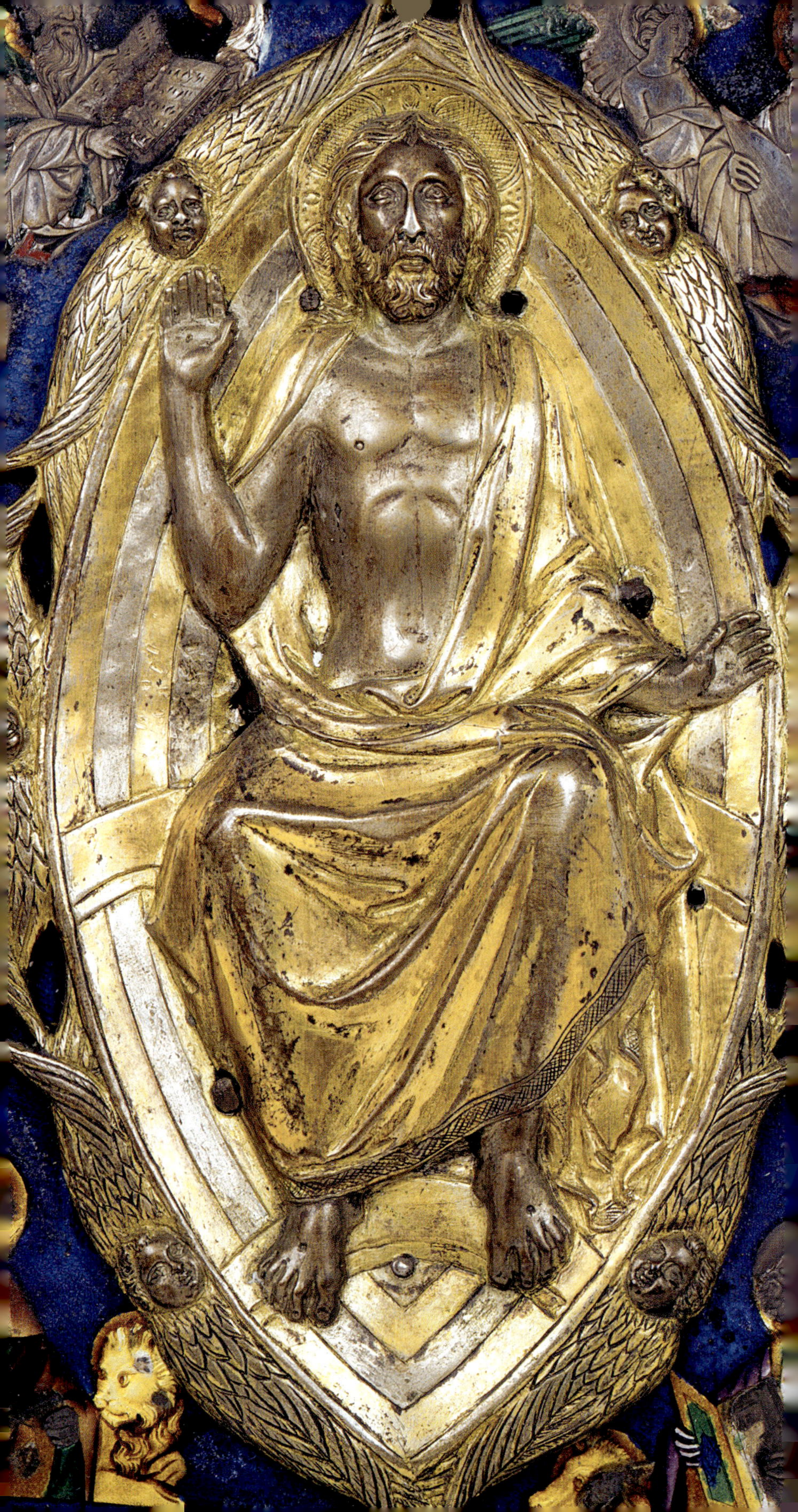

# Art Works to Admire

*Veronica Randon*

Sienese goldsmith, *Pax*, ca. 1390-1400, Forechapel

The maxim that every museum is the fruit of its own history and of the civilization that produced it holds true also for Siena's Civic Museum, whose uniqueness lies in the fact that it has always been housed in the same building and that this building was erected for the specific purpose, which it still maintains, of being the seat of the city's government.

With its impressive decorations made up of the extensive, major fresco cycles which have adorned its walls through the centuries, the Palazzo Pubblico nonetheless constitutes today not only a context of unparalleled beauty, but also a container so charged with artistic meaning and evidence as to represent with its authoritativeness a strong pole of attraction already in and of itself, sometimes overshadowing the perception of the prestigious art objects on display inside it.

Attentive visitors who wish to dwell on the contents of the showcases, the furnishings, or the paintings hanging in the various rooms, can at the same time immerse themselves in a parallel course through the museum that is paradigmatic of the evolution of a heritage of art whose constitution was not linear and homogeneous, but complex and stratified. The works preserved in the Palazzo Pubblico and making up the collections of the Museo Civico are not limited just to the enlightened patronage of those who have governed Siena over the centuries, but are the result of complex socio-political phenomena and individual initiatives that have followed each other over the centuries. Retracing the history of the collections and the various art works on display in the palace today, however, means noting also that the museum is not a static organism unchanging through time, but is in constant evolution, revealing in the forming of its various collections and the succession of arrangements in which they have been displayed the development of its identity and the changing taste of various ages.

Unfortunately, the art works on display in the Civic Museum today can furnish only a timid idea of the artistic and ceremonial splendor which over the years characterized the government of Siena and its magistracies and can only partially be reconstructed on the basis of the surviving documentation. Numerous documents attest through the centuries to the presence in the palace of frescoes, paintings and art objects, now lost due to various factors, among them the wear and tear of time, the cessation of their function, and the transformation of the rooms for which they were created. While some very famous works have been lost, like the *Virgin and Child Enthroned in Majesty* painted by Duccio for the old Chapel of the Nine in 1302, a veritable model for Sienese painting after it, the invaluable collection of painted covers of the record books of the Biccherna, the tax office, have survived and are now in the nearby Archivio di Stato, where they were moved in the nineteenth century. Nonetheless, art works of undeniable prestige are still in the palace today, testifying to the prestigious patronage of the Commune of Siena. Among these are a *Pax* made of embossed and enameled copper, once used in the liturgy of the palace chapel; the fifteenth-century *Plaquette* showing the she-wolf and twins made by Giovanni di Turino; and two precious late fourteenth-century painted wooden boxes, currently on display in the Sala dei Pilastri.

In the course of time, the museum has also taken on the role of repository of valuable pieces coming from other parts of the palace, such as the sinopia underdrawing for the fresco of the *Virgin and Saints* painted by Giovanni Antonio Bazzi, known as Sodoma, for the Cappella di Piazza, or the *She-wolf with the Twins* by Giovanni di Turino which once topped the column next to the entrance to the Palace, or from the rest of the city, like the *She-wolf and Twins* made by someone in the circle of Neroccio di Bartolomeo de' Landi, originally on the column in Piazza Postierla, or the bronze hitching rings by Guidoccio Cozzarelli which once graced the façade of the palace of the Magnifico Pandolfo Petrucci. Emblematic in this regard is the history of the fifteenth-century Fonte Gaia by Jacopo della Quercia which, after it was replaced in 1868 by the algid copy made by Tito Sarrocchi, was recomposed by Corrado Ricci in a theatrical installation on the Loggia dei Nove for the great exhibition of early Sienese art in 1904, where it stayed until the late 1980s, when it was moved for conservation reasons into the Santa Maria della Scala museum complex.

Starting in the second half of the eighteenth century,

when Grand Duke Leopold suppressed many religious institutions, and later with further suppressions, of the lay companies and those under Napoleon, bringing enormous amounts of church property under state control, the Palazzo Pubblico became a great storehouse of art works of various sorts, for the most part religious in nature. A more recent offshoot of this phenomenon can be seen in the recent suppressions of charity institutions like the San Marco orphanage, with their most important and valuable art works coming into the civic collections in the early 1970s. Examples of these are the four paintings adorning the coffin stand belonging to the lay company of Sant'Onofrio, a key work for reconstructing the artistic personality of the Sienese painter Bartolomeo di David, the four hunting scenes by the Flemish artist Philipp Peter Roos (known as Rosa da Tivoli), and the very fine painting by Bernardino Mei of *Saint Bernardine of Siena in Ecstasy*, commissioned by the Company of Sant'Onofrio de' Mendici. On deposit from the Butini-Bourke home for poor women are the four paintings from the coffin stand belonging to the Company of Santo Stefano ai Pispini, a masterpiece of the early maturity of the Sienese artist Ventura Salimbeni, and from the Istituto Tommaso Pendola, the large canvas by Sebastiano Folli entitled *Noli me tangere*.

In 1835, the prestigious collection belonging to Pompeo, Federico, and Leopoldo Spannocchi was left to the Sienese community. This collection, dismantled and currently divided between the Pinacoteca Nazionale and the Civic Museum, consists mainly of paintings from northern Europe and northern Italy. As specified by the learned eighteenth-century abbot Girolamo Carli, the collection, brought as a dowry by Countess Caterina Piccolomi della Mondella, the last descendant of her branch of the family, to her marriage to Giuseppe Spannocchi, had been partially assembled in Mantua by her ancestor, General Enea Silvio Piccolomini, following the imperial sack in 1630 of that city and of the celebrated "heavenly gallery" of the Gonzaga dukes, while a small core of the collection was made up of paintings already present in the Piccolomini family palace in Siena. The six delightful little scenes attributed to Cristofano Rustici, of the months of November, May, October, June, September, and January represented by delicate genre scenes, probably were part of this latter group.

The Spannocchi collection, however, is not an isolated case of donation of art works by private parties.

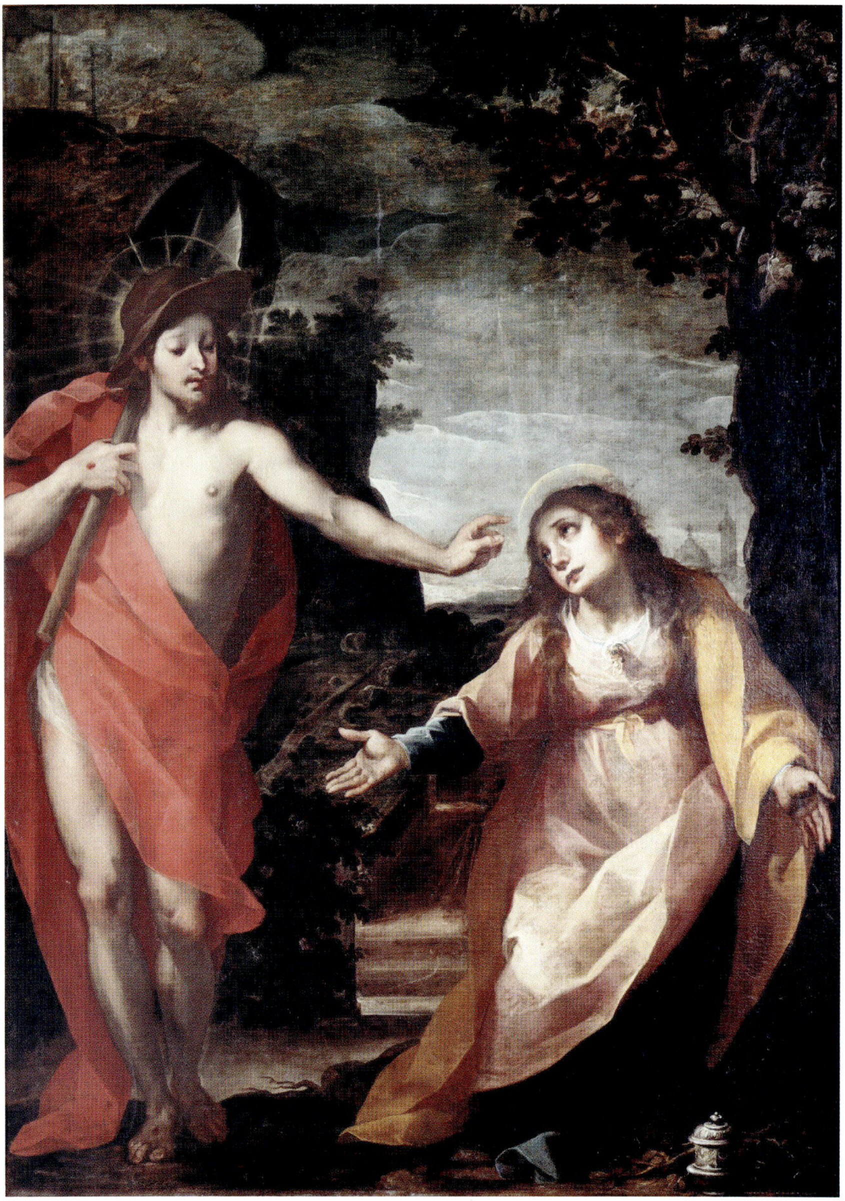

For a long period of time, it appears that it was a common practice on the part of Sienese families, often residing far from their homeland, to pay tribute to their origins by giving valuable art objects to the city. In this way, works of unquestioned prestige have come into the collections of the Civic Museum, such as the paintings of *The Battle of Ponte a Valiano* by Gaetano Lapis, called Carraccetto, or *Gideon Choosing his Soldiers* by Johann Heinrich Schönfeld, donated by the Tondi family from Gubbio and the Petroni family from Naples, respectively.

Sebastiano Folli,
*Noli me tangere*,
16th-17th centuries,
Picture Gallery

As time passed the custom was extended also to individuals who wished to leave to the community a memento of themselves or of their ancestors. An example of this is the pike used during the siege of Siena by the Captain of the Republic Marcello Palmieri, donated by his descendant Palmiero Palmieri.

Since the 1860s when the museum was opened to the public, limited in the beginning to the monumental apartments, until today, the number of art objects housed in it, which over the course of time became much more varied in type, has been further increased by purchases made in the course of the twentieth century on the flourishing antique market with enlightened foresight by the city administration.

Starting in the early twentieth century, when the idea took shape of turning the public building into exhibition space with the definitive transfer of the public offices still occupying its most prestigious rooms on the first floor, the acquisition of new collections began to be more rational and orderly, with an eye to creating a permanent display of art objects representative of the city and its historical, cultural and artistic image.

In this perspective, around 1935, the Topographic Museum was set up in the rooms of the Captain of the People, consisting of prints, drawings and paintings of Sienese subjects and illustrious figures taken mainly from the collections of the Biblioteca Comunale degli Intronati, to which they have recently been returned, as well as scale models reconstructing the ancient fountains and entire neighborhoods of the city.

This was joined in the 1950s by the Numismatic Museum, which brought together the valuable collections of coins, seals, and medals from the time of ancient Rome to the nineteenth century belonging to the Biblioteca and originally in the collections of the erudite Fedro Bandini and Giuseppe Porri, and a similar core collection from the Accademia dei Fisiocritici, making it one of the most complete in Tuscany, despite the fact that it was removed from display in 1976 and placed in the museum's storerooms.

It was only around the middle of the 1980s that the Civic Museum was given its definitive arrangement, which it preserves still today, albeit slightly modified due to modern exhibition concerns, in full respect of its complex identity, emblematically represented by its collections and its history.

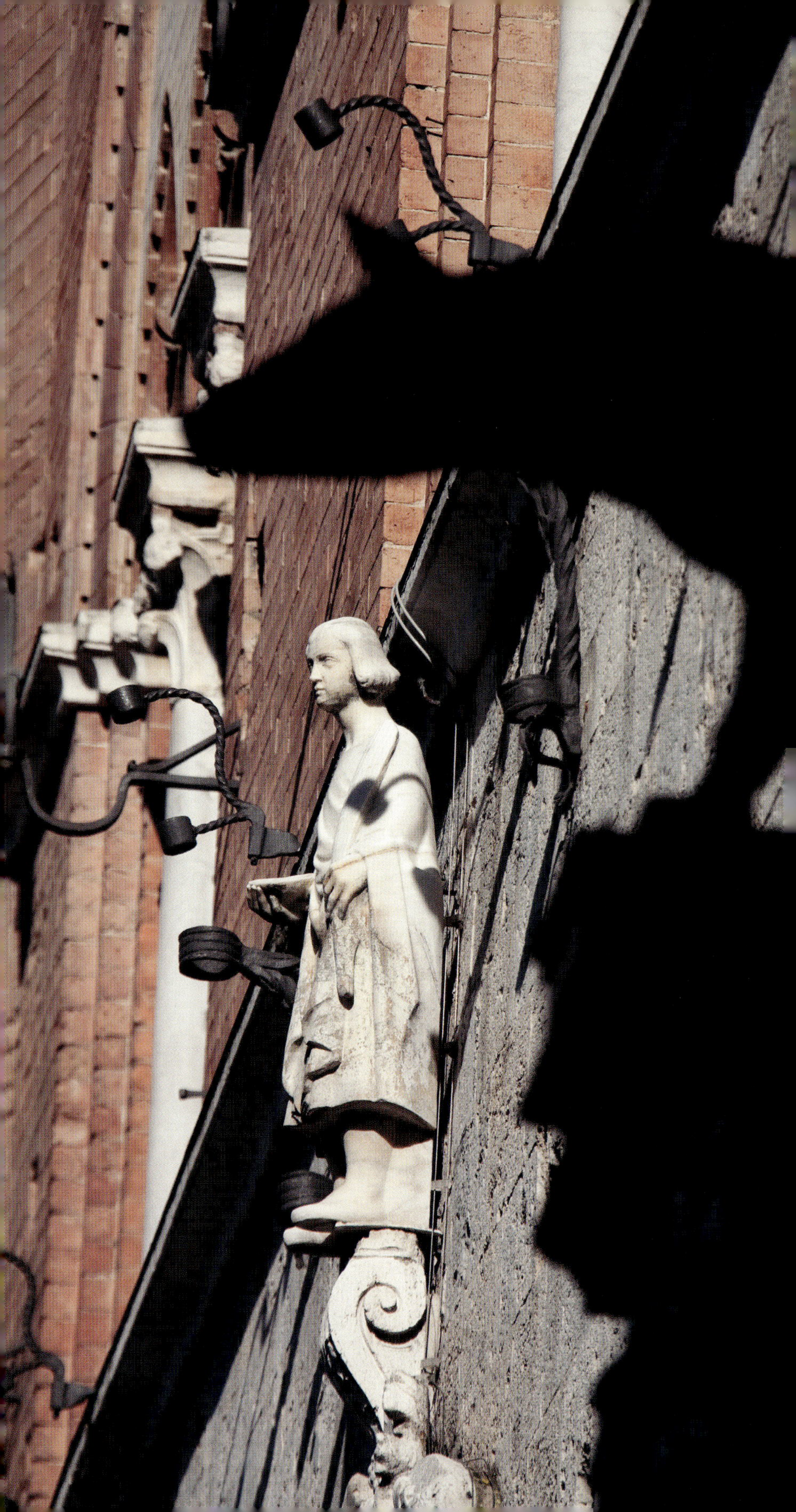

## The Construction of the Palazzo Pubblico
# A Perfect Combination of Architecture

*Letizia Galli*

A close-up view of the Palazzo Pubblico façade with the silhouette of the stone she-wolf on the corner of the building, and in the foreground a statue of Saint Ansanus, protector of the city, on the tympanum of the entrance portal

The Palazzo Pubblico closes like a stage backdrop the circle of Piazza del Campo, crowned by the patrician palaces that surround it.
Nothing is left to chance in this extraordinary specimen of early fourteenth-century urban planning, starting with the passageways that lead into the great open space of the plaza, almost all little entryways, squeezed between the palaces, like gaps in a wall. Already, walking through these, one begins to taste the fullness of the Campo, its light and colors which change with the varying hours of the day and night, embraced by the unmistakable skyline of the ancient buildings.

**Piazza del Campo**

This public square was born as a vast free, open space – called at the time the "campus fori," the "field outside" – and this it has remained. Enclosed within the city walls around the middle of the twelfth century, it was paved only in the first half of the fourteenth century (1327-1349), as the conclusion of the project to give a definitive urban arrangement to this part of the city, which was intended as the "secular" and civic pole of Siena's social fabric, almost as a counterbalance to the religious pole anchored by the tall, imposing edifice of the cathedral.
The incline of the square, slightly downhill, follows that of the terrain, which slopes down from the cathedral. Its characteristic shell shape is defined by the Palazzo Pubblico, which closes it off at the bottom, in the center of which the lines of the nine sections come together.
The division of the pavement into nine sections reflects the make-up of the governing body, the Government of the Nine, who chose this pattern for that purpose.
The current appearance of the palaces around the square is varied, from the ancient D'Elci and Sansedoni palaces built of brick and topped by crenellation,

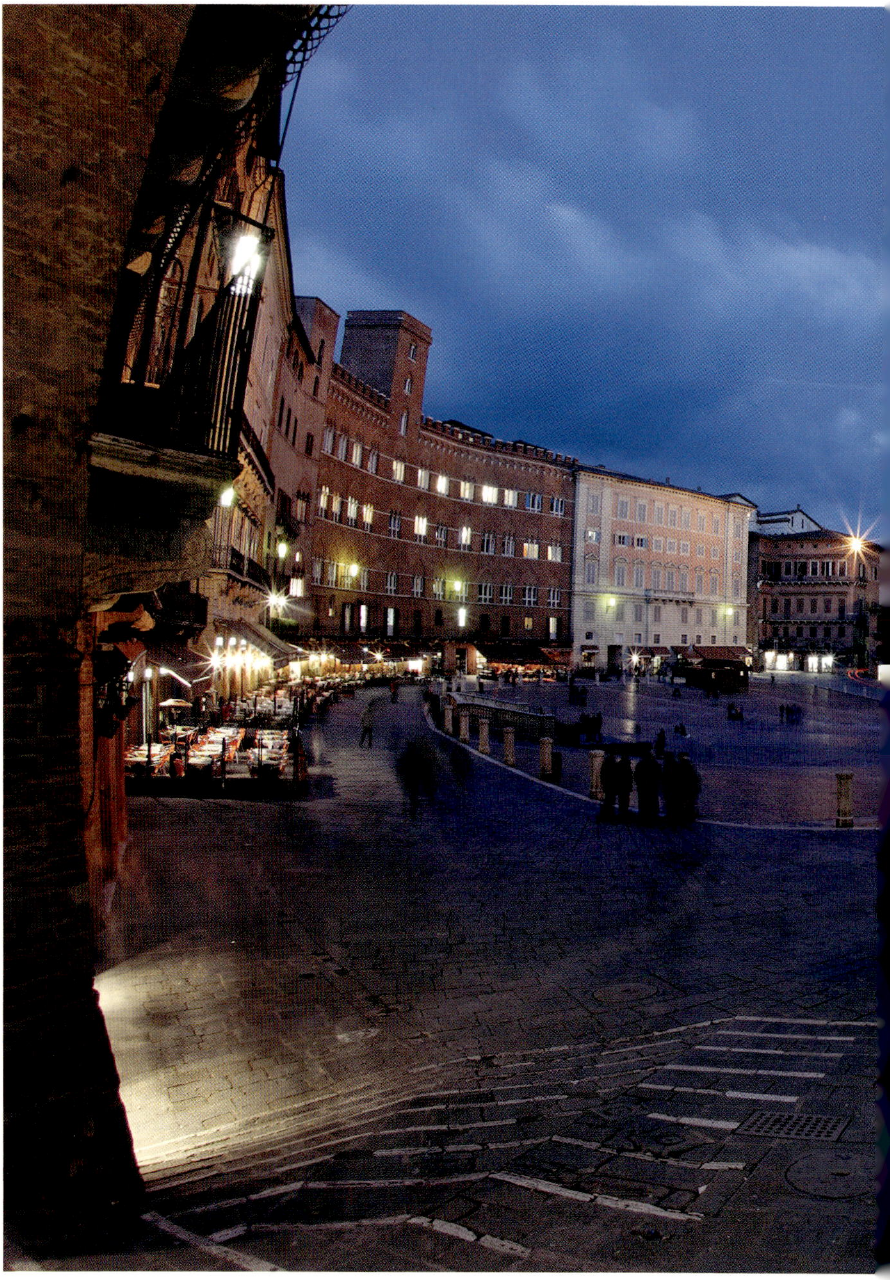

to the colored eighteenth-century renovated facades of the Casino dei Nobili and Palazzo Chigi Zondadari. But this has not always been the case, and here too nothing was left to chance.

A directive of the *Costituto* of 1297 forbade, for example, the construction of wooden balconies on the sides of the palaces overlooking the Campo, and required the use of stone colonnettes on the windows, to avoid any disturbing elements in the overall harmony.

An evocative view of Piazza del Campo from the Costarella entrance to the square

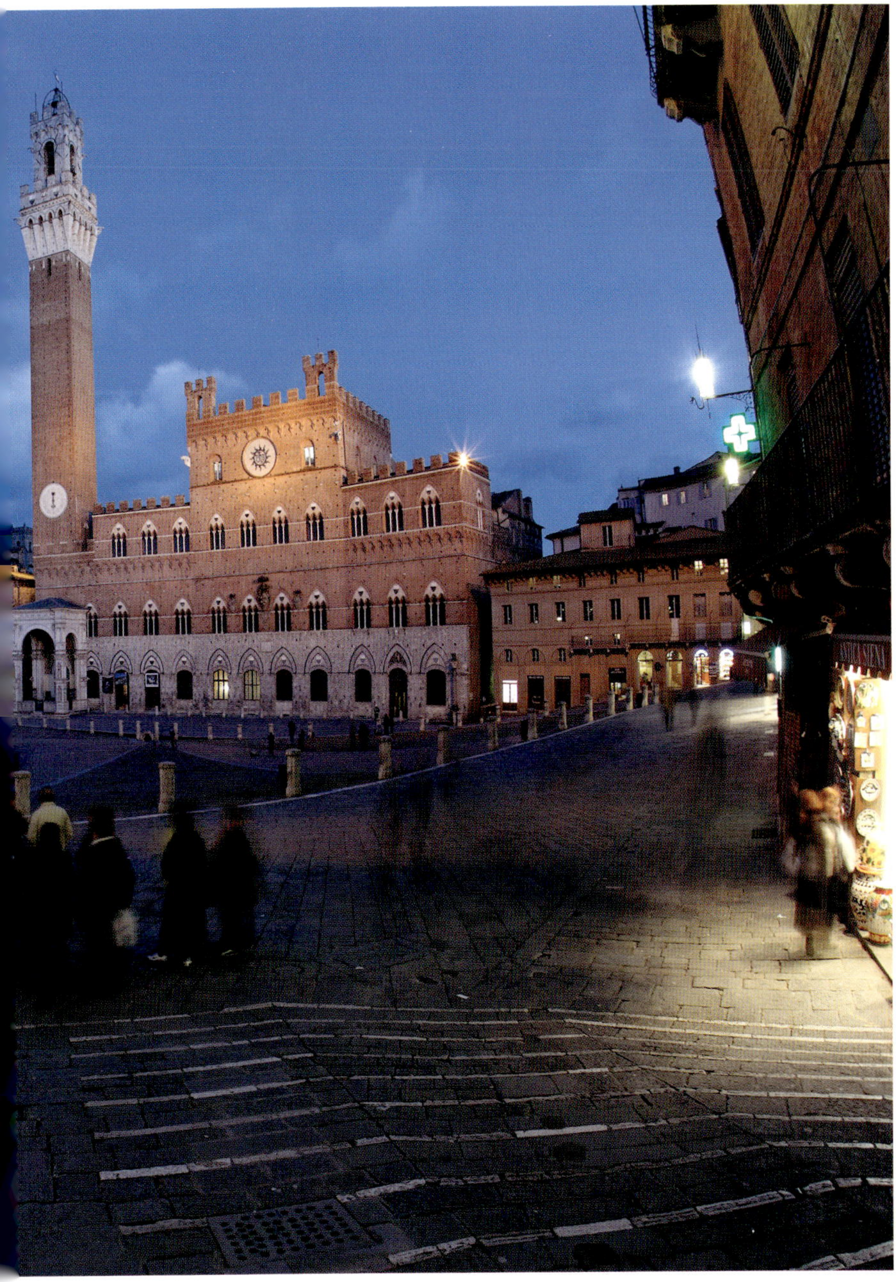

## The Palazzo Pubblico

The idea of building the Palazzo Pubblico began to take shape around 1280, given the need for a public place to hold meetings of the officials of the commune; until then, public business had been conducted in churches or private homes, chosen on each occasion. The Council of the Bell, the highest government body, for example, met in the church of San Cristoforo, and other meetings

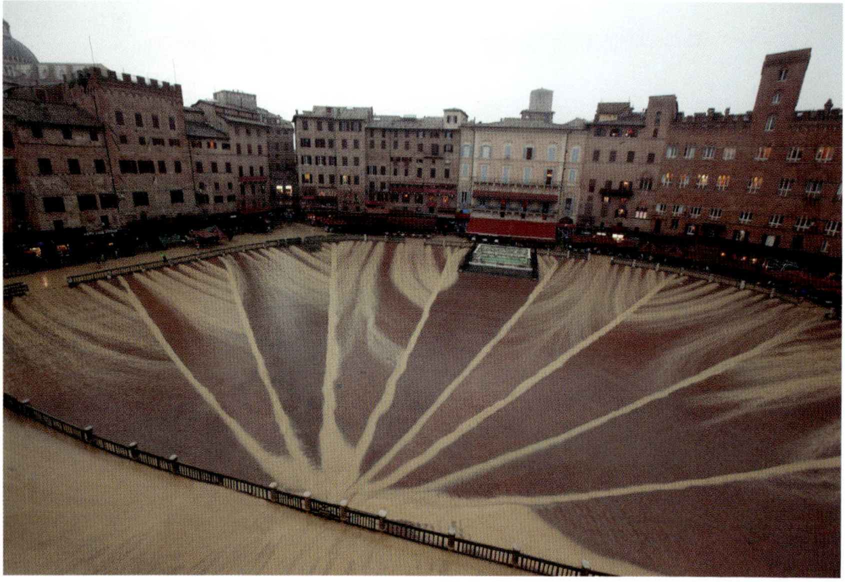

were held in the palaces of powerful Sienese families like the Tolomei or the Ugurgieri.

In order to have a building of its own, in 1293 the Commune of Siena began buying the houses of private citizens adjacent to the Bolgano, a building which was already public and housed the mint, and the customs house; both of these were at the bottom of the Campo between the streets called Malborghetto (currently Via Dupré) and Malcucinato (now Via di Salicotto).

In 1297-1298, work was begun to remodel the old Bolgano. By 1305, construction was complete on the tall central section of the palace, flanked on the right by the wing of the Nine and on the other side by the Palazzo del Podestà with the Torre del Mangia. In 1310, the Nine settled into the palace, which could be said to be finished when the travertine battlement on top of the Torre del Mangia was completed (1348) and the large porch on the back set up (1350).

Thus it only took fifty years to transform a group of private buildings into one of the biggest Gothic civic buildings in Italy.

In civic architecture between the late thirteenth and the first half of the fourteenth century, the innovation of Siena's Palazzo Pubblico marks the transition from the fortress to the palace. The crenellation remains to evoke a fortress, but defense towers had practically no doors, while Siena's Palazzo Pubblico has ten on the front, and had another ten on the back.

The other new element, architectural and decorative at

Piazza del Campo during the days of the Palio. A thunderstorm has washed dirt from the racetrack into the grooves marking off the nine sections of the pavement, emphasizing their shape.

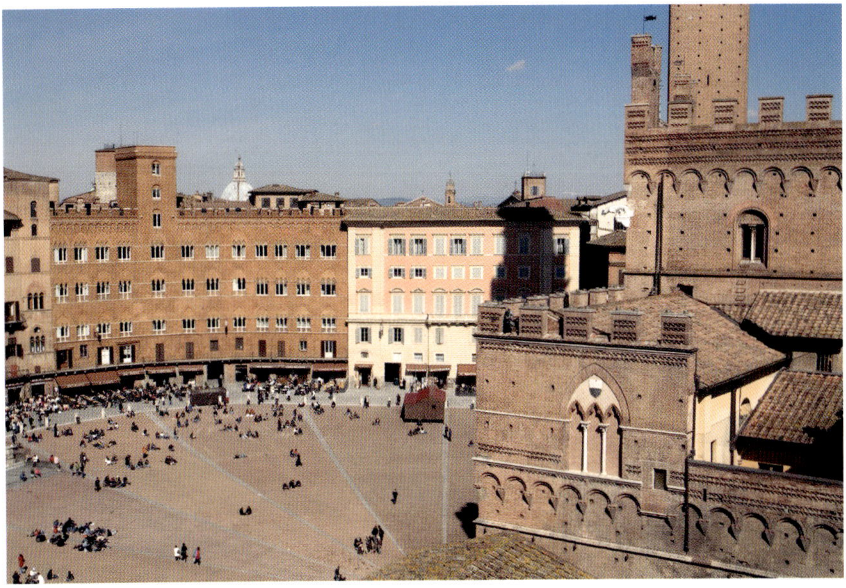

The palaces ringing the square.
Most prominent are Palazzo Sansedoni and Palazzo Chigi Zondadari.

the same time, is the Sienese three-light window. This is based on strict geometric forms: an equilateral triangle on top of a square, with the pointed arch fitting inside the triangle. The Palazzo presents two rows of triforate windows, with a matching set on the back of the building. The strict geometry is accompanied, however, by the open airiness that these windows, divided delicately into three sections by slender colonnettes, give to the front of the palace, together with the sequence of portals, in a masterful balance of closed and open, of inside and out.

The same sober, measured aspiration to architectural rigor, mediated by the characteristically Sienese predilection for elegance, beauty, and chromatic variance – think of paintings by Duccio and Simone Martini – finds full expression in the division of the façade, with its gray stone on the ground level and brick on the upper part, embellished by the delicate border of blind archlets.

All this – innovation, taste, beauty – cannot be associated with one precise name. The documents are no help in identifying the name of an architect who might have created a unified plan, as the organic, harmonious arrangement of the whole would suggest. The names of the "operari" (superintendents) follow each other over the years in the records of payments and appointments, and some certainly appear more often than others, but no one personality emerges over all the others, except perhaps one "Maestro Giovanni," identified as a miniaturist and calligrapher, who could perhaps have been the

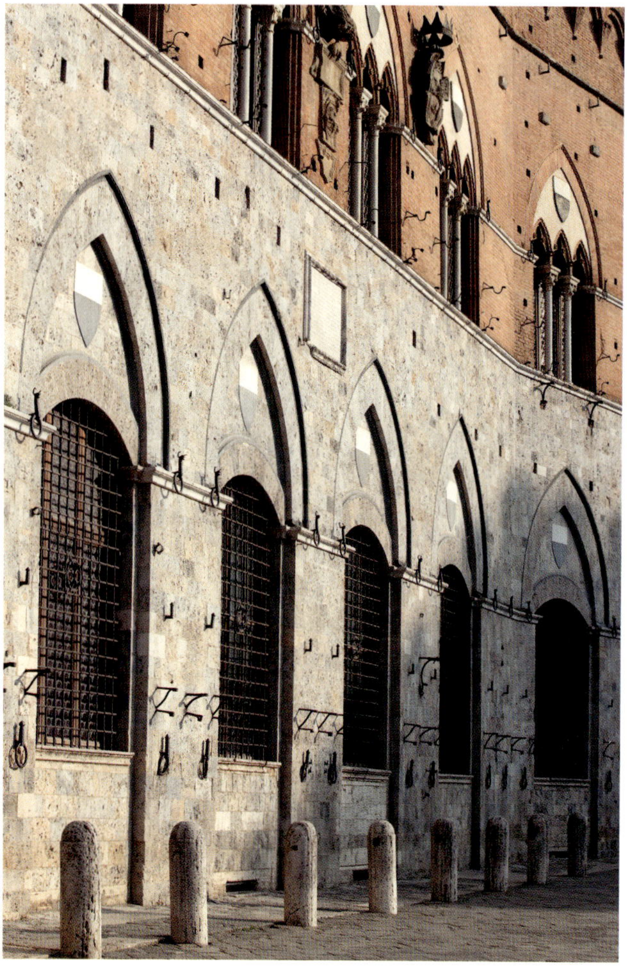

The sequence of portals, some now transformed into windows, across the palace front.

author of the plans, but really too little is known about him. Whoever it is, one or more than one, the designer of the Palazzo Pubblico was in any case a product of the early fourteenth-century cultural climate of Siena, the expression of a lively environment open to outside influence, whether from France or Arabia, the fruit of the Via Francigena pilgrimage route or the vast and profitable economic affairs of the Sienese merchants.

The palace's appearance has not changed greatly over the centuries.

In 1352, it was decided to build the small chapel at the foot of the Torre del Mangia, dedicated to the Virgin Mary, as a sign of thanksgiving for the end of the terrible plague of 1348, which decimated the population of the city. This is a little marble jewel, open on three sides, reflecting both late Gothic and Renaissance taste. The first phase of work was finished around 1376, but the sculptor and architect Antonio Federighi worked on it

Sano di Pietro, *Saint Bernardine Preaching in Piazza del Campo*, 1448, Siena, Museo dell'Opera

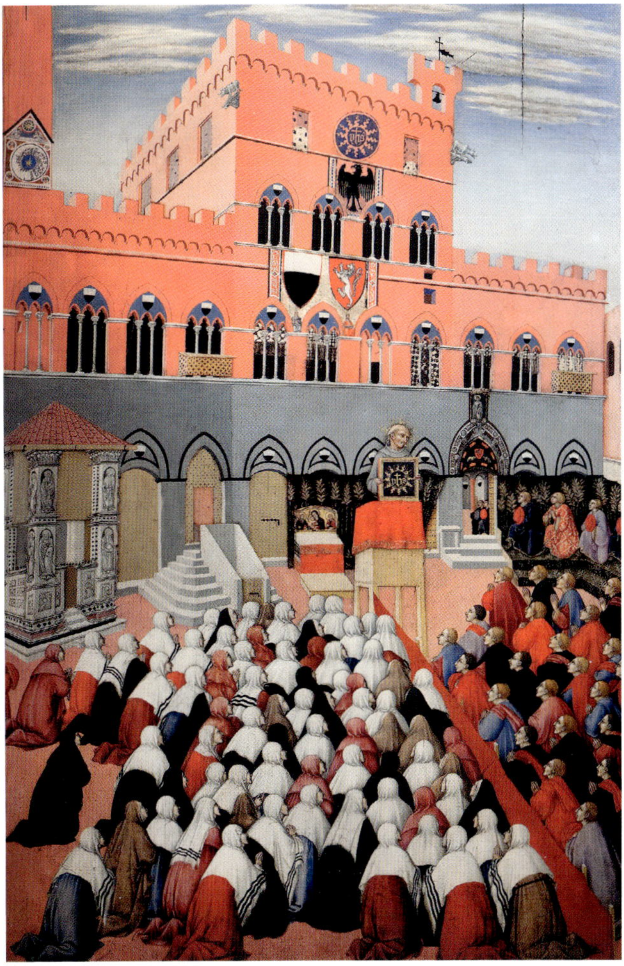

again at the height of the Renaissance (1461-68), providing both structural and decorative contributions in a classicizing style, modifying the round arches that support an architrave adorned with facing pairs of gryphons and vase motifs, and embellishing the pendentives with niches and vegetable garlands.
The final important intervention on the façade of the palace was done in the late seventeenth century (16980). The Roman architect Carlo Fontana raised the side wings of the palace on either side of the tall central section, to which he added a small sail-over belfry on the left side. Inside, Fontana built the grand staircase linking the floors of the building on the Malborghetto side.

## The Salt Storerooms

A vast exhibition space for temporary shows has been recovered inside Palazzo Pubblico from the cellars located

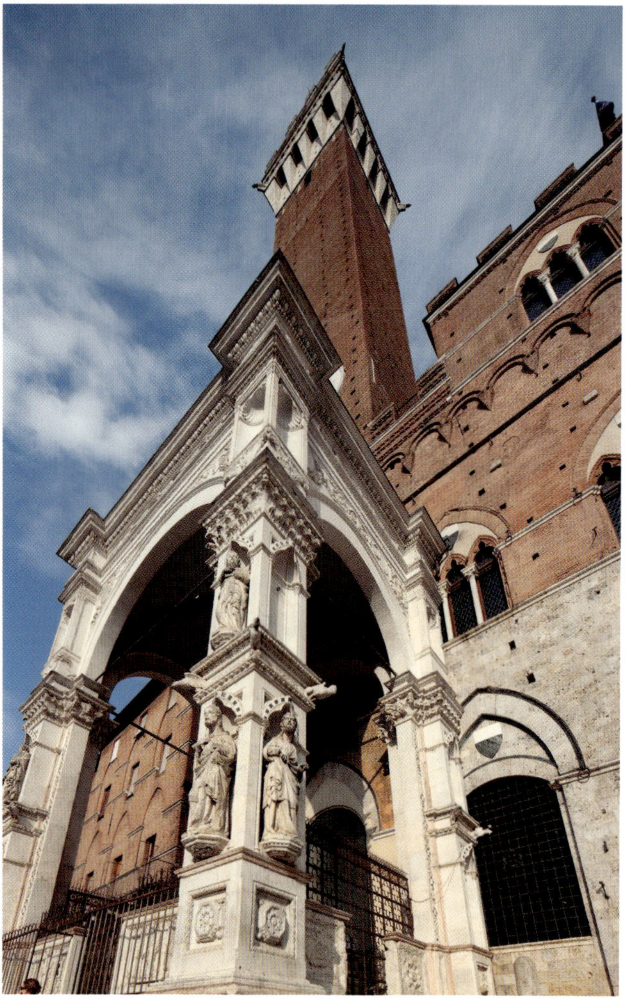

An unusual angle on the Chapel at the foot of the Torre del Mangia

between level of the Campo and the Piazza del Mercato level below it in back. These enormous rooms under the Torre del Mangia and the Cortile del Podestà were originally occupied, at least in the lowest part, by the commune of Siena's salt warehouses, which were forgotten for centuries and remained for a long time abandoned underground space.
The restoration project, handled by Terrosi, Manganelli, Nepi, Valacchi architects in 1974-78, uncovered the foundations of this part of the building, characterized by enormous pilings and buttressing walls, and a huge ancient cistern, located on the edge next to the Piazza del Campo, used to collect the rainwater running off the palace, which was then diverted into the underground water system created in medieval Siena.
The recovered space, entered through the same portal as the museum, now consists of two levels connected by a

The salt storerooms

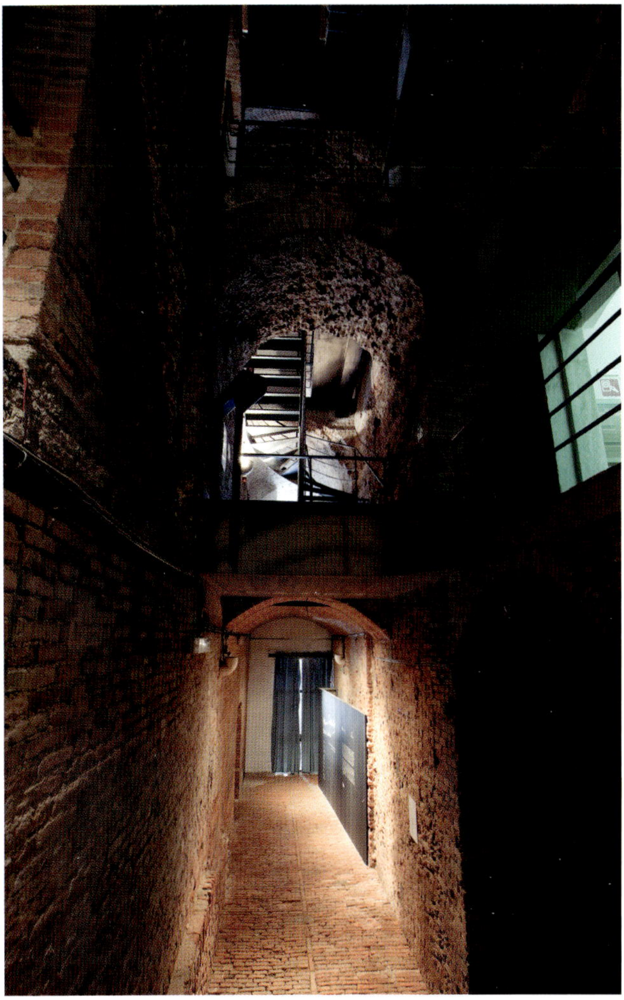

modern staircase. The stairs, placed between the central body of the palace and the Cortile del Podestà, occupy the space that must once have been an interior passage-way between the Campo and the Marketplace, not too different from the other one, also lost, between Via di Salicotto and the square below, which divided the Podestà's palace from the Palazzo della Campana.

## The Prison and the Palazzo della Campana

On the left side of the Palazzo Pubblico, next to the Torre del Mangia, along the Via di Salicotto, is a big building which echoes the style of the Palazzo Pubblico. Since the middle of the sixteenth century it has housed the city theater, but it was built at the same time as the seat of civic government.
In 1327 the communal government decided to build a

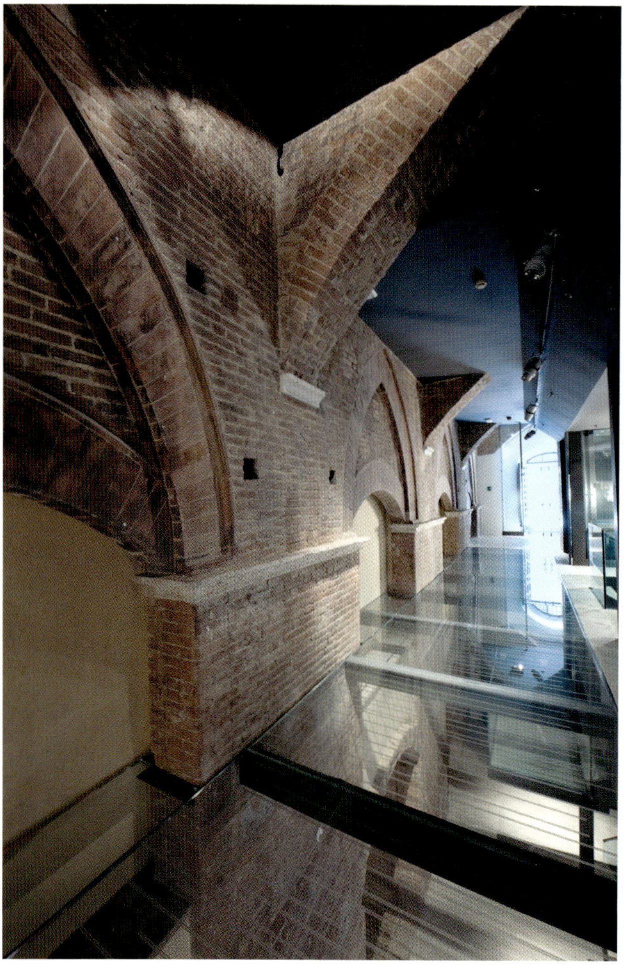

The large Gothic arches of the back wall of the Palazzo Pubblicom recovered on the interior of the Teatro dei Rinnovati

prison on a piece of land behind the Palazzo Pubblico. Until that moment, as had been the case for meetings of the government officials, the custom had prevailed of renting space or even rooms in private buildings to house prisoners.

In 1330, the prison was finished. It was a low, isolated building, presumably all on one floor, situated between Via di Salicotto and the so-called "Foro Boario" (cattle market), the current Piazza del Mercato, overlooked by the back of Palazzo Pubblico. In the meantime, plans had been drawn up to finish the palace, with the addition of the Podestà's wing on the left at the foot of the Torre del Mangia. In the enthusiasm of this moment, when the Sienese people's creative fervor for urban planning reached its peak, the decision was made to begin a new building phase for the entire civic complex, focused on the new prison building.

The need had been felt for some time to have an adequate

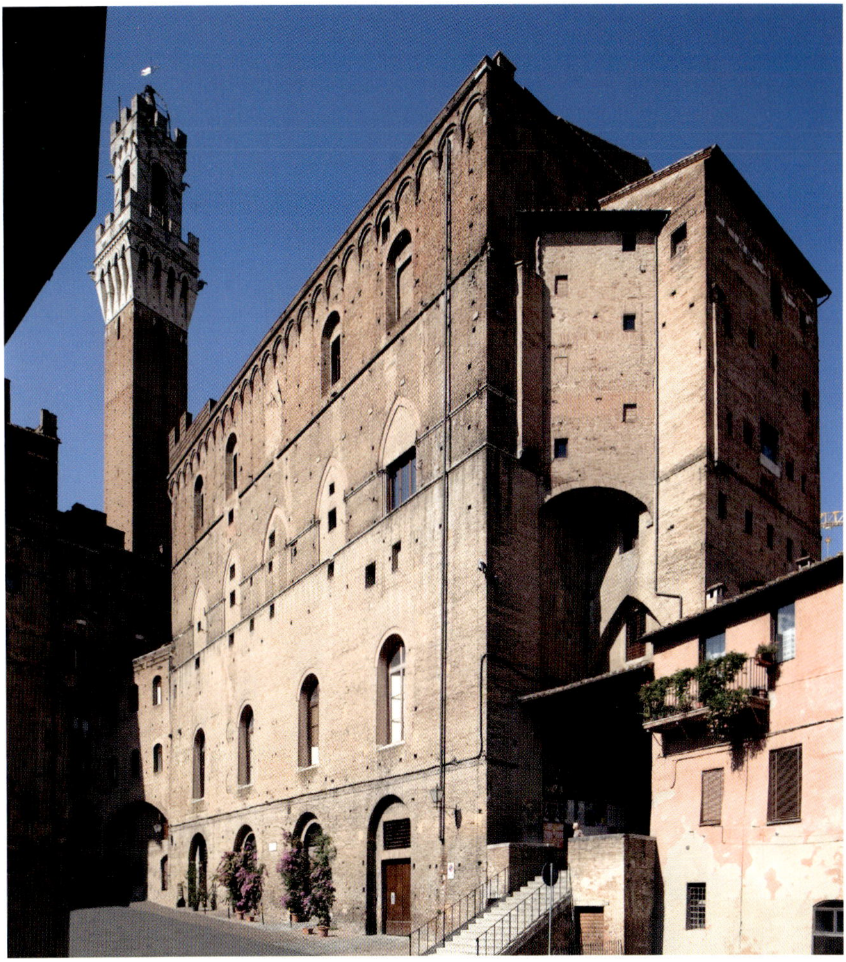

The Palazzo della Campana, now the home of the Teatro dei Rinnovati, seen from the Piazza del Mercato

place to hold meetings of the General Council, the highest civic body and certainly the one with the greatest participation, called also the "Council of the Bell" because a bell was rung to signal to members that it was time to meet. In 1339 it was decided to raise and expand the prison building to make one great 'container,' that is to say a vast empty space which could, to put it simply, hold a lot of people.

The building, called from that moment on the "Palazzo della Campana" ("the bell building"), was constructed to harmonize completely, in terms of shape and finishing details, with the adjacent Palazzo Pubblico. It was given a row of triforate windows on its two main sides and crenellation at the top, which was destroyed by fire in the eighteenth century; a large portal connected it, by means of a bridge, with the Palazzo del Podestà. In 1343, work was finished.

Thc Gothic portal, made of brick and datable in the first

half of the fourteenth century, was recently rediscovered during the restoration of the Teatro dei Rinnovati in 2009. This was a large pointed arch piercing the outside wall of the Palazzo della Campana. The arch has now been incorporated into the wall of the theater auditorium, but the upper part of the left jamb and the frame of the archivolt, decorated with rosettes and dentils, are clearly visible. During this same restoration work, which is also visible inside the theater, the back wall of Palazzo Pubblico, datable between 1325 and 1331, was uncovered. This wall, long forgotten and hidden behind partition walls and whitewash, with its four high portals at the base and triforate windows in the upper section, is in perfect harmony with the remaining back façade of the town hall, overlooking Piazza del Mercato, which was designed and built, down to the tiniest details, to match the main façade.

## The Teatro dei Rinnovati

In 1555, after a long siege, the Republic of Siena fell under Florentine dominion, ruled by the Medici family, and became a part of the Grand Duchy of Tuscany.
One of Cosimo I de' Medici's first acts upon taking official possession of the city in 1561, when among other things he reformed the principal bureaucratic functions of the ancient state of Siena, was to decree that the General Council would go back to meeting in the Sala del Mappamondo in Palazzo Pubblico. What at first sight might seem to be a marginal decision, above and beyond its strong political significance (since it effectively deposed the governing body most representative of Sienese communal liberty), in fact marked the end of the Palazzo della Campana as the symbol of social and civic life in the city. Since the palace was a large building, totally enclosed and with an empty interior, the new rulers decided to turn it into a theater, which Siena lacked. Thus the ancient Palazzo della Campana became what is now the Teatro dei Rinnovati.
Assigned until the early nineteenth century to a learned academy in Siena, the Accademia degli Intronati, it was built first of wood and later of masonry, to a design by Carlo Fontana (1668), before he worked on the Palazzo Pubblico.
After its interior was completely destroyed by two fires (in 1742 and 1751), it was rebuilt and renovated twice in the middle of the eighteenth century and restored

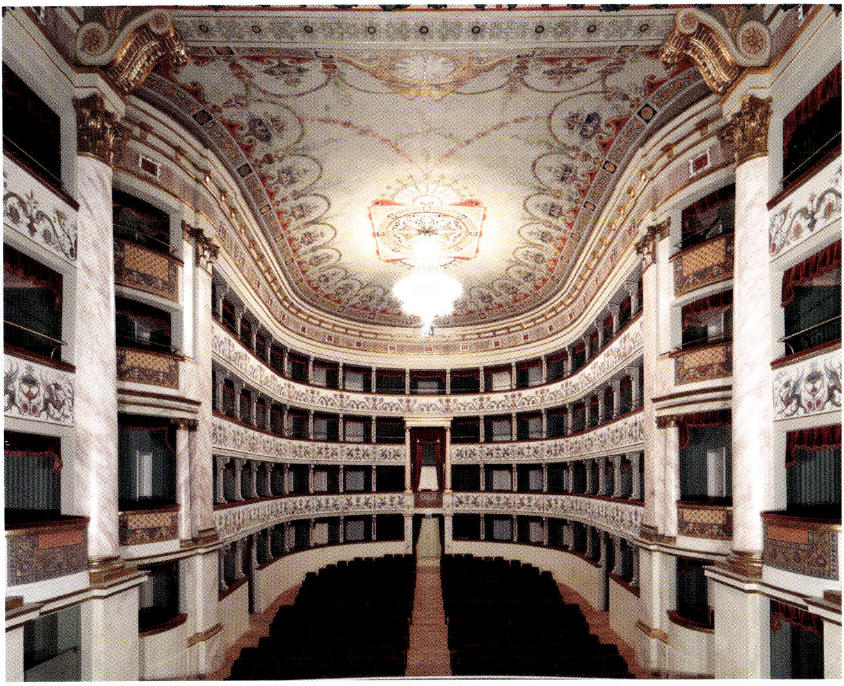

The interior of the Teatro dei Rinnovati

again after it was damaged in a disastrous earthquake (1798).

In the beginning of the nineteenth century, management of the theater was handed over to the owners of the boxes, who came together to form the Accademia dei Rinnovati, hence the theater's name which it still preserves, even though ownership passed into the hands of the City of Siena in 1935.

The appearance of the Teatro dei Rinnovati, recently the object of major technical upgrades and preservation measures mentioned above (directed by architect Ettore Vio in 2009), is still that of an elegant, refined eighteenth- or nineteenth-century theater. The layout of the stalls and boxes follows essentially that established by the famous architect Antonio Galli Bibiena in 1752, especially in the bell shape of the floor plan of the auditorium, adopted for optimal acoustics and views of the stage.

The decoration is later in date. What we see today is essentially the decorations painted by Cesare Maffei and Giorgio Bandini in 1853. The parapets of the boxes are adorned with flowers, ribbons, fantastic animals, dragons, birds. and anthropomorphic herms. The ceiling has a more complex decorative scheme, with the perimeter marked off by arches of vegetable garlands emerging from vases to frame monochrome medallions of mythological scenes and figures, surrounded by floral and animal motifs.

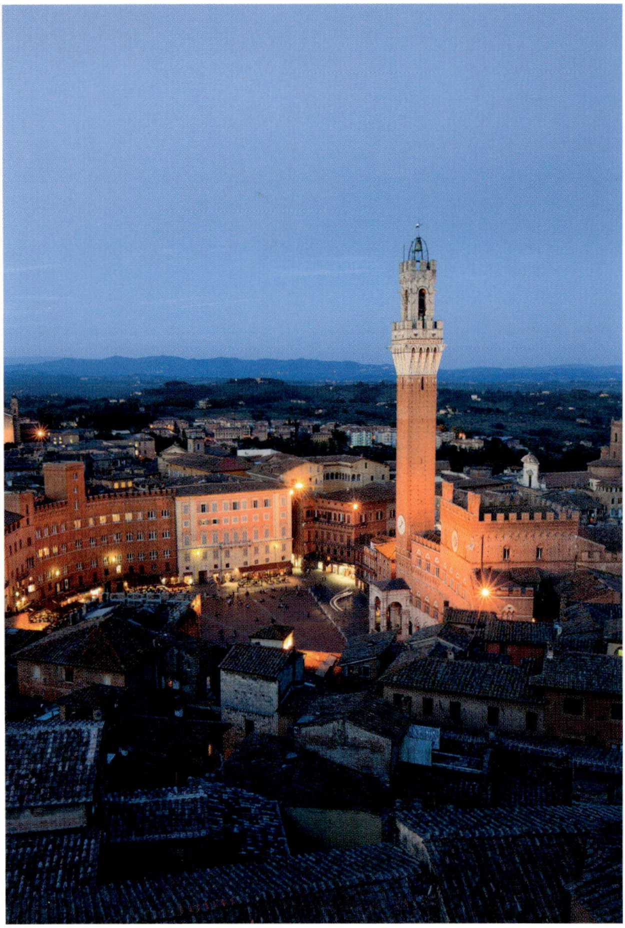

The Torre del Mangia and the Palazzo Pubblico at sunset

## The Torre del Mangia

Much has been written about the historical, political and anthropological significance of the Torre del Mangia and what it means and has meant to the Sienese.
The decision to build a tower of this kind certainly, at that time, transmitted a message of power. A sign of power with a dual aspect, from the governors to the citizens and to their rival factions, and seen from outside, an explicit signal of force and even of audacity from a city that wanted to show just how rich and important it was. The fact that such a strong sign of power is also a work of undeniable architectural and aesthetic value is due to the refinement and taste of the Sienese who, as we know, were particularly sensitive and attentive to the beauty of their city.
An early Sienese chronicle tells that in 1325, the Sienese began building a tower on the corner of what was then called Via di Malcucinato and is now Salicotto.

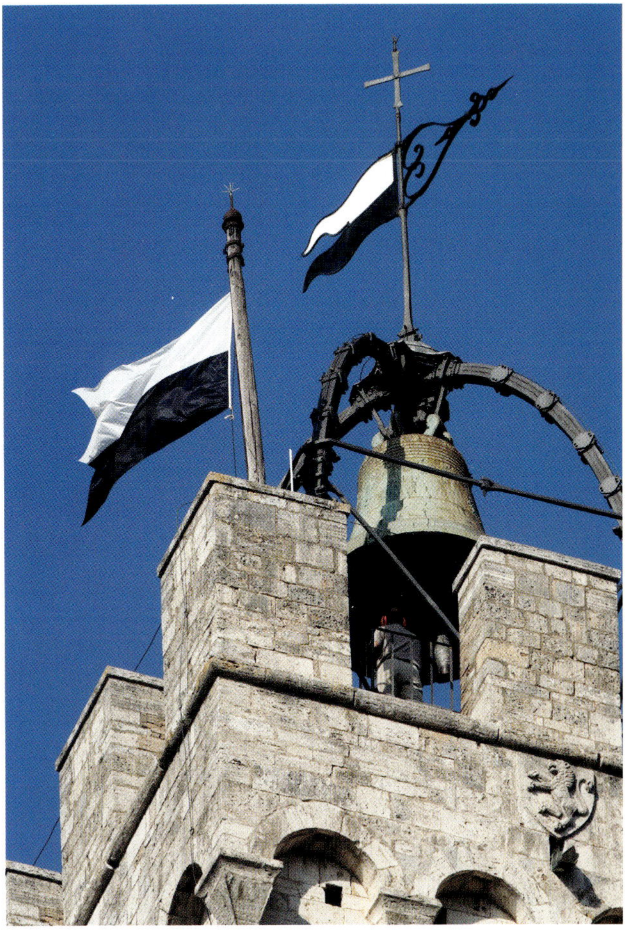

The battlements of the Torre del Mangia showing the "Big Bell"

In reality, historians tend to move a few years later, to around 1338, the date when construction began on the tower. By that time, the building of Palazzo Pubblico, begun in the closing decades of the thirteenth century, was certainly almost completed, at least as far as the exterior was concerned.
Just as was the case with the Palazzo Pubblico, we do not know the name of the architect of the Torre del Mangia, and in fact there probably was not just one person behind the design. Various craftsmen worked on the construction as master builders (*capomastri*). The name has been mentioned of Agostino di Giovanni, a well-known and respected of mid-fourteenth-century Sienese sculptor, as well as of two brothers from Perugia, Minuccio and Francesco di Rinaldo, even if we know that at least eight so-called "operari turris" (superintendents of the tower) took turns working on the tower over a period of about ten years.
It did not take long to build. Payments are reported from

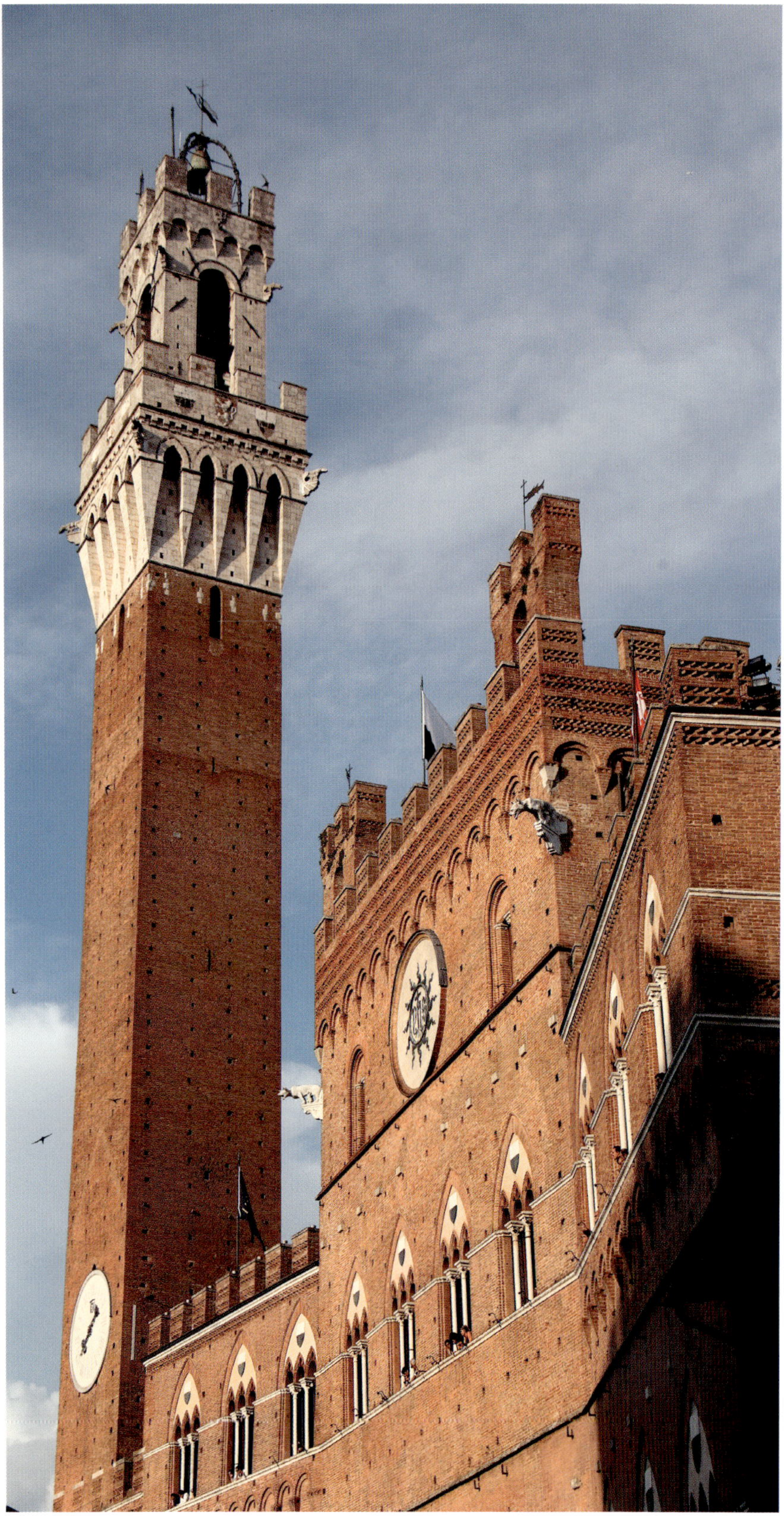

The Palazzo Pubblico and the tower seen from the Casato curve

1338 to 1349. It must have been finished in 1348, because the resolution was passed to have the "new bell… of the Nine Lords" cast to be put in it. But this is not the large bell which can be seen, even from a distance, at the top of the Torre del Mangia. It was replaced in 1666 with the one which the Sienese immediately called the *Campanone* (Big Bell) because of its size, also familiarly referred to as *Sunto*, because it was dedicated to Our Lady of the Assumption.

*Sunto* has one tone, dull and deep, due to a sort of cut on the bottom edge which distorts its sound, but its unmistakable tolling marks the most important moments in Sienese life even today, especially those connected with the Palio, and it is deeply loved by the people of this city.

One thing is sure, at any rate: above and beyond questions of who may or may not have designed it, the Torre del Mangia is an architectural gem, because of its size and type of construction, especially in the context of the time it was built.

With its 87 meters of height (102 if measured to the top of the lightning rod), it rests, without foundations, on a base of tufa rock, which is particularly stable and elastic, then rises up with its simple, austere brick face initially resting on the adjacent structures. The first two floors of the Palazzo are continuous with the bottom section of the tower; one of the two gothic windows is still partially visible, while the other has been hidden by the chapel. From this point, the tower soars freely upwards to its crown. The grand, beautiful silhouette of the battlements decorating and finishing the top represented at that time, along with the tower's height, the true signs distinguishing it from any other tower in the city, with the refined solution of the white travertine contrasting with the red brick walls and the heraldic reference of the eight she-wolves at the corners, the symbol of possession and power on the part of those who commissioned the tower and of the entire city.

With the completion of the tower, the overall look of the entire palace was complete.

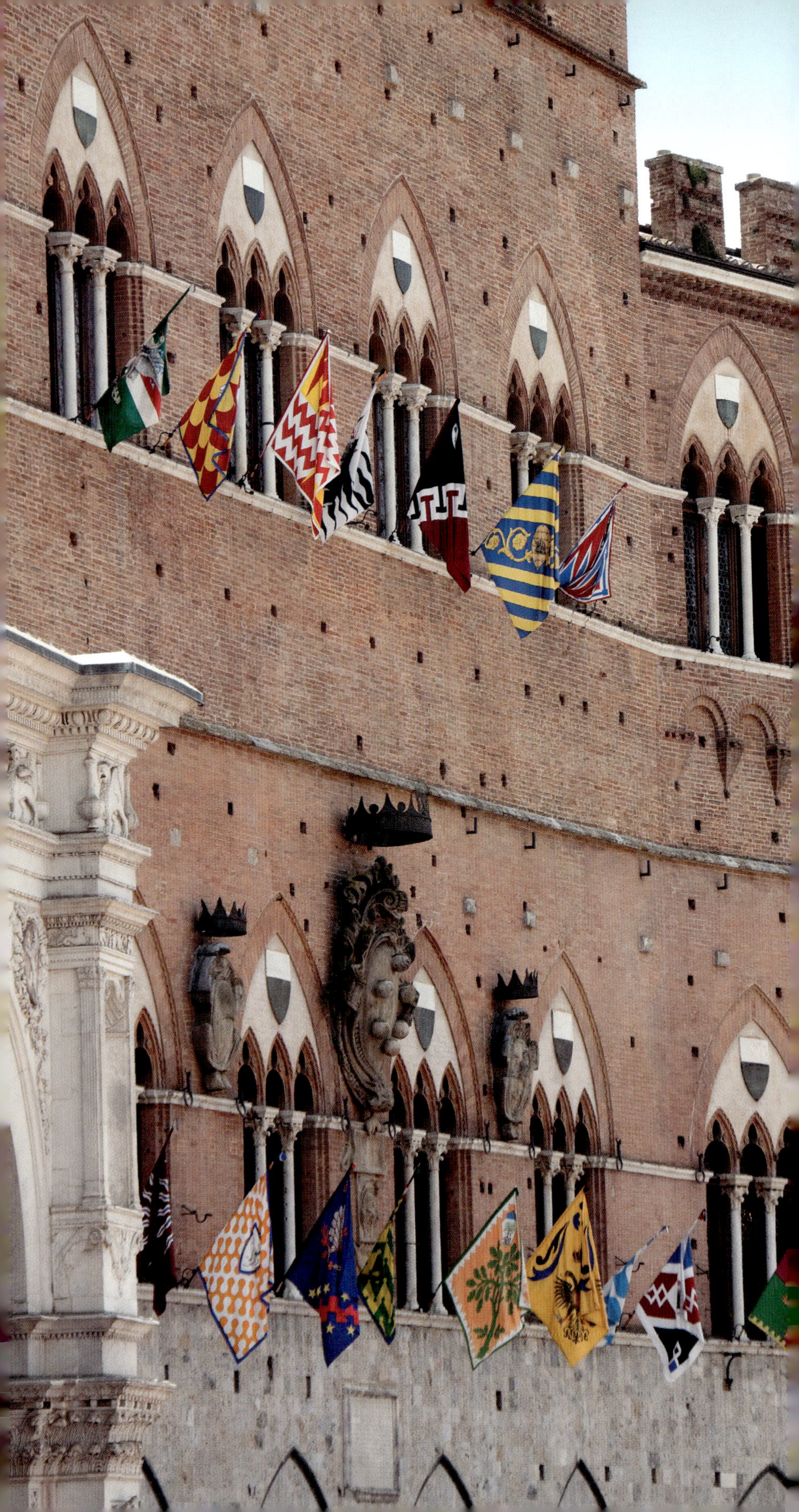

# The Palio and the Palace
# Protagonist behind the Scenes

*Letizia Galli*

The flags of the seventeen contradas hanging in front of the windows of Palazzo Pubblico

The organization of the Palio is a complex machinery whose main gears are the seventeen contradas (town districts) and whose engine is the City of Siena.
The Palazzo Pubblico plays a leading role as the site of some of the principal rituals, not all of which place on the eagerly awaited dates of 2 July and 16 August, the days of the Palio.

## Drawing the Names of the Contradas

Every year, on the last Sunday in May, the Palio season begins with the display from the windows of the first floor of Palazzo Pubblico of the flags of the seven contradas who have the right to run the July race.
Three more flags will be added to these seven, the three contradas whose names are drawn in the presence of the mayor and the captains of the ten contradas that participated in the race run in July the year before, to complete the core of ten who will run this year.
The same operation takes place for the August Palio, usually the second Sunday after the race in July.
The façade of the palace is enlivened by the bright colors of the contradas and the flags waving in the breeze. The atmosphere heats up with the sound of the palace trumpets, whose clarion call announces that the flags of the lucky contradas are about to be displayed. The tension of the wait is brief but intense, and all eyes in the packed Piazza del Campo are on those two Gothic windows and the colors of the tip of the flag that emerges suddenly from the darkness of the room, met by shouts and leaps of joy and hugs all around among the members of the chosen contradas.
The flags of the seven contradas excluded from this race hang gloomily from the windows of the floor above. Next year they will be the seven who run by right, but this year they are left out of the game.
The very same ritual and the very same reactions are repeated on the second Sunday in July, when the contradas for the August Palio are drawn; because every

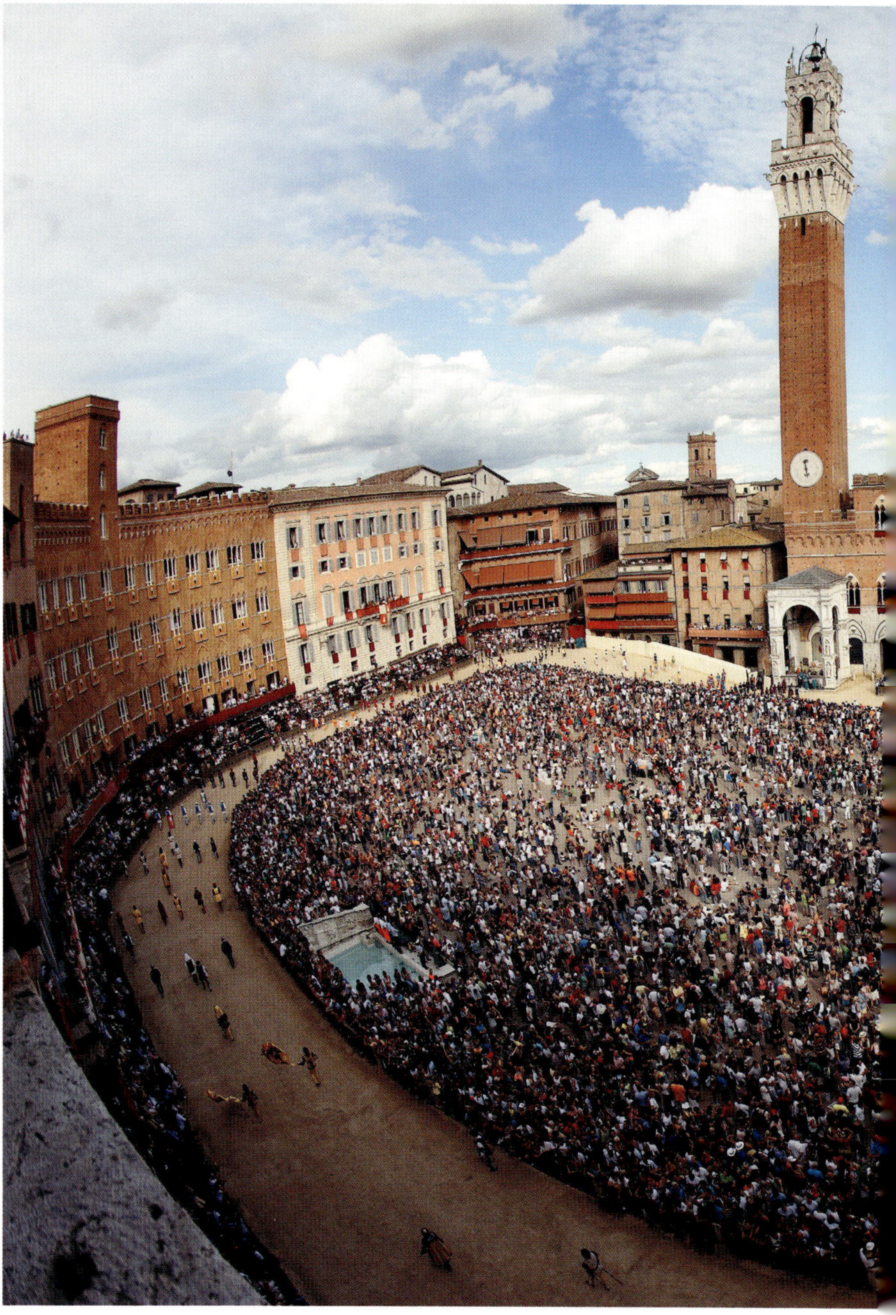

An aerial view of Piazza del Campo during the historical parade before the running of the Palio

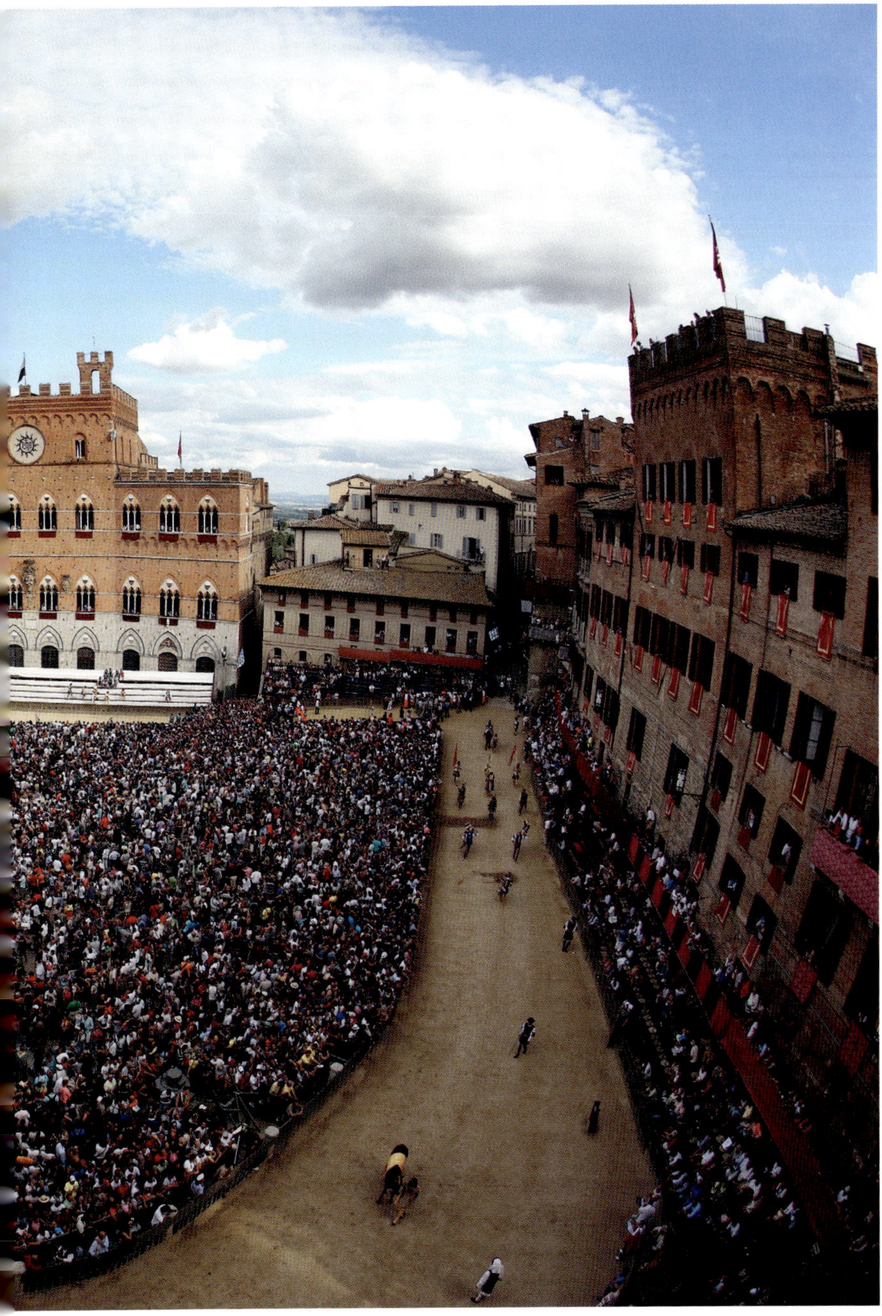

Palio is a story unto itself, and the July Palio is something completely different and separate from the August race.
Only again, the Palazzo Pubblico is the protagonist. The captains of the participating contradas, gathered together in the palace, choose the ten horses they consider best suited to the race, which are still kept in the Entrone. People continue to crowd into the space in front of the palace waiting for the horses to come out – this is one of the most eagerly-awaited moments of the four days preceding the Palio. The luck of the draw, more or less benevolent, will determine the contrada's fate in the Palio, but not only that. The quality of the horse assigned by lot to the contrada affects also the choice of its rider, who is paid by the contrada, and also all the web of relations, pacts, alliances and negotiations, some open, some secret, that the contradas set in motion up to the final moment before the race.
When the mayor comes out of the palace and takes his place on the podium together with the captains, an unreal silence falls over the square. Time seems suspended, a frozen moment, but in reality everything takes place in little more than half an hour. The names of the horses are placed in one box and those of the contradas in another. The innocent hands of two young children draw the names, one of the horse, the other of the contrada, which are paired together. The first minutes of silence then give way to songs, curses, joy or desperation according to the first impression of the horse assigned by fate to the contrada.
Slowly, just as it had filled up, the Campo empties out.

## Registering the Jockeys

In the four days of trials, the Palazzo Pubblico remains practically empty, behind the scenes, half-hidden by the imposing podium erected in front of it, where the groups chosen to represent the contradas in the pre-Palio parade will take their place after the procession on the afternoon before the race. In reality, the mayor continues working inside the palace, managing all the operations connected with the festivities. The rest of his job, the political and administrative duties, is held in abeyance.
The palace becomes alive again on the morning of the Palio. Before the running of the sixth and final trial, called the "provaccia," Mass for the jockeys is celebrated in front of the Cappella di Piazza located right at the base of the

Torre del Mangia, one of the few occasions on which the chapel is officiated, attended by the jockeys and captains of the participating contradas and by a vast number of the faithful.
Later, in the room adjacent to the mayor's office, on the ground floor of the palace, the jockeys are registered: another meeting, official and ritual at the same time, between the municipal administration and the protagonists of the race. This meeting is not open to the public, but it attracts a small crowd of contrada members who stand in wait in front of the entrance of the Sala delle Lupe. Its purpose is to specify some rules for the race both by the mayor and by the official starter. Essentially, however, it repeats an ancient, traditional act which is that of the "segnatura" (writing down") of the jockeys, in other words the official registration of the jockey who will ride for the contrada that has selected him. Every captain, when the mayor calls out the name of his contrada, holds up and shows to everyone present the jacket the jockey will wear during the race and states the jockey's name and nickname. This moment is important because, just as it is not possible to change horses once they are assigned, after this official act the jockey cannot be changed either.

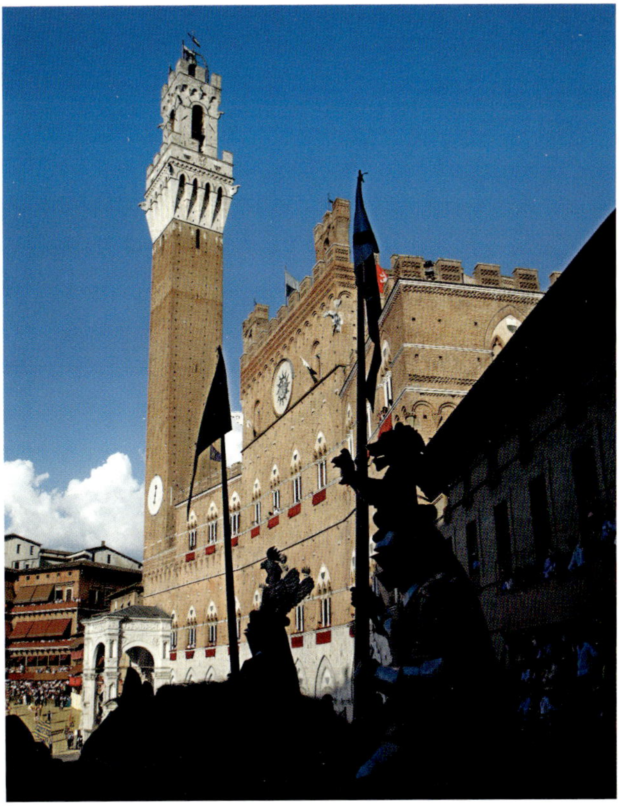

The Palazzo Pubblico behind the silhouettes of the men-at-arms in the historical parade

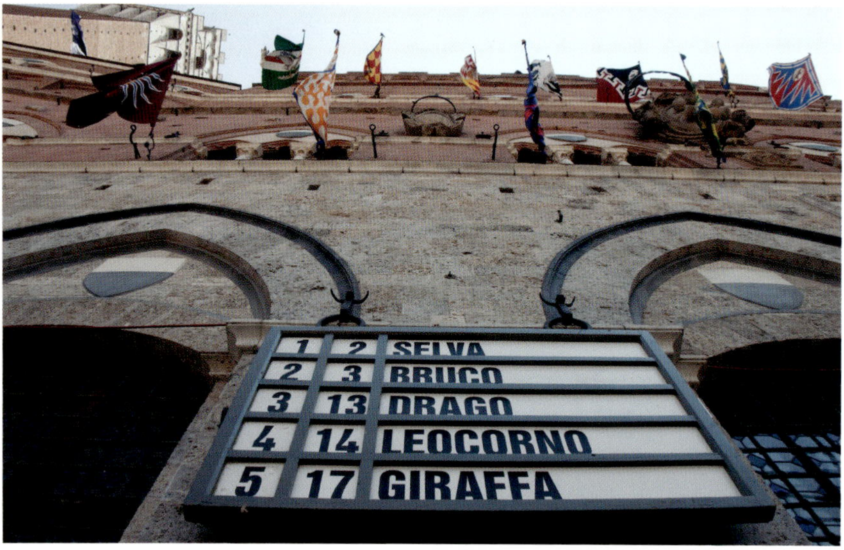


Board placed on the front of the Palazzo Pubblico to display the horses' numbers and the names of the contradas assigned to them by lot

## *Sunto* and the Flag of Victory

During the long afternoon that precedes the race, the Palazzo Pubblico only carries out its institutional duties, welcoming into its beautiful rooms the many guests who are invited every year to watch the Palio from the Gothic windows of the palace.
Meanwhile *Sunto*, as the Sienese call the big bell on top of the Torre del Mangia, marks the time with its deep slow ringing as the brightly colored, elegant historic parade makes its solemn progress around the Piazza del Campo.
The horses and jockeys who will race, and who participate in the parade nonetheless, gather together in the *Entrone*, cloistered and protected, closed off from the outside world, where the final deals are struck before the race.
Sunto implacably keeps ringing until a few instants before the great door of the *Entrone* swings open to let the jockeys and horses file out. And just as that tolling stops, so does the heart of every Sienese stop beating. From this moment on, everything is terribly serious.
The race itself is short, little more than a minute. But the preceding phase, the line-up at the starting rope, can take a long, even a very long time. The wait is exhausting, seemingly never-ending, in which everything hangs suspended, awaiting that one minute of pure madness. Then, with the firing of the gun, it is all over, and in the "regular" chaos which takes over, amid the unbounded joy of the winners and the desperation

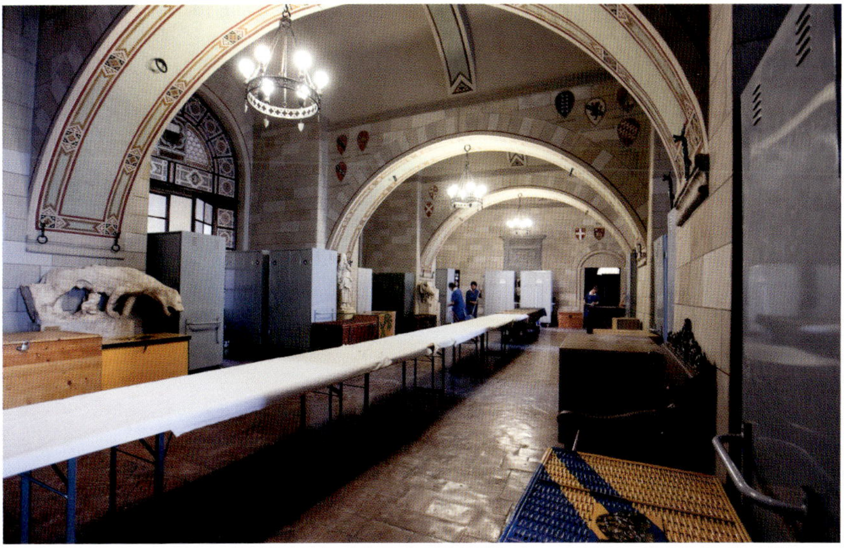

The Hall of the She-wolves with the baskets and cupboards of the contradas, ready to welcome the costumed participants in the parade on the afternoon of the Palio

of the losers, one banner alone is hung out of the central window of the Palazzo Pubblico: the flag of the victorious contrada.

## The Prize Banner

A few days before the Palio, the marvelous prize everyone is fighting for, the "drappellone," or long banner, is secretly brought into the Town Hall. This is the so-called "cencio" (rag) of painted white silk, which will be awarded to the winning contrada. The city administration decides each time who will paint it; leading contemporary artists, both in Italy and abroad, such as Guttuso, Folon, Cremonini, and Fromanger, have been asked to try their hand at this project. The main iconographical theme is established, which is always different, but some rules remain unchanged. Among these is the obligation to represent Our Lady (of Provenzano for the July Palio, of the Assumption in August), the symbols of the contradas participating in that race, the coats of arms of the Terzi (thirds) into which the city is divided, and the arms of the mayor currently in office. In the days preceding the presentation of the Palio banner to the city, it is safeguarded in the mayor's office, far from indiscreet or curious eyes, because it will only be revealed to the public during an official ceremony in the Cortile del Podestà, called familiarly by the Sienese the *Entrone* (Big Entrance), and judged by public favor, which is unaffected by the signature, more or less prestigious, of the artist who painted it – because the impact

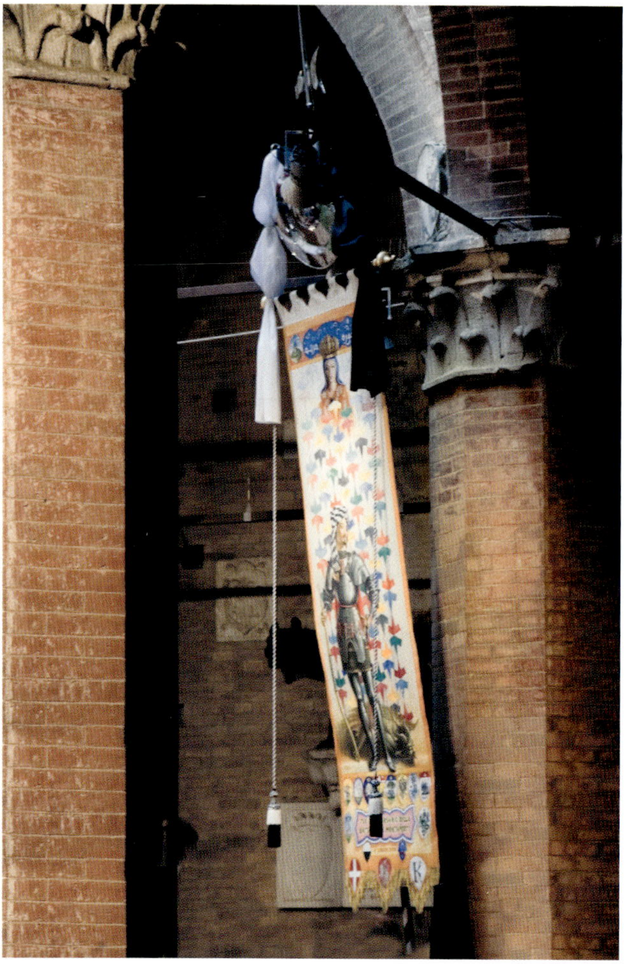

The banner painted by the artist Ali Hassoun for the 2 July 2010 Palio is presented in the *Entrone*

of the Palio banner in that moment is a thunderbolt, a sudden falling in love. One either likes it or not, greeting it with applause or boos if it does not immediately strike the right emotional chord.

**Drawing Lots for the Horses**

Four days before the Palio, on the morning of 29 June for the July race and of 13 August for the one in August, the Palazzo Pubblico is the center of all the operations concerning the race.
This is the day that the horses are assigned by lot to the participating contradas.
From the early morning hours, the evocative sound of horse's hooves can be heard on the gray stone of the city